RETHINKING THE PUBLIC

Innovations in research, theory and politics

Edited by Nick Mahony, Janet Newman and Clive Barnett

This edition published in Great Britain in 2010 by

The Policy Press
University of Bristol
Fourth Floor
Beacon House
Queen's Road
Bristol BS8 1QU
UK

Tel +44 (0)117 331 4054
Fax +44 (0)117 331 4093
e-mail tpp-info@bristol.ac.uk
www.policypress.co.uk

North American office:
The Policy Press
c/o International Specialized Books Services (ISBS)
920 NE 58th Avenue, Suite 300
Portland, OR 97213-3786, USA
Tel +1 503 287 3093
Fax +1 503 280 8832
e-mail info@isbs.com

British Library Cataloguing in Publication Data
A catalogue record for this book is available from the British Library.

Library of Congress Cataloging-in-Publication Data
A catalog record for this book has been requested.

ISBN 978 1 84742 416 7 hardcover

Cover design by The Policy Press
Printed and bound in Great Britain by Cromwell Press Group, Trowbridge

Contents

Notes on contributors

Clive Barnett is a Reader in Human Geography at the Open University, Milton Keynes. He is author of *Culture and democracy* (Edinburgh, 2003), co-author of *Geographies of globalization* (Wiley Blackwell, 2010), co-editor of *Spaces of democracy* (Sage, 2004) and *Geographies of globalisation* (Sage, 2008).

Gurpreet Bhasin recently completed her PhD at The Open University. She is a historical geographer, interested in public spaces, discourse, politics and the media in colonial India. She also has a background in international relations and has recently worked as a consultant in the Department of Geography at The Open University.

Clive Gabay is studying at The Open University for his doctorate on the multiple agencies, inclusions and exclusions of alter-globalisation networks. He has a Masters degree from Birkbeck College, University of London, and has worked for a number of human rights and international development non-governmental organisations.

Richenda Gambles is studying for a doctorate at The Open University. Her research seeks to locate a 'structure of feeling' relating to the first few years of parenting and she uses this framework to reflect on the position and power of policy in people's lives. She has also worked as a journalist, an associate lecturer at The Open University and a lecturer in social policy at the University of Oxford.

Liza Griffin is a Senior Lecturer in Politics at the University of Westminster. She studied at The Open University for a doctorate on good governance, scale and power in the European Union. She has published on the management of marine resources and is interested in debates about power and space in relation to the governance of sustainable development.

J. Simon Hutta is in the final stages of his PhD thesis at The Open University on lesbian, gay and trans people's experiences of city spaces in relation to activist politics of safety in Brazil. Before this, he studied psychology and cultural studies at the Free University Berlin and the University of California, Santa Cruz. His research interests include security, citizenship, sexuality and the experience of space.

Eleanor Jupp is a Research Fellow in Urban Policy and Social Inclusion in the Department of Planning, Oxford Brookes University. She gained her doctorate on public space and community organising in disadvantaged neighbourhoods from the Department of Geography, Open University, in 2006. Before this she worked as a policy adviser and consultant for non-governmental organisations and government on issues of neighbourhood renewal, social inclusion and the built environment.

Nick Mahony is an ESRC Post-Doctoral Fellow at the Centre for Citizenship, Identities and Governance at The Open University, where he is active in the Publics Research Programme. For his doctorate, Nick compared participative experiments organised by governmental, popular media and social movement experiments. He continues to explore the publics and forms of politics mediated by contemporary participative experiments, most recently by engaging with industrial, arts and academic experiments to trace how this field is shaping up more broadly.

Janet Newman is a Professor of Social Policy and Director of the Publics Research Programme within the Centre for Citizenship, Identities and Governance at the Open University. Her research centres on the cultural politics of governance, new formations of citizenship, and professional and organisational change. Her most recent book, with John Clarke, is *Publics, politics and power: Remaking the public in public services* (Sage, 2009).

Jessica Pykett is a Research Associate at the Institute of Geography and Earth Sciences, Aberystwyth University, where she is researching the politics of governing through 'behaviour-change' policies and the ascendance of libertarian paternalism in the UK. Prior to this she was a Research Fellow in the Department of Geography at The Open University, working on the pedagogical nature of state practices. She studied for a PhD on the geographies of education and citizenship at the University of Bristol.

Scott Rodgers is a Lecturer in Media Theory at Birkbeck, University of London. His research focuses on the intersections between studies of mediated communication and approaches to cities and urban politics. He is currently working on translating his doctoral thesis into a book that explores the unravelling relationship of the newspaper and the city, and the implications this has for emerging configurations of urban life.

ONE

Introduction: rethinking the public

Nick Mahony, Janet Newman and Clive Barnett

The idea of 'the public' as a singular entity, circumscribed by bonds of national solidarity and expressing itself in a unified public sphere, has become increasingly problematic. New media and information technologies are undercutting traditional notions of the public sphere, opening up a range of innovative possibilities for public communication. New objects of public concern are emerging: for example, around environmental issues, human rights, trade justice and access to the global 'commons' of scarce resources. And many of these issues are in turn summoning up new subjects of public action that articulate local and national scales of activity with transnational scales. At the same time, shifts in the political landscape are intensifying efforts by government and non-governmental actors to summon up figures of the active citizen, the responsible community and the choice-making consumer, all of which potentially challenge models of the public as a privileged scene of collective agency. In many nation states, such summonings seem to displace the classical values of publicness in the name of individual or community responsibility; and they are associated with the rolling out of public policies that are increasingly focused on regulating how personal lives should be lived.

In trying to make sense of these shifts, we are confronted with a bewildering set of normative claims. Indeed, both academic and policy writings on publics and the public sphere tend to be long on assertions and injunctions and weak on empirical substance. New media, it is claimed, have already displaced the value and relevance of 'old' communication technologies in sustaining democracy (see, for example, www.e-democracy.org; Leadbeater, 2008). New strategies of governance that empower individual persons rather than treating 'the public' as an undifferentiated unity are offering opportunities for independence and self-development that were unthinkable under the paternalistic welfare state (see, for example, Diamond et al, 2008). New ways of engaging citizens in public dialogue and debate, whether by public or commercial institutions, are offering an immediacy and sensitivity to difference that were impossible under old norms of representative democracy). New contentious struggles demonstrate the irrelevance of forms of politics bounded by the nation state (Drache, 2008). These claims are presented here in simplified form, but what is striking is that in most cases the depiction of new possibilities is presented as transformations that *have already taken place*: the normative slides uneasily into the descriptive.

The contributions to this volume both complicate such accounts and offer a critical distance from their normative underpinnings. The book is based on the work of a group of scholars clustered around the Publics Research Programme at The Open University.[1] This group was engaged over two years in intensive discussions about how their individual studies might provide a collective intervention into contemporary theorisations of publics and publicness. Their studies draw on theoretical work across a range of disciplines, including cultural studies, human geography, development studies, politics, sociology and social policy, inflected through post-colonial, feminist, social movement and other critical theory perspectives. While much of the literature on these topics draws on normative theories of the public sphere (Habermas, 1989), the main contribution of this volume is its empirical grounding in theoretically informed doctoral and post-doctoral social science research. The grounded cases in this volume examine some of the processes through which new formations of publicness and new forms of public action are emerging.

This empirical grounding enables us to show how appeals to 'new' publics (in media discourses and by governmental actors and social movements) are cross-cut by older institutional, political and cultural practices. We explore some of the paradoxes inherent in contemporary governmental strategies that appeal to communities rather than states, persons rather than citizens. We offer analyses of how print media both constitute local, urban publics and open up transnational formations, including, historically, that of pan-Islamism. We show how challenges to the public/private distinction have produced new terrains of governmental action as well as new spaces of agency. We engage with contemporary struggles – over the sustainability of natural resources, over global justice claims or around the politics of community – showing how formal and informal politics, institutional and cultural practices are entangled. Our contributors trace the complex interleaving of global, national and local formations of publics and representations of the public interest. They also highlight the importance of paying attention to the historical context in which different publics are summoned, or different issues are raised as public matters. Finally, we draw attention to what we term a politics of mediation, showing how claims about publics and publicness are mediated through discursive, material and institutional practices.

But what do we mean when we speak of 'the public'? Our approach here starts from assumption that a public is not best thought of as a pre-existing collective subject that straightforwardly expresses itself or offers itself up to be represented. Rather, we are interested in elaborating on how publics, in the plural (Calhoun, 1997), are called into existence, or summoned. On this understanding, '[p]ublics are called into existence, *convened*, which is to say that they are sustained by establishing relations of attention whose geographical configurations are not given in advance' (Barnett, 2008, emphasis in original). This emphasises how publics are formed through processes of *address* (Warner, 2002; Iveson, 2007) and implies that the precise spatial dimensions and socio-cultural composition of a public cannot be determined in advance of the actions and activities through which it makes its presence felt. In short, it implies focusing on the processes through which publics *emerge* (see also Angus, 2001). We theorise this process of public emergence by distinguishing analytically between the objects, mediums and subjects of publicness (Barnett, 2008). Publics emerge around particular objects of concern, that is, around specific issues (Dewey, 1927; Marres, 2005). They emerge by articulating these issues through particular mediums, and in distinctively public mediums that combine intimate and anonymous registers of address (Barnett, 2003). They gather together and draw on the agency of plural, multiple social subjects variously affected by issues at hand (Warner, 2002). Our approach to thinking about the emergence of publics, then, leads us to think about the participants in public action in a particular way. Rather than thinking of these as the already constituted citizens of a territorial nation state, or as the idealised deliberators of rational conversation, we focus in this volume on the actors whose ongoing practices shape and sustain the spaces and sites of publicness.

Publics are not only summoned, but are also *assembled*: made up from the uneasy and impermanent alignments of discourses, spaces, institutions, ideas, technologies and objects. The notion of assembly draws attention to the ambiguities and unsettled qualities of any emergent formation of publicness or public action: 'publics are fluid and mobile, being assembled at particular moments for particular projects' (Newman and Clarke, 2009, p 20). Of course, this thought can be applied to underwrite both highly pessimistic and highly optimistic interpretations of contemporary dynamics of public action (Newman and Clarke, 2009). On the one hand, there is a pessimistic narrative. It is common to hear that public institutions are in decline, and that any sense of a collective public solidarity bounded by the nation state is becoming unsustainable. For example, Marquand (2004) speaks of the 'decline of the public' under a process of 'incessant marketisation', which has 'generated a culture of distrust, which is corroding the values of professionalism, citizenship, equity and service like acid in the water supply' (2004, p 3). Consumerism is often highlighted in such narratives of decline (Needham, 2003; Lawson, 2009). Similar themes, but within a different analytical frame, are pursued by Devine and colleagues (2009) in the tellingly titled *Feelbad Britain*. In public and policy debates across Europe and the US, commentators worry that inward migration and increasing diversity threatens the national solidarities on which public cultures and public institutions are assumed to depend (Alesina and Glaeser, 2004; Clarke, 2007b). Accounts of the roll-out of 'neoliberal' logics of rule suggest that public sensibilities and loyalties are progressively undermined by and replaced by market rationalities (cf Newman, 2006; Barnett, 2009). The intensification of efforts by governments and non-governmental actors to summon up the figures of the active citizen, the responsible community or the choice-making consumer elicits concern that the collective and unifying dimensions of public solidarity are being displaced by more partial and divisive modes of agency (Barnes et al, 2007; Clarke et al, 2007; Neveu, 2007; Carrel et al, 2009).

On the other hand, the sense of publics as flexible and mobile also underwrites a more optimistic narrative in which the classical features of nationally bounded public spheres are now seen to be proliferating across different scales. So, for example, the emergence of transnational politics mobilised around global issues has been interpreted as offering the possibility of a resurgence of progressive public action politics (for example, Dryzek, 2006; Drache, 2008; cf Fraser, 2007). At a different scale, a governmental focus on 'local community' is presented as opening up new opportunities for public engagement and citizenly action (see, for example, publications of the UK Department for Community and Local Government at www.communities.gov.uk, and Mooney and Neal, 2009, for critique). In these optimistic narratives, attention is focused on the potential of new communications technologies to re-energise public action, transform democracy or reform public services; on the problematisation of new objects of public concern, such as climate change or human rights; and on the emergence of new subjects of public action, such as the 'queer' subjects of gay and lesbian mobilisations or the subjects of the politics of 'new life' (Robins, 2005).

While there might be something to each of these narratives, there is a tendency in both to let normative evaluation race ahead of descriptive and explanatory analysis. In this volume, by focusing in detail on different examples of the emergence of publics in diverse contexts, we seek to underscore the sense that the purpose of emphasising the variable qualities of publics is to keep in view that processes of assembling, convening and summoning publics is always cross-cut by calculations, forces and strategies that are resolutely *political*:

> Things, people, and issues get made public by a variety of means, but all of them involve processes of making visible matters of connective concern. Publicness is historically and socially variable – the combinations of things, sites, people, ideas and the rest are not permanently or intrinsically public: their construction as public matters involves political struggles to make them so. They may also be de-publicised, and de-politicised (taken out of recognisable public concern). (Newman and Clarke, 2009, p 2)

In the next section, we elaborate on four related dynamics of the emergence of publics that the chapters in this volume, taken together, draw into view as playing important roles in shaping the politics of public action.

Framing the analysis: personalising, representing, mediating, becoming

The contributions to this volume draw on a range of contemporary theoretical approaches from across the social sciences and each one engages with detailed empirical case analysis. The chapters present work on the 'new' media, on spatial configurations of power and on the transformations of governance as well as research based on queer theory, post-colonial theory and feminist theorisations of the reordering of public, private and personal. Read as a whole, there are four related themes that run across the chapters that, we would suggest, help orient future analysis of the reconfigurations of public life around understanding processes of emergence: the personalisation of publics; the processes of claims making and representation through which public action is articulated; the practices of mediation through which claims are assembled into publics; and the emphasis on publicness as a dynamic process of becoming.

Personalising publics

A recurrent theme across the chapters in this volume is that of the personalisation of public life. Most theorisations of the public focus on the distinction between the public and private – its history, validity and various forms (see Squires, 1994; Weintraub and Kumar, 1997; Guess, 2001; Staeheli and Mitchell, 2008). We pay particular attention in this volume to a more complex folding together of the public, the private and the personal. The concept of the personal cuts across any stark, binary framing of the public and private as opposed values. One of the contributions of feminist critical theories is to challenge the bracketing of personal issues as private ones, to be kept away from or sequestered from the properly sober, deliberative and rational conventions of the public realm (Young, 1990; Benhabib, 1996; Lister, 2003; Fung, 2004; Krause, 2008). These theoretical challenges, closely associated with the claims of so-called 'new' social movements, have brought matters such as sexuality, parenting, care and domestic violence into public view, making them objects of public debate and potentially at least of policy action. Such issues are addressed in this volume in various chapters. For example, in Chapter Ten, Simon Hutta analyses the articulation of rights claims by gay and lesbian activists in Brazil, involving the explicit politicisation of personal identities through various forms of informal and formal public action. Eleanor Jupp's analysis in Chapter Six focuses on the mobilisation of 'community' as a liminal space between public and private, highlighting the tacit and embedded forms of personal knowledge and their activation in engagement with governmental projects.

At the same time, the fracturing and proliferation of publics through the politicisation of personalised identities from 'below' has generated an increasing concern, an anxiety even, from 'above' to regulate and mobilise various personal capacities for the greater public good (see Clarke, 2004). Concern among politicians and policymakers with respecting and responding to the diverse needs of members of 'the public' reflects a shift in the rationalities of public policy towards the personal (van Berkel and Valkenburg, 2007; Needham, forthcoming); citizens are viewed less and less as passive pawns to be efficiently provided for and more and more as active queens able to express demands (see Le Grand, 2006). This confluence of bottom-up and top-down personalisation is addressed by Chapters Three and Seven. Chapter Seven examines the transformation of schooling in the UK in the last decade, showing how contrasting projects of personalisation and citizen education work with and against each other. Chapter Three examines how governmental projects seek to tap into personal capacities and everyday resources in seeking to address macro-policy issues of public health and childcare. In short, personalisation emerges from these chapters as a strategy for 'governing the social' (Newman, 2001; Rose, 2004; Clarke, 2007a), in which empowerment, engagement and participation are meant to be attuned and responsive to the diversity of personal capacities and needs of an inherently differentiated public.

The personalisation of publics, as it unfolds through the chapters in this volume, turns out to be a focus of contradiction and paradox. It marks the success of second-wave feminism's claims that 'the personal is political', bringing into view a series of claims to public attention around personalised issues and in personalised registers. But this is matched by an extension of the reach of state-directed public policy initiatives into the regulation of all sorts of facets of personal life. It is a feature of this latter trend that such initiatives are often framed around subject positions, such as the individual, the consumer or the community, that displace wider notions of public solidarity. Calls for concerted public action around, for example, improving 'school standards' or enhancing childcare provision are not necessarily made in the name of a singular public, nor straightforwardly meant to sustain a public sensibility.

Of course, the personalisation of public action that we have just touched on is not only a matter of a multiplication of the issues that are considered to be properly public objects of concern. This multiplication is related to, even emerges through, shifts in the mediums through which claims for public attention are articulated. Contemporary public spheres are shaped by a diverse range of emotional and affective registers. While this is not a wholly novel phenomenon, it is a mark of the fracturing (in both theory and practice) of unitary public spheres and the proliferation of multiple, overlapping publics (Young, 1990; Warner, 1991; Phillips, 1993). If publics are spoken of and spoken for in a range of personalised grammars and registers, this challenges the rational/irrational distinction that marks the separation of public and personal. It implies that public life might be becoming reconfigured around the image of the expressive subject capable of knowing its own interests and being able to effectively articulate them too. This brings us to the second theme running through the analysis of emergent publics in the chapters in this book: the processes of claims making through which publics are addressed, summoned and transformed.

Representing publics

Where a public is thought of as, or can be made to appear to be, a singular, collective entity, then speaking for and about it can seem straightforward, a matter of expressing its voice – the institutions of representative democracy necessarily depend on successfully pulling off this appearance. It is, of course, also the case that activists and campaigners have an interest in pulling off the same trick, of being able to elide the gap between the claims they make to express the interests of certain constituencies and the status of those claims as claims. This observation, by now standard in social and cultural theory, is not, it should be said, best understood as an epistemological conundrum or a disobliging attack on the scandal of speaking for others. Taking seriously the claims-making processes through which public action emerges and is sustained not only helps us to understand the irreducibility of representative practices to public formation, but also helps to transform the understanding of the concept of representation itself – understood now as an inherently performative process of fragile and imperfect claims making (Saward, 2006; Moss and O'Loughlin, 2008). This conception of representation as claims making is important for the understanding of emergent publics because it draws attention to the importance in many forms of public action of multiple practices of simultaneously giving voice to others by speaking in one's own voice – of claims of representativeness that might appeal to a basis in authentically embodying a particular identity, for sure, but might also take the form of giving testimony, or bearing witness, or simply being present in a public place. In short, we are suggesting that one thing that makes a wide diversity of communicative practices stand out as public actions – from mass mobilisations in public protests to individual contributions to 'vox pop' media events, new forms of citizen journalism enabled by the web and mobile phone, and the generation of survey data representing public opinion – is their performance as representative. That is, claims seek to embody, affirm, give voice to, bring to light, speak for and make visible particular issues, interests or identities in the hope of eliciting some form of response – whether of recognition and acknowledgement, or of more concerted action.

The chapters in this book evidence the range of forms that claims making takes in forming new publics and contesting the dimensions of existing publics. Such claims may take the form of unifying, expressive claims to give voice, hoping to forge relationships and identifications; they may be mobilising, provoking forms of social action; or they may be more justificatory, sustaining forms of authority for concerted public action (see Chapters Two and Nine of this volume). These claims may be made on behalf of marginalised, previously 'silenced' constituencies, as elaborated in Simon Hutta's analysis of queer activism in Brazil (Chapter Ten); they may be made on behalf of those deemed unable of speaking for themselves, such as future generations, the young (as in Jessica Pykett's account of educational governance in Chapter Seven), or those suffering unjust imprisonment and torture; and they may be made in the name of non-humans, such as endangered species, or, as in Chapter Eight, via the plural representation of fish in contested governance of natural resources. This latter dimension of claims making – the representation of and through non-human actors (Latour, 2005; Eckersley, 2009) – is important not least because it reminds us that processes of public representation necessarily pass through some medium or other.

Mediating publics

This brings us to the third theme running through the analysis of emergent publics in the chapters in this book: the importance of practices of mediation in summoning and assembling publics. Publics are put together through various combinations of devices, procedures, things and mediums (Latour and Weibel, 2005). This helps us put into perspective the much-discussed role of 'the media' in shaping and constituting publics. The chapters in this book underscore the importance of understanding the difference that the materialities of media practices make to public formation. So, for example, Chapter Four discusses how the classical role of the urban metropolitan newspaper as a public medium is being reconfigured by new assemblages of production and distribution technologies and the proliferation of new cultural technologies of dissemination – the web, iPods and mobile phones. Chapter Five brings a historical perspective to the same issue, showing how the medium of 'print' is embedded in different practices and sites of interaction, conjuring different publics that stretched from the urban through the colonial-national territory to the transnational. Chapter Two tracks how genre conventions drawn from a particular medium – whether that of a TV show, a participatory governance experiment or a social movement gathering – are translated across contexts with unpredictable consequences for the shapes and dimensions of publics addressed and assembled.

The volume as a whole demonstrates the significance of a range of mediating practices encompassing, but also stretching beyond, conventionally defined media. Richenda Gambles' analysis in Chapter Three of the personalisation of welfare rationalities focuses on the reconfiguration of state–citizen relationships made possible, in fact and fantasy, by web-based media. Chapter Eight focuses on a complex of institutional, organisation and technological mediation through which conflicts over 'European' public resources are worked through (cf Barry, 2001) and Chapter Nine unravels the complex relations of authorisation, delegation and naming involved in bringing into view a transnational public mobilised around issues of poverty alleviation. Thinking in terms of mediation broadly understood, rather than 'the media' narrowly understood, helps us understand how important media practices are to public formation while avoiding the trap of conflating 'the public sphere' with 'the media'.

Becoming public

The mediated aspect of publicness is closely related to the importance of processes of representation in constituting publics. The philosopher Jacques Derrida (1992, p 88) argues that 'the public' can show no sign of life 'without a certain medium'. 'The public', he argues, does not, cannot and should not be expected to speak in its own voice, in the first person. Rather, it is only cited, spoken for, ventriloquised. Or, to put it another way, publics are always in the making. Linking the distinctive reconfigurations of public representation to the acknowledgement of the importance of mediation in public formation brings us, then, to the final theme running through this volume: the sense that publics are formed through processes of becoming – that they are always emergent, rather than mere expressions of pre-existing interests, issues and identities. It is here that analytical attention might be best focused, and it is this emphasis on becoming and emergence that marks out this volume. Rather than using pre-existing models to evaluate the publicness of this or that new formation, or simply championing new formations as reinventing all the potential of the public sphere, the contributors to this volume attend closely to the events, practices and processes through which publics come into view, sustain themselves over time and extend themselves over space.

In so doing, they flesh out the argument sketched here that publics emerge around the problematisation of combinations of subjects, mediums and objects of action, care and concern. These subjects include new 'queer' identities (Chapter Ten) and children (Chapter Seven), distinctively collective identities like 'community' (Chapter Six) and complexes of global solidarity (Chapter Nine). Mediums include electronic and print modes of public address (Chapters Three and Four), socially and culturally differentiated print cultures (Chapter Five) and more or less deliberative forums, meetings and participatory experiments (Chapters Two and Six). Emergent objects of public action analysed here include new practices of care (Chapter Three), non-territorialised resources (Chapter Eight) and global poverty (Chapter Nine). These processes of becoming underpin each of our other themes, forming the integrating spine of the book.

Structure of the book

The chapters in this book are varied in their focus, but each aims to do three things. First, each offers a brief sketch of an empirical research study, and in doing so challenges normative conceptions of how publics should be mobilised or public issues addressed. As such, they offer important empirical and analytical resources for other researchers and help reframe the relationship between theory, methods and political engagement. Our contributors show how particular theories and methods help frame the topic concerned, bringing some frames into view but occluding others. They draw on a range of methodologies and theoretical resources, but rather than summarising these in a formal way (as for a PhD or refereed paper), the editors have encouraged them to experiment with writing in ways that draw connections between theory and evidence, using extracts or vignettes from their data to give a flavour of the empirical substance of their larger projects.

Second, each chapter is concerned with how publics are convened or summoned; how new objects of public action emerge; or how public action is itself mediated, and with what consequences. This concern with subjects, objects and mediums offers one framing for the book, with these categories cutting across and being themselves reworked in specific chapters. But it is important to note how these concerns have often flowed from the personal and political commitments of our contributors. The question of how to hang on to 'politics' while being engaged in research is partly answered by different forms of reflexivity offered by different contributors. But it is also evident in the theoretical resources on which they have drawn, resources that challenge an image of processes and their effects as finished projects – that mistake momentary forms as fixed formations. Such perspectives, we think, open up rather than close down the possibilities of continued engagement with the issues raised by their doctoral work.

Third, each chapter opens up important questions about the paradoxes at stake in attempts to rethink the politics of the public. Here we engage with dominant notions of both decline and proliferation; that is, we challenge the idea that the possibilities of public life have been erased by neoliberal logics that privilege individual subjects rather than foregrounding publics and publicness. But we also distance ourselves from over-optimistic and premature excitements about the proliferation of emergent publics made possible by web-based technologies and emergent political struggles. We seek to navigate our way through these pessimistic and optimistic narratives because they tend to suppress the political agency involved in emergent publics.

In Chapter Two, Nick Mahony begins from the normative proposition – in the Power enquiry of 2006 and elsewhere – that the polity and the public sphere are in crisis and that this crisis needs to be addressed through enhancing opportunities and modes of participation. In each of his three case studies (of a participative budgeting exercise, a TV game show and a social movement gathering), he shows how claims are made about the value of direct forms of participation over a discredited and unresponsive form of institutional politics.

In Chapter Three, Richenda Gambles provides an analysis of Mumsnet. She positions her study in claims about the value of web-based technologies to facilitate social interaction and thereby offer new forms of support to parents and parents-to-be, forms of support that reduce parental dependence both on professionals and on other family members. In the face of the presumed disembedding of women from traditional forms of family and community, there is a suggestion that new forms of community might be produced through online, peer-based interactions.

In Chapter Four, Scott Rodgers addresses the distinction between old and new media by exploring how new media technologies enter into the settings of supposedly 'old' media organisations. In focusing on how *Toronto Star* editors negotiated new forms of visual display and online technology, he highlights the tenuous practices and material settings that make up sites of public action, and in turn questions sweeping claims about the political potential of, or otherwise the threats posed by, new media.

Gurpreet Bhasin continues the theme of mediation in Chapter Five, showing how colonial publics emerged, functioned and were made effective in late 19th- and early 20th-century Delhi through print media. What were then 'new' media practices, she argues, served to create important links, networks and circuits of discussion, not only between British and Indian arenas, but also an emerging 'pan-Islamic' movement. Based on archival research, this chapter presents a gripping account of new voicings, silencings and conflicts.

In Chapter Six, Eleanor Jupp presents an enthnographic study of community activism in the UK, showing how local women and officials mediated the governmental turn to 'community' through their work with teenagers and their families. She situates her analysis in feminist critiques of the public/private dichotomy, suggesting how the changing context produces reconfigurations of public/private, male/female and state/citizen in the 'contact zones' and 'liminal spaces' worked by local activists.

In Chapter Seven, Jessica Pykett continues the analysis of changing configurations of UK governance, focusing on schooling as a site in which competing discourses are mediated by local professionals and through spatial practices. The drive towards personalisation re-imagines education as a personal goal rather than a public good. However when considered alongside current policy directives on citizenship education, the rationales, practices and effects become much less straightforward. Young people, she suggests, are constituted as private persons *and* as public citizens.

In Chapter Eight, Liza Griffin shifts the scale of analysis to the European Union's (EU) governance of global resources. She traces contestations over definitions of 'the public interest' in fisheries management, showing how publics (as subjects and objects) are summoned, convened and mediated. Her chapter draws our attention to the sustainability of part of the 'global commons' of natural resources, especially in the face of perceived crises. She shows how different stakeholders mobilised different claims to represent the public interest and how controversies over such claims tested the limits of the governance institutions of the EU.

In Chapter Nine, Clive Gabay takes as his focus global justice struggles and the possibility of progressive politics. His particular focus is on the Global Call to Action against Poverty, which, he suggests, comprises a multiplicity of public actors and objects. The contingent and unfixed qualities of any idea of an emerging global public produces problems of naming and categorising: the process of naming, he suggests, produces a premature fixity that fails to resolve the messiness of the publics who are summoned. He offers a stringent critique of the 'unthinking globality' that closes down any kind of relational and processual analysis.

In Chapter Ten, Simon Hutta explores the possibilities of political world making on the part of marginalised actors, focusing on the emergence of the lesbian, gay, transgender and bisexual movement in Brazil. He points to the heterogenous enactments of the 'first wave' of the gay movement, and to the conflicts and confrontations these later produced. He uses his account both to challenge the 'publics/counterpublics' distinction in the work of Fraser and Warner and to offer in their place the notion of 'paradoxical publics' and their generative potential.

The concluding chapter revisits the four themes we have introduced here – those of personalising, representing, mediating and becoming – and assesses what the volume as a whole contributes to the project of 'rethinking the public'.

Together, these chapters highlight innovations in research, theory and politics. The contributions offer an opportunity to rethink the public, public communication and public action in a post-national, globalising, digital and mediatised world, but a world in which new divisions and lines of inequality are becoming increasingly significant. Liza Griffin contributes to work on the global commons that cannot be contained within national boundaries or controlled by national governments, and that requires new transnational institutions and regulatory practices. Nick Mahony shows how images of the local, national and transnational speak to different publics, while Gurpreet Bhasin traces how nationalism, colonialism and pan-Islamism offered contested boundaries of the public sphere in colonial Delhi. Scott Rodgers highlights the importance of understanding the relationship between local milieu and the more widely distributed circulatory space that urban media inhabit. Clive Gabay traces the ways in which actors invoke global discourses and institutions when engaging in national politics. Richenda Gambles, Simon Hutta, Eleanor Jupp and Jessica Pykett demonstrate the importance of situated localised sites of practice as the scenes of mobilisation and national governance. The spatial imaginaries of publicness and public action are, it seems, being reconfigured; and as our contributors show, questions of identity and belonging, difference and diversity, and citizenship and cohesion continue to offer competing images and claims of public legitimacy.

Note

[1] For further information on this programme, see www.open.ac.uk/ccig/ programmes/publics and www.open.ac.uk/socialsciences/emergentpublics.

References

Alesina, A. and Glaeser, E. (2004) *Fighting poverty in the US and Europe*, Oxford: Oxford University Press.

Angus, I. (2001) *Emergent publics: An essay on social movements and democracy*, Winnipeg: Arbeiter Ring Publishing.

Barnes, M., Newman, J. and Sullivan, H. (2007) *Power, participation and political renewal: Case studies in public participation*, Bristol: The Policy Press.

Barnett, C. (2003) *Culture and democracy: Media, space and representation*, Edinburgh: Edinburgh University Press.

Barnett, C. (2008) 'Convening publics: the parasitical spaces of public action', in K. Cox, M. Low and J. Robinson (eds) *The Sage handbook of political geography*, London: Sage Publications, pp 403-17.

Barnett, C. (2009) 'Publics and markets: what's wrong with neoliberalism?', in S. Smith, R. Pain, S. Marston and J.P. Jones III (eds) *The Sage handbook of social geography*, London: Sage Publications, pp 269-96.

Barry, A. (2001) *Political machines: Governing a technological society*, London: Athlone Press.

Benhabib, S. (ed) (1996) *Democracy and difference: Contesting the boundaries of the political*, Princeton, NJ: Princeton University Press.

Calhoun, C. (1997) 'Plurality, promises, and public spaces', in C. Calhoun and J. McGowan (eds) *Hannah Arendt and the meaning of politics*, Minneapolis, MN: University of Minnesota Press, pp 232-59.

Carrel, M., Neveu, C. and Ion, J. (2009) *Les Intermittencies de la démocratie formes d'action et visibilités citoyennes dans la ville*, Paris: L'Harmattan.

Clarke, J. (2004) 'Dissolving the public realm? The logic and limits of neo-liberalism', *Journal of Social Policy*, 33(1), pp 27-48.

Clarke, J. (2007a) 'Introduction governing the social', *Cultural Studies*, 21(6), pp 837-47.

Clarke, J. (2007b) 'Diversity versus solidarity? Social divisions and post welfare societies', Paper presented at the TISSA conference on 'Migration, minorities and refugees: social work under conditions of diversity', Messina, Sicily, August 28-31.

Clarke, J., Newman, J., Smith, N., Vidler, E. and Westmarland, L. (2007) *Creating citizen-consumers: Changing publics and changing public services*, London: Sage Publications.

Derrida, J. (1992) *The other heading*, Bloomington, IN: Indiana University Press.

Devine, P., Pearman, A. and Purdy, D. (eds) (2009) *Feelbad Britain*, London: Lawrence and Wishart.

Dewey, J. (1927) *The public realm and its problems*, New York, NY: Henry Holt and Company.

Diamond, P., with Public Service Reform Group (ed) (2007) *Public matters: The renewal of the public realm*, London: Methuen.

Drache, D. (2008) *Defiant publics: The unprecedented reach of the global citizen*, Cambridge: Polity Press.

Dryzek, J. (2006) *Deliberative global politics: Discourse and democracy in a divided world*, Cambridge: Polity Press.

Eckersley, R. (in press) 'Representing nature', in S. Alonso, J. Keane and W. Merkel (eds) *The future of representative democracy*, Cambridge: Cambridge University Press.

Fraser, N. (2007) 'Transnationalizing the public sphere: on the legitimacy and efficacy of public opinion in a post-Westphalian world', *Theory, Culture and Society*, 24(4), pp 7-30.

Fung, A. (2004) 'Deliberation's darker side: six questions for Iris Marion Young and Jane Mansbridge', *National Civic Review*, Winter, pp 47-54.

Geuss, R. (2001) *Public goods, private goods*, Princeton, NJ: Princeton University Press.

Habermas, J. (1989) *The structural transformation of the public sphere*, Cambridge: Polity Press.

Iveson, K. (2007) *Publics and the city*, Oxford: Blackwell.

Krause, S. (2008) *Civil passions: Moral sentiment and democratic deliberation*, Princeton, NJ: Princeton University Press.

Latour, B. (2005) *Reassembling the social: An introduction to actor-network theory*, Oxford: Oxford University Press.

Latour, B. and Weibel, P. (eds) (2005) *Making things public*, Cambridge, MA: MIT Press.

Lawson, N. (2009) *All consuming*, London: Compass.

Le Grand, J. (2006) *Motivation, agency and public policy*, Oxford: Oxford University Press.

Leadbeater, C. (2008) *We-think: The power of mass creativity*, London: Profile Books.

Lister, R. (2003) *Citizenship: Feminist perspectives* (2nd edn), Basingstoke: Palgrave Macmillan.

Marquand, D. (2004) *Decline of the public*, Cambridge: Polity Press.

Marres, N. (2005) 'Issues spark a public into being: a key but often forgotten point of the Lippmann-Dewey debate', in B. Latour and P. Weibel (eds) *Making things public*, Cambridge, MA: MIT Press, pp 208-17.

Mooney, G. and Neal, S. (eds) (2009) *Community: Welfare, crime and society*, Maidenhead: Open University Press.

Moss, G. and O'Loughlin, B. (2008) 'Convincing claims? Representation and democracy in post-9/11 Britain', *Political Studies*, 56(3), pp 705-24.

Needham, C. (2003) *Citizen-consumers: New Labour's marketplace democracy*, London: Catalyst Forum.

Needham, C. (forthcoming) *Personalising public services*, Bristol: The Policy Press.

Neveu, C. (ed) (2007) *Cultures et pratiques participative: Perspectives comparatives*, Paris: L'Hartmann.

Newman, J. (2001) *Modernising governance: New Labour, policy and society*, London: Sage Publications.

Newman, J. (2006) 'Restating a politics of the public', *Soundings: A Journal of Politics and Culture*, 32, pp 162-76.

Newman, J. and Clarke, J. (2009) *Publics, politics and power: Remaking the public in public services*, London: Sage Publications.

Phillips, A. (1993) *Democracy and difference*, Pennsylvania, PA: Pennsylvaina University Press.

Robins, S. (2005) *Rights passages from 'near death' to 'new life': AIDS activism and treatment testimonies in South Africa*, IDS Working Paper 251, Brighton: Institute for Development Studies.

Rose, N. (2004) 'Governing the social', in N. Gane (ed) *The future of social theory*, London: Continuum International Publishing Group, pp 167-85.

Saward, M. (2006) 'The representative claim', *Contemporary Political Theory*, 5(3), pp 297-318.

Squires, J. (1994) 'Private lifes, secluded places: privacy as political possibility', *Environment and Planning D: Society and Space*, 12, pp 387-401.

Staeheli, L.A and Mitchell, D. (2007) *The people's property: Power, politics, and the Public*, New York, NY: Routledge.

van Berkel, R. and Valkenburg, B. (2007) *Making it personal: Individualising activation services in the EU*, Bristol: The Policy Press.

Warner, M. (1991) 'The mass public and the mass subject', in C. Calhoun (ed) *Habermas and the public sphere*, Cambridge, MA: MIT Press, pp 377-401.

Warner, M. (2002) *Publics and counterpublics*, New York, NY: Zone Books.

Weintraub, J. and Kumar, K. (eds) (1997) *Public and private in thought and practice*, Chicago, IL: University of Chicago Press.

Young, I.M. (1990) *Justice and the politics of difference*, Princeton, NJ: Princeton University Press.

TWO

Mediating the publics of public participation experiments

Nick Mahony

Public engagement experiments are currently proliferating. State-commissioned experiments have included citizens' juries, citizens' councils, deliberative polls and consensus conferences; media experiments have used 'voting' and plebiscites in many different kinds of television programmes or entailed the creation of online political 'games'; social movement practitioners have experimented with the orchestration of translocal political events and used internet technologies to help cultivate temporary alliances for bursts of political activism. These and many other apparently novel approaches to public engagement are already being investigated by researchers concerned with either state, media or social movement politics (see, for example, Barnes et al, 2007 and Goodin, 2008 for an exploration of state experiments; for media experiments, see, for example, Livingstone, 2005 and Riegert, 2007; for social movement experiments, see, for example, Holloway, 2002 and de Sousa Santos, 2007). While rigorous and extensive, this scholarship has not so far compared different kinds of experimentation and therefore explored relationships of similarity and difference between these forms of emerging practice. This gap in the literature is significant: state, media and social movement practices have not so far been viewed as part of a single extended field of practice and the emergent properties of this field have not so far been investigated. As experiments increasingly compete with each other for people's attention, the task of comparing how different experiments across different domains are designed, mediated and participated in becomes more important. And as boundaries between state, media and social movement practices and the publics that they appeal to become less easy to discern, so it becomes more important to study these dynamics and their effects.

Practices that work to engage and involve publics as participants in politics are not in themselves novel. However, with the legitimacy and authority of voting, elections and institutional politics on the wane (Mair, 2006; Stoker, 2006; Hay, 2007), it is becoming increasingly important to research new sites and ways of mobilising people as political actors – especially if contemporary transformations in politics and forms of public action are to be understood and engaged with.

The PhD (Mahony, 2008) on which this chapter draws was designed to begin to address this issue by investigating public participation experiments instigated by state, media and social movement actors in order to explore and compare how publics are brought into being by different kinds of participative events. Drawing on this research, this chapter highlights the ways in which three different contemporary experiments have enacted forms of public participation to interrupt certain pre-existing forms of institutional politics. Pinpointing some of the different forms of public conduct that were privileged during these different experiments, the chapter highlights how the apparently 'new' publics of these experiments were actually called up by invoking various pre-existing norms of public action.

It is useful to introduce the three experiments that were investigated for this research before continuing any further. Harrow Open Budget was a local government event promoted as a kind of participatory budgeting experiment that would involve the public directly rather than via established representative channels. Convened in Harrow's municipal leisure centre on a Sunday afternoon in October 2005, 250 residents were enrolled to discuss topics including social care, traffic congestion and waste management. Participants were arrayed in groups of 10 around banqueting tables and provided with refreshments, facilitators and wireless key-pads. After each of the five 30-minute policy discussions, participants were invited to use their key-pads to vote on different pre-constituted policy 'options' with music and lighting effects used to signal the beginning and end of 10-second bouts of public polling.

Vote for Me was a popular media experiment commissioned by the broadcaster ITV in the run-up to the 2005 UK general election. It set out to find an 'ordinary' member of the UK public to stand for Parliament in the 2005 general election; at the peak of its popularity, this week-long, week-night serial attracted an audience of over a million people. The aim of this show, according to one of its press releases, was to renew the UK's parliamentary democracy by offering the British people a new, more accessible and more relevant way of engaging with politics. Inspired by the popularity of shows such as X Factor and Pop Idol, the programme featured a panel of 'expert' judges and invited contestants to participate in a sequence of challenges designed to test their capacities as potential MPs. During the 'live' finals, viewers were offered the opportunity to vote for, and ultimately decide on, who should be supported to stand in the next general election. Seven finalists were whittled down via a series of viewer polls over the series of four 30-minute programmes, with the winner of this election announced in the final climactic moments of the show's fifth and final episode.

The third participative experiment that was explored for this research was the 4th European Social Forum. This was convened by a multiplicity of European social movement organisations and activists and attracted approximately 20,000 participants. The event took place over four days and nights in May 2006 in a sprawling conference centre facility in the suburbs of Athens, Greece. A festival atmosphere was created on this site with a programme of over 280 themed political seminars and workshops and 100 cultural activities. In common with other Social Forum ventures, this event was ambitious in that it was explicitly set up to challenge hierarchical forms of organisation and to challenge various forms of social, economic, political and cultural inequality. The overall aim, according to the publicity material, was to facilitate collective resistance and generate alternatives to 'neoliberal' forms of globalisation.

These initiatives are apparently quite distinct. Their publicity materials held out the possibility of interrupting rather different pre-existing forms of institutional politics; they offered prospective participants different ways of conducting themselves as a public; and they set out to challenge different established norms of public action. Two other crucial differences were also evident. Each privileged a different scalar imaginary of politics – ranging from 'local' to 'national' to 'translocal' or 'transnational'; and the substance of the political aims that were related to each experiment were also rather different. But the aim of this chapter is to draw out potential *similarities* by exploring the mediating practices that shaped the outcomes of each event. The chapter draws attention to mediating practices inherent in the publicity materials through which publics were summoned (section one); to the processes of convening and facilitating 'new' publics (section two); and to the translation work of participants themselves (section three).

In trying to make sense of these different practices, I turned to a range of literatures. The first section of the chapter draws on the work of literary and public sphere theorist Michael Warner (2002) to illuminate the some of the more contradictory qualities of the publics summoned up through publicity materials. Section two uses the work of sociologists of experimentation to reflect on the particular forms these events took and on the practices of facilitation. Finally, section three uses scholarship on 'translation' to examine how people interacted during the bouts of participation that were opened up during each event.

Recognising the publics of participative experiments

Rather than presume that the publics of the events discussed in this chapter somehow already existed, my research set out to explore the practices, processes and relations through which their publics were brought into being. The work of Michael Warner (2002) underpinned this approach. For Warner:

> A public might be real and efficacious, but its reality lies in just this reflexivity by which an addressable object is conjured into being in order to enable the very discourse which gives it existence. (Warner, 2002, p 67)

As Barnett (2008) notes, Warner's theory of public action underscores the temporality of public-making processes and how such processes depend for their success on establishing and re-establishing 'relations of anticipation, projection, response and reply' (2008, p 9). According to Warner, public-making processes should not be understood primarily in technical terms but rather as *poetic*:

> Public discourse says not only "Let a public exist" but "Let it have this character, speak this way, see the world this way". Then it goes

> in search of confirmation that such a public exists, with a greater or
> lesser success – success being further attempts to cite, circulate and
> realize the world understanding it articulates. Run it up the flagpole
> and see who salutes. Put on a show and see who shows up. (Warner,
> 2002, p 114)

For Warner, two postulates enable all public-making projects. The first is that
public-making projects must be based on some kind of shared social base that
prospective participants share. Only then can a public initiative locate and address
its public as a social entity. A social base may be a shared social space or habitas,
a shared topical concern or simply a pre-existing communicative genre or form
held in common by a particular group. It is the process of designating some kind
of shared social base that enables public confidence in a performance, confidence
that a public will relate to something real and will move along a 'real path'.

Public-making processes, if they are to work, must also promise to enable
forms of self-organisation and participation. This is the second of Warner's two
enabling postulates.

> Whether faith is justified or partly ideological, a public can only
> produce a sense of belonging and activity if it is self-organized [...]
> Belonging to a public seems to require at least minimal participation,
> even if it is patient or notional, rather than a permanent state of being.
> (2002, pp 70-1)

There are considerable tensions between Warner's two postulates. Such tensions are,
he argues, inherent to public-making processes and are actually *constitutive* of these
forms of action. Indeed, Warner's claim is that it is actually the inherent instability
of these entities that lends them their generative potential. These instabilities lend
public-making projects an unpredictability and ambivalence, leading Warner to
characterise publics as 'an engine for (not necessarily progressive) social mutation'
(2002, p 113). Warner's framework was immensely useful for understanding the
qualities of the publics summoned in the three public participation experiments
investigated in this chapter. His theory of public action offered a way of accounting
for the apparently contradictory ideas of the public that were found circulating
in the publicity materials. On the one hand, each event's publicity promised that
these experiments would allow participants to self-organise and direct politics
for themselves. On the other hand, these materials also related and aligned each
event to various pre-existing organisations, sets of ongoing public projects, specific
pre-constituted political aims and already-familiar forms of public conduct.

For example, the publicity material of Harrow Open Budget suggested that this
experiment would bring a form of politics into being that would be conducted
on the public's own terms. The material used informal and vernacular forms of
rhetoric, promoting an anti-elitist standpoint. It also alluded to the possibility
that this experiment would facilitate bottom-up, spontaneous and indeterminate

forms of political organisation. 'It's *your* money, it's *your* Harrow – have *your* say' (italics in original), the text on the website exclaimed.

Using statistics to support the idea that electoral politics in Britain was suffering from a crisis of legitimacy, Vote for Me's publicity cast the viewing public as a sovereign political actor. It promised an experiment that would give them *direct* access to the political process by offering UK citizens the opportunity to select an 'ordinary' person to stand as a prospective parliamentary candidate. It stressed that volunteers wishing to take part in this political talent contest would 'only be eligible if they have no affiliation with any political party that qualifies for election broadcasts'. The material invoked the idea that this experiment would somehow be 'authentic' and 'untainted' because it would outlaw any contestants taking part who had formal party political allegiances.

The 4th European Social Forum was an experiment that also appealed to a public that was apparently not represented by more established institutions or career politicians. This time, however, rather than being a local or national public, the public that was summoned was translocal, transnational and global. It was a public with a loosely associated set of political ideals and positions – anti-war, anti-imperialist, environmentalist, anti-neoliberal, feminist, egalitarian, libertarian – that was simply in need of a forum through which to plan and conduct self-organised forms of political action.

Despite how each event's publicity emphasised the need for public autonomy, each also affiliated and thereby aligned these processes to particular pre-existing organisations, institutions and sets of already established political aims and projects. The Harrow Open Budget experiment was related to the project of making the local council's pre-existing public policy framework more effective in practice. Vote for Me was presented as a way of reinvigorating and re-legitimising pre-existing modes of parliamentary politics. The 4th European Social Forum assembled a particular constellation of already-established social movement organisers and was shaped by pre-existing projects and forms of political agency.

My research therefore found that the publicity material for each event held out the possibility of two, contradictory-feeling, forms of public action: one that was self-directed, spontaneous and therefore indeterminate; and one guided by pre-existing organisations and geared towards developing already-ongoing public projects and pre-constituted sets of political aims. For the purposes of analysis, it was useful to disentangle and distinguish these two forms of public action. In the publicity material itself, however, these ideas were interwoven, articulated with one another and even fused.

One of the ways that such interweaving was traceable was in the *naming* of these initiatives. So, for example, the name 'Vote for Me' works to interweave ideas from two different lexicons, one continuous with the practices of representative democracy ('Vote') and one summoning up an interruption of these conventions by naming 'Me' as the autonomous subject around which representative processes need to be organised. These two ideas of political organisation were also articulated in the *forms of practice* that were privileged. One theme was that of the importance of adapting pre-existing practices. In publicity for the 4th European Social Forum, for example, social movement actors were encouraged to pursue and extend the pre-existing agendas and ideas of these groups. But there was also an emphasis in these same materials on autonomous action and on the need to transcend prior commitments and allegiances through intensive bouts of inter-personal interaction. When it came to summoning up particular *roles* for participants, different understandings of political organisation were fused. In the case of Harrow Open Budget, for example, publicity cast prospective participants as independent and capable of self-organisation *and* as actors mobilised to take forward pre-constituted sets of ideas and established forms of practice. Despite being interwoven, articulated and fused in these and other ways, considerable tensions remained between the ways in which publics were addressed and the ideas of public action promised. However, thinking with Warner, the coexistence of these apparently distinct forms of address and action can be recognised as constitutive of the public appeal, make-up and forms of enactment offered by each experiment.

What my analysis shows is the presence of Warner's two 'enabling postulates' in each of these experiments. Despite the differences between each event – in the publics summoned, the form of politics espoused and the spatial and temporal dynamics – this has enabled me to highlight commonalities in the mediation work performed by the publicity materials associated with each event. Each set of publicity material interwove, articulated and fused two apparently contradictory ideas of public action while, at the same time, summoning up and appealing to publics with very different sets of characteristics.

Convening and facilitating participative experiments

The focus on publicity materials in the previous section offered one dimension of my analysis of mediating practices. To investigate how the three events described above were actually convened and facilitated in practice, I then conducted bouts of participant observation research in each setting. This was analysed using the work of scholars concerned with the sociology of experimental practice.

Millo and Lezaun (2006) suggest that to construct an event as an experiment first requires a gap to be marked out between what its inside and what its outside is. To do this, boundaries are put in place that differentiate between the complexity of the world 'outside' and what is part of, or 'internal' to, the experiment itself (2006, pp 181-2). Through these means, what is marked as 'external' to the experiment can be lent the status of turbulence, interference or noise. In the case of the political experiments that are the focus of this chapter, it is evident that boundaries were put in place to construct each experiment as a self-contained event. For example, these demarcation practices rendered each place specific and time limited. They could then be constituted as experimental enclaves for new ways of doing things – enclaves for innovation temporarily bound off from the norms of conventional politics and the routines of everyday life.

The Harrow Open Budget experiment was enacted over the course of a Sunday afternoon in the borough's municipal sports hall, in a location detached both from the local town hall and from participants' own homes. It was designed as a high-tech meeting space, very different from conventional public meetings and similar in some respects to a contemporary ask-the-audience-type game show. Vote for Me was fronted by Jonathan Maitland, a presenter with a history in consumer affairs programmes. The line-up of 'expert judges' selected for this programme comprised John Sergeant, Kelvin McKenzie and Lorraine Kelly – media figures who have each built their reputation on their capacity to relate to 'ordinary people'. Contestants were also showcased in a studio that was more Pop Idol than Question Time, with all of these presentational strategies working to constitute this experiment as an extraordinary event: a television experiment different from traditional institutional politics as well as an event that promised to interrupt viewers' ordinary everyday routines and roles. The 4th European Social Forum took place in a very large conference complex that could assemble approximately 20,000 people drawn from a myriad of activist groups on a single site. This signalled that this experiment was different from institutional politics as practised by political parties and organisations such as the International Monetary Fund or G8 and also different from single-issue social movement politics. The design of the assembly enabled participants to come together and to pursue many different activities and ways of participating in parallel, from political seminars to music concerts, and from networking events to film screenings. The event was set up to showcase the unity *and* the diversity of those enrolled as participants.

When it came to exploring the sets of organisational practices used to facilitate and mediate bouts of participative activity in each setting, the two distinct and apparently contradictory ideas of public action that were invoked in each event's publicity were once more in evidence, though again interwoven, articulated and fused in distinct ways in each setting. This finding highlighted further similarities between the processes and practices used to construct each event. Comparing the ways in which each experiment was convened and facilitated enabled me to highlight evidence of a similarly structured and sequenced three-phase facilitation process. Phase one comprised *naming and framing*. In each case, naming and framing practices specified some of the basic characteristics of the experiment, including the organisations or groups that would be involved, where participation would take place, how much time would be given for participation, how participation would be managed, the number of participants who would be able to take part, and crucially, the task or topic around which these activities would be oriented. In Harrow Open Budget, for example, naming and framing practices worked to specify that bouts of public policy discussion would last no more than 30 minutes and would take place in the main sports hall of Harrow's municipal leisure centre around banqueting tables in groups of no more than 10 people. Naming and framing practices also specified that there would be five main bouts of discussion and that each of these would be geared to the discussion of particular 'local' public policy topics such as 'waste management', 'traffic congestion' and 'social care'.

A facilitation guide specified that a participant's role was to 'listen', 'respect' the opinions of others, 'talk honestly' and act as if they had been 'nominated to speak on behalf of the wider community' (Harrow Open Budget Discussion Guide, 25 October 2005). Similar naming and framing practices were found in each of the other two experiments.

The second phase of these facilitative regimes comprised *participation work*. While they differ considerably, in each experiment multiple public performances were enacted through such work, with different roles and scripts for different performers. In the Vote for Me experiment, for example, participation work entailed either performing as a competitor or as a viewer. During this series of five nightly programmes, viewers were asked to assess contestants' performances, to consider their potential and to elect their preferred candidate via a series of telephone polls. In the process, contestants were invited to perform variously as 'authentic', 'ordinary' and 'representative' members of the UK public and as 'professional', 'credible' and potentially effective Members of Parliament.

The third and final phase of these facilitative regimes invited participants to *generate results, conclusions and endings*. In each setting, this entailed participants generating forms of closure that would round off bouts of participative activity. Again, this varied in each experiment; in the Harrow and Vote for Me experiment, this took the form of the declaration of 'results', while in the 4th European Social Forum event, participants were invited to negotiate a series of 'next steps' with one another, thus consolidating what had been either agreed (or disagreed) on during a particular participative session. On other occasions, this simply involved participants sharing contact details to facilitate further networking and action planning.

At each of the three phases described above, those who were enrolled or summoned as participants were invited both to self-organise and, at the same time, invited to work towards the realisation of pre-constituted public projects. In common with other forms of public experimentation (Barry, 1998), these processes appealed to participants by offering them sensory, embodied and performative as well as more argumentative forms of interactive practice. All of these processes entailed forms of projection. However, according to Pinch (1993, p 28), all experiments are preceded by forms of projection – projections not only about how practices are likely to work but also about what people's desires and capacities are. These projections were different in each case. Harrow Open Budget was an experiment that tested participants' desire and capacity to work as a public in collaboration with its council on the task of thinking through and deciding on local public policy and budgetary priorities. Vote for Me tested the desire and capacity of the viewing public to use a particular reality television format to select a prospective parliamentary candidate from 'ordinary' members of the UK population. The 4th European Social Forum, meanwhile, tested participants' desire and capacity to resist and generate alternatives to 'neoliberal' globalisation via a four-day event. 'Black boxing' is the name that Pinch (1993) and others (see for example Latour, 1987) have given to practices that freeze certain kinds of projected human action into technologies or other kinds of material practice. In the context of the public experiments being analysed here, black boxing could be used to describe how a range of different forms of projected participant action were frozen into the facilitative designs that were used to organise and manage these events.

This section has brought to the fore some of the ways that organisational practices and facilitative designs were used to manage three public participation experiments. The mediation work performed by these practices is significant for a number of reasons: it marked out certain places and moments for publics to convene for participative events; it interwove, articulated and fused invitations to enact apparently contradictory forms of public action; it foregrounded particular objects of public concern, and privileged certain forms of conduct and public subjectivity.

Public interactions

As well as investigating the publicity material and the assembly design of each experiment, my research also generated material that allowed participants' interactions to be analysed. In the case of Harrow Open Budget and Vote for Me, I drew on transcripts of verbatim interactions, while in the case of the European Social Forum, I relied on my experience as participant observer.

When it came to exploring this material, it was helpful to draw on literature on *translation*. In contemporary linguistics, Steiner (1998) has used the idea of translation to describe the creative and interpretative work that is implicit in every act of communication. Communication, for Steiner, is not about the transfer of ideas but is instead an act that is inventive and even transformative. Sociologists Bourdieu and Wacquant (1992) use the idea of translation to underline how webs of social relations and the authority of different translators affect communication. Another influential group of scholars within the discipline of science and technology studies uses translation to characterise the processes through which actors bring ideas and/or objects into relation to one another. Such practices, according to Callon, inevitably entail 'mutual definition and inscription' (1991, p 143) with mediators therefore being any actors with the capacity to 'translate' and 'redefine' (Latour, 1993, p 81).

In the context of my research, the idea that participants acted as translators captures some of the creative ways that they performed and responded to the boundaries that had been set. When faced with situations that summoned them to act in specified ways or to work with pre-defined ideas, they were observed translating and negotiating these injunctions in a multiplicity of inventive and sometimes transformative ways. This is not to say that anything was possible or to say that all of the interactions that were observed were always benign or 'progressive'. During Harrow Open Budget, my transcript showed that participants expressed a wide range of views about the sets of pre-constituted policy options that they were presented with and asked to choose between. Analysis of the discussion highlighted some of the ways in which participants elaborated, critiqued and proposed alternatives to these options. For example, they contested many of the underlying assumptions that were inscribed into the pre-constituted options and sought to relate what were presented (for example, in discussion of waste management policies) as 'local' policy issues to broader national and even global political debates. In these and other ways, the framing of the policy 'options' that they were invited to discuss was frequently questioned and challenged. Many of those enrolled as participants also went on to propose alternative policy options that were quite different from those they were originally invited to discuss.

The transcript of Vote for Me also showed participants contesting the ideas of the public that were privileged in this event's publicity and design. On several occasions, for example, candidates seeking public support contested the authority of the Vote for Me process either by attacking the impartiality of the judges or by questioning the transparency of its editorial approach. The eventual outcome of this exercise also unsettled some of the assumptions about the public that were mobilised in this event's publicity. Rodney Hylton-Potts won on a platform of policies that included promises to end all UK immigration and to castrate all those convicted of paedophile offences. His election (through a public vote) challenged the idea that those participating in this experiment, either as contestants or viewers, would somehow necessarily be more benign and progressive than either career politicians or mainstream political parties.

The 4th European Social Forum, in common with other Social Forum activities, was particularly ambitious in that it was explicitly set up as an experiment that aimed to challenge – through the very enactment of the event itself – political relations of domination and subordination that pertain in the world 'outside'. One way it tried to do this was by offering participants opportunities to organise and convene meetings around campaigns or topics that they were particularly active in or interested in pursuing with others. Simultaneous translation facilities were also on offer so that no one language had a privileged status during Social Forum meetings. Compared with the other experiments, a large amount of time was also set aside for open discussion. On many occasions, these meetings were observed to be working well, offering opportunities for robust discussions, the formulation of proposals and agreements for future collaborations between different participants. However, the boundaries of this apparently open and creative space were also challenged as participants tussled over what a principle of participative equality should mean in practice. During one meeting, for example, participants debated the political effectiveness of bouts of open-ended dialogue in the face of conflicts such as the wars in Iraq and Afghanistan and the threat of global warming. As a result, some called for a stronger and more institutionally unified form of Social Forum leadership and for a system of collective representation. Responding to such challenges, other participants defended the Social Forum ethos. These were passionate about the value of continuing to use the Forum to attempt to work with and through differences in a participative and inclusive way. A tension was therefore evident between vanguardist and rather more pluralist tendencies. Such conflict points to some of the different understandings of public action that were circulating; however, they also foreground the active work of translation (of the meaning of equality, of norms of public debate and so on) in this setting.

What my research highlights is how those acting as participants in these experiments become mediators and translators during the bouts of interaction that they were engaged in, negotiating forms of action within the parameters of each event. They actively translated and thereby sometimes transformed the ideas and injunctions that they were presented with during these experiments. This indicates that alongside understanding mediation as a form of practice enacted by different kinds of organisations through their publicity materials, facilitation practices and technologies, mediation also needs to be understood as a creative activity on the part of those enrolled as participants.

Conclusion

The research drawn on in this chapter investigated, close up and in detail, the practices and processes through which the publics of three contemporary participative experiments were brought into being. Investigating these experiments as events, I have shown the value of paying attention to the mediating role of publicity materials, facilitative practices and participants' own interactions. This approach opened up the possibility of comparing the ideas of public action, the notions of the political and the projections of participants' desires and capacities in three experiments that were, ostensibly at least, very different. This approach also allowed participants' interactions to be explored, opening up the possibility of analysing how participants negotiated, via processes of translation, the apparently contradictory ideas of public action in circulation in each event.

Despite their apparent differences – one a governmental initiative, one a media event and one a social movement gathering – I have shown how this research brings into view affiliations between the processes of summoning, performance and translation enacted in each setting. Each was constituted as an interruption to a particular form of pre-existing institutional or organisational politics. The three experiments were not cast in their publicity materials as supplements to pre-existing political processes, but rather as showcases for entirely new and more publicly responsive ways of conducting politics. However, once we follow Warner and recognise publics as 'fictional', publics cannot be assumed to be entities that are simply waiting to be called on, mobilised and brought to voice. If publics are instead understood as entities that must be summoned into existence and then channelled, the constitution, performance and voice of these entities – what I have termed processes of mediation – become a matter of struggle. Mediation processes, in public participation events and elsewhere, are significant because they work to shape the publics and the forms of politics that are (and are not) enacted during these events. The matter of how publics are constituted, how they perform and what they do and say, and what 'new' politics actually means, is a matter of intense social and political contestation across this field.

Each experiment worked hard to bring into being particular forms of public conduct, with each doing this in the name of particular versions of the public good. All three made strong normative claims about the value of public participation in the face of an assumed crisis of institutional politics. However, each of the three brought to the fore rather different political agendas. In each case, tensions arose as a result of participants being required to enact forms of self-organisation and, at the same time, to have regard for already-ongoing public projects.

Other contemporary studies have shown how participative experiments work through, and in relation with, norms and expectation linked to pre-existing milieus (Baiocchi, 2003; Davies et al, 2006; Barnes et al, 2007). My contribution here is to further substantiate the idea that publics are not free-floating entities. The publics called on and brought into being by the experiments discussed were presumed to already have strong connections and allegiances to different already-existing webs of social relations, political projects and forms of conduct. At the same time, however, I have shown how the public subjects called on to participate were also presumed to have the desire to self-organise, act autonomously and perform politics in ways that were not predetermined in advance of bouts of public participation. By comparing how these tensions were played out in apparently very different settings, my research raises questions about the divisions of public labour inscribed in different participative experiments. More research will be needed to identify, compare and evaluate mediating practices in a range of other sites; however, what I have done here is to begin to map, describe and reflect on how it is possible to mediate relations of public authority through different kinds of experimental events.

What focusing on mediation does is draw attention to the contingency of different kinds of experiments and, especially, the unpredictability of participants' translation practices. The significance of this research is therefore not simply that it highlights the heterogeneity of the contemporary field of public participation experiments, but, rather more importantly, it also shows that such experiments are unlikely to result in a single technical fix to the 'problem' of how to involve (plural) publics in public governance and politics more generally. If this research underscores the idea that the constitution of publics and the constitution of politics are both matters of intense struggle, with the legitimacy and authority of established forms of institutional politics apparently on the wane, the forms that participative experiments take are likely to continue to diversify.

Mediation, in this chapter, has referred to much more than the issue of which media are deployed in these settings. What are conventionally referred to as 'the media' are, of course, significant (see Chapters Four and Five in this volume). But my use of the term 'mediation' denotes the mediating role of ideas and facilitative practices; the mediating role of those enrolled as participants themselves as they engage in creative processes of translation; and the mediation work that establishes (or re-establishes) relationships between publics and pre-existing 'authorities'. As experiments of the kind explored here continue to claim to be able to engender forms of political renewal, so it will become more and more important to be able to recognise and engage with the politics of these forms of public mediation. Looking across this field of practice, this will mean continuing to ask questions such as who is testing or trying to demonstrate what through these kinds of experiments; who is learning from these events; how the boundaries to the events are fixed (and transgressed); how the 'results' of these experiments are generated and disseminated; and what the repetition of experiments of this kind might be working to pre-figure.

The participative experiments that have been highlighted here hint at the possible emergence of novel ways of performing public accountability and political inclusion. If publics are understood as entities that can potentially be summoned up and enacted in an infinite variety of ways, these experiments cannot be dismissed simply on the basis that they do not include some kind of 'representative' sample of 'the public'. There simply is no single way of representing the public. Representations are 'claimed' (Saward, 2006), new forms of democracy are 'enacted' (Saward, 2003). The question of how a legitimate public needs be constituted (its size, geography, characteristics, capacities, desires, the resources that need to be made available to it if it is to participate effectively) for it to have political authority is one that is currently being tussled over through precisely the kind of experiment I have considered here (see also Chapters Nine and Ten in this volume).

A further challenge for researchers concerned with these developments will be that of finding ways to distinguish 'progressive' from more 'reactionary' participative experiments. Or, put another way, to differentiate between benign and malign public summonings and performances. Meeting this challenge will entail continuing to try to develop ways of mapping, comparing and analysing the distinct but interrelated forms of mediation enacted by different kinds of public participation experiments. It will also entail continuing to develop approaches that bring empirical material into relation with debates in contemporary normative theory.

It is inevitable that I, as a researcher, am also a mediator in conducting academic work of this kind, and thus take on a public role (Bourdieu, 1988, 1990), however small. My personal aim as an aspiring researcher in this field is to help fashion a progressive politics of public mediation.

References

Baiocchi, G. (2003) 'Emergent public spheres: talking politics in participatory governance', *American Sociological Review*, 68(1), pp 52–74.

Barnes, H., Newman, J. and Sullivan, H. (2007) *Power, participation and political renewal*, Bristol: The Policy Press.

Barnett, C. (2008) 'Convening publics: the parasitical spaces of public action', in K. Cox, M. Low and J. Robinson (eds) *The Sage handbook of political geography*, London: Sage Publications, pp 403–17.

Barry, A. (1998) 'On interactivity: consumers, citizens and culture', in S. MacDonald (ed) *The politics of display: Museums, science, culture*, London: Routledge, pp 98–117.

Bourdieu, P. (1988) *Homo academicus*, Stanford, CA: Stanford University Press.

Bourdieu, P. (1990) 'The Scholastic point of view', *Cultural Anthropology*, 5(4), pp 380-91.

Bourdieu, P. and Wacquant, L. (1992) *An invitation to reflexive sociology*, Chicago, IL: Polity Press.

Callon, M. (1991) 'Techno-economic networks and irreversibility', in J. Law (ed) *A sociology of monsters: Essays on power, technology and domination*, London: Routledge, pp 132-64.

Davies, D., Wetherell, M. and Barnett, E. (2006) *Citizens at the centre: Deliberative participation in healthcare decisions*, Bristol: The Policy Press.

de Sousa Santos, B. (2007) *Democratizing democracy: Beyond the liberal democratic cannon*, London: Verso.

Goodin, R. (2008) *Innovating democracy: Democratic theory and practice after the deliberative turn*, Oxford: Oxford University Press.

Hay, C. (2007) *Why we hate politics*, Cambridge: Polity Press.

Holloway, J. (2002) *Change the world without taking power*, London: Pluto.

Latour, B. (1987) *Science in action: How to follow scientists and engineers through society*, Harvard University Press: Cambridge, MA.

Latour, B. (1993) *We have never been modern*, Harvard University Press: Cambridge, MA.

Livingstone, S. (ed) (2005) *Audiences and publics: When cultural engagement matters for the public sphere*, Bristol: Intellect Books.

Mahony, N. (2008) 'Spectacular political experiments: the constitution, mediation and performance of large-scale public participation exercises', Unpublished PhD thesis, Centre for Citizenship, Identities and Governance, Open University.

Mair, P. (2006) 'Ruling the void? The hollowing out of western democracy', *New Left Review*, 42.

Millo, Y. and Lezaun, J. (2006) 'Regulatory experiments: genetically modified crops and financial derivatives on trial', *Science and Public Policy*, 33(3), pp 179-90.

Pinch, T. (1993) 'Testing – one, two, three ... testing!: towards a sociology of testing', *Science, Technology and Human Values*, 18,(1), pp 25-41.

Riegert, K. (2007) *Politicoentertainment: Television's take on the real*, New York, NY: Peter Lang.

Saward, M. (2003) 'Enacting democracy', *Political Studies*, 51(1), pp 161-79.

Saward, M. (2006) 'The representative claim', *Contemporary Political Theory*, 5(3), pp 297-318.

Steiner, G. (1998) *After Babel: Aspects of language and translation*, Oxford: Oxford University Press.

Stoker, G. (2006) *Why politics matters: Making democracy work*, Basingstoke: Palgrave MacMillan.

Warner, M. (2002) *Publics and counterpublics*, New York, NY: Zone Books.

THREE

Going public? Articulations of the personal and political on Mumsnet.com

Richenda Gambles

The growth of interactive online communication is often associated with an opening up and extending of communicative options and possibilities, and a key aspect or example of this is the sort of communication that focuses on topics of a personal or intimate nature. In this kind of communication, people are encouraged and enabled to go public with personal feelings or experiences and this, in turn, can tap into, shape and potentially transform public understanding and debate – what was termed 'personalising publics' in the introduction to this volume.

This optimistic reading suggests that interactive online communication has the power to enable personal feelings, concerns and experiences to become more publicly known, recognised and taken up in public and political contexts. Yet it is worth reflecting on what of the personal might be closed off in relation to the public or political, or how the personal and political might be rearticulated in these processes in more troubling kinds of ways. This is considered here with reference to Mumsnet.com, an interactive parenting website that has exploded in fame and popularity in the UK in recent years. This chapter reflects on what is made public through Mumsnet and considers, in the process, how it might work to produce new articulations of the personal and political and what might be at stake through these new articulations.

In exploring Mumsnet, I draw on the work of Shani Orgad (2005), who has looked at interactive websites for people experiencing breast cancer. Orgad argues that interactive websites that focus on the discussion of deeply personal issues offer important spaces to 'go public' with personal feelings and experiences. Yet, she suggests, such sites encourage people to rely on personalised and privatised strategies for making sense of and working through their experiences, rather than encouraging them to speak to or call up the public–political realm. In reflecting on Mumsnet, I argue that dynamics between the public, political, personal and private are rather more blurred, and indeed mutually constitutive, than Orgad's analysis would suggest. With attention to this blurring and mutual constitution, I consider how the personal and political is articulated on Mumsnet and think about how this relates more generally to the public, political and personal of contemporary understandings and experiences of parenting.

Mumsnet and its public, political and personal significance

I first became aware of Mumsnet in the context of my PhD research, which focused on the first few years of first-time parenting in the UK. This research considered the ways in which parental understandings are experienced through, shaped by and shaping of contemporary policy discourses as well as popular cultural representations of parenting. I chose to focus on the first few years of first-time parenting because it is a site, moment or experience of personal, public and political significance. Becoming a parent, particularly for the first time, is a moment of profound personal change and transition (Wetherell, 1995; Thompson and Kehily with Hadley and Sharpe, 2008), and yet this personal change and transition occurs in the context of much contemporary political and public attention relating to parenting. This suggests that personal experiences and political or public discourses are likely to be mutually constitutive of each other (Lewis and Fink, 2004).

In relation to the UK government, parenting has become a site of intense interest and intervention (see also Chapter Six of this volume). This has been evident through extensive policy activity relating to parenting, including the development of parental leaves, parental rights to request flexible working, affordable childcare and Sure Start initiatives, and the extension of midwife and health visitor services (Home Office, 1998; DCSF, 2007; DfES, 2007). The development of policies and initiatives focusing on parenting has been attributed to a range of factors. These include a desire to better support parents in the bringing up of their children and to encourage or, if necessary, to coerce, parents to take up certain economic and moral responsibilities in relation to their parenting (see Featherstone, 2004; MacLeod, 2004; Gillies, 2005, 2007; Williams, 2005). This focus – seen by New Labour as essential for the well-being of children and wider society more generally – can be linked to what Furedi (2002) has called 'parental determinism', in which good or bad parenting is seen as the key determinant in the behaviour and development of children.

Parenting, including the first few years of parenting, is also, of course, the subject of wider public discussion. It pervades the UK news media as well as other forms of popular culture, such as parenting books, magazines, television programmes and websites (MacLeod, 2004; Hardyment, 2007). This suggests that the media and popular culture contribute extensively to the mediation – but also production and transformation – of norms and expectations relating to parenting as well as what might be viewed as appropriate forms of public-political action. Parents get a lot of their knowledge of policy initiatives as well as ideas about parenting more generally from the media. Politicians, in turn, get much of their knowledge and understanding about parenting experiences from the media and popular culture, as well as evoking the media itself to justify new policy developments and initiatives. Beverley Hughes MP, then UK Minister for Children, Young People and Families, made reference, for example, to the popular television programme Supernanny in a speech about parenting:

Government too must extend the opportunities for parents to develop their expertise; the popularity of Supernanny exemplifies the hunger for information and for effective parenting programmes that parents often express to me. (Beverley Hughes, MP, in a keynote speech to the Institute for Public Policy Research, July 2006, cited in Gill and Jensen, 2008)

Harriet Harman MP, then UK Minister for Women and Equality, indicated her intention to create a website for parents to debate issues they want politicians to notice, which 'would be modelled on the success of Mumsnet, the website with topics ranging from nanny problems to breastfeeding techniques' (*The Observer*, 2006).

My research draws on three distinct data sources: selected New Labour policy documents relating to the first few years of parenting; interviews with first-time parents; and media and popular cultural representations including parenting manuals, the television show Supernanny, contemporary 'chick lit' novels relating to parenting and the interactive parenting website Mumsnet.com. Through my analysis of these different data sources, I worked to locate something of a contemporary mood or sensibility relating to contemporary understandings and experiences of becoming and being a parent, and to make more visible the ways in which the personal, political and public are shaping of each other in the formation of these sensibilities.

My decision to use governmental sources, popular culture and personal narratives reflected my use of Raymond Williams' structure of feeling approach (Williams, 1961, 1977). Structure of feeling is a concept that seeks to capture a 'mood, sensibility or atmosphere associated with a specific period or generation' (Lewis and Fink, 2004, p 58). It refers to the 'actual living sense of a culture' where 'official consciousness of a period, as codified in legislation and doctrine, interacts with the lived experiences of that period, and defines the set of perceptions and values common to a generation' (Macey, 2000, p 366). For Williams, structure of feeling is both a theoretical concept and a methodological approach in which legislation or policy can be read alongside popular cultural texts so as to get a nuanced and dynamic reading of a mood or sensibility of a period (Williams, 1961, p 70). Williams coined and developed the concept – and its associated approach – to explore and locate something of a cultural essence associated with a particular period or issue that, he argues, is 'as firm and definite as "structure" suggests' yet something that 'operates in the most delicate and least tangible parts of our activity' (Williams, 1961, p 64). In this context, I argue that this structure of feeling approach invites attention to, and can be used to explore and develop, a more nuanced reading of public and political sentiments by recognising and reflecting on the ways in which these can emerge from, and feed into, personal and privatised feelings, dispositions and experiences.

Mumsnet is a particularly rich data source because it is both a popular cultural representation of parenting and, through enabling people to participate and interact, a space through which to explore personal narratives, strategies and negotiations associated with becoming and being a parent. Another key reason for focusing on Mumsnet is that during my research it became a personal space for me due to my (troubled) experiences of becoming a parent. In the year prior to writing this chapter, I experienced three miscarriages and, through my familiarity with Mumsnet in the context of my PhD, I became personally involved in interactive discussions in the context of venting and dealing with my disappointment and grief. While writing this chapter, I wondered whether it would be seen as appropriate to include discussion of my own troubled experiences of becoming a parent and my subsequent engagements with Mumsnet. Perhaps it was too personal and private for discussion in an academic – and by implication a public and political – genre in which the personal of the researcher is often (but not always, as seen in many chapters in this book) under-discussed or even swept aside?

Yet Mumsnet, for me, has been a particularly personal public and my personal use of the site has shaped and influenced the way I explore and understand it. Indeed, it is the very combination of my personal engagements with Mumsnet, alongside my interest in and commitment to a feminist politics emphasising the connectivity of the personal and political, that has sharpened my attention to the concerns I raise in this chapter: that of the importance of considering the connectedness between the public, political, personal and private as well as what might be at stake, politically and personally, through the opening, recognising or failure to recognise, such connections. Because of my personal engagements with Mumsnet and my emotions and feelings relating to my experience of miscarriage, it also became apparent that I had begun to somewhat re-inflect Williams' structure of feeling concept. When Williams wrote of a structure of feeling he was talking about a collective mood or feeling of a generation or period. While I use this meaning, I also explore feelings at a more personal and emotional level and so explore further the ways in which a public mood or set of sentiments is also one that penetrates and is shaped by more personal or intimate feelings and dispositions.

Mumsnet as a personal public

Mumsnet is an interactive website best known for its talk boards where parents or parents-to-be (or more accurately mothers and mothers-to-be) meet and discuss a whole range of experiences of interest and concern to them. What is immediately obvious from browsing through the Mumsnet site and its talk boards are the many different aspects and challenges associated with parenting. Articles and posts on all manner of topics are covered, including advice and suggestions about baby names, condolences and support for people who have suffered miscarriages or still-births or have had problems conceiving, and tips and discussions about how best to tackle child development and behavioural issues ranging from breastfeeding to potty training or children's interaction with other children. There are also multiple posts about childcare and when or whether to go back to paid employment following the arrival of a child, posts on sibling relationships and reviews of products and paraphernalia that claim to aid in the raising of children. Mumsnet, I argue, can thus be regarded as a personal public in two distinct but overlapping ways.

First, Mumsnet can be viewed as a personal public because of the *processes* of participation it enables and encourages. As an open-access website, it can be read by anyone who has access to the internet; and becoming a member and contributing to discussions is a quick and easy process. Mumsnet has several thousand members – in 2007, an interview with one of Mumsnet founders, Justine Roberts, noted that Mumsnet had 60,000 members and was receiving 250,000 hits a month (*Telegraph*, 2007) – and can be seen as a dialogic space in which people get together and share knowledge, understandings and challenges relating to being or becoming a parent. Orgad has suggested that this type of interactive online communication can offer a positive, transformative experience in which the sharing of personal narratives can enable personal experiences to become publicly visible, rather than just a private set of feelings or experiences (Orgad, 2005, p 12 online version). In making this claim, she draws attention to the process of online communication in which participants can publish their accounts in 'a direct, straightforward and simple way … with minimal (if any) editorial intervention' (Orgad, 2005, p 15 online version). This means that users have control of what gets depicted as well as the tone of these depictions, and this generates an articulation of 'real' and diverse experiences in a publicly accessible forum. Orgad also notes that unlike much of the mass media, where 'multiple experiences are commonly bundled into one representative figure … the online space can accommodate multiple stories and voices' (2005, p 18 online version). This suggests that the processes of online interactive communication have the capacity to make public the wealth and diversity of what might otherwise be regarded as personal or private experiences.

Second, Mumsnet can be seen as a personal public because of the public and personal significance of the *content* to which it speaks, in this case of being or becoming a parent. The subheading or strap line on the website is 'by parents, for parents' and a central orientation of Mumsnet is that parents are the real experts because of their own personal experience of parenting. This is demonstrated clearly through the title a book compiled by Mumsnet founders, *Mums on babies: Trade secrets from the real experts* (Foster et al, 2003), which is described as the first in a series of Mumsnet guides to parenting and features selected extracts from Mumsnet discussions. In the Introduction, the book claims to offer 'a vast archive of expertise – collected the hard way – by thousands of real parents' (Foster et al, 2003, p x). This online forum and its spin-off books can be seen as a site through which parents can meet, chat and swap stories and advice, and where parents can support each other, and learn from, negotiate and make sense of their parenting experiences in interaction with each other. In doing so, Mumsnet emphasises the importance of lay expertise or knowledge in relation to parenting. This is seen as being of particular value in a context of conflicting and competing advice and information. Mumsnet is thus portrayed as offering a place for parents to sound off, learn from each other and gain personal support and advice. This is seen as all the more necessary in 'our increasingly atomised modern western world' (Foster et al, 2003, p x), where mothers do not always have a friend or relative to hand. Indeed, they suggest that:

> Whatever the parenting poser you are facing, the chances are that one of Mumsnet's members will have been there already. Their advice is offered in a rather different tone of voice to the tablets of stone delivered by the parenting gurus: not so much 'do this because it's the right way' as 'this worked for me, maybe it could work for you'. (Foster et al, 2003, p x)

This suggests the positive potential of online communication – both in terms of its process as well as its content – in that experiences of parenting can be discussed, shared and debated in interaction with others through Mumsnet as a personal public forum.

Mumsnet as a political public

I argue that, as well as being a personal public, Mumsnet is a *political* public, not least because of the activities generated by the website. Mumsnet is presented as an identifiable community that 'swing[s] into formidable and effective action should any member need help' (*Times Online*, 2008a). Examples given in this newspaper article range from Mumsnetters rallying round, to find a replacement doll for a mother whose child was inconsolable without it, to support for people suffering domestic abuse, losing their children to cot death or experiencing post-natal depression. Indeed, people make personal use of the site to deal with and talk through the day-to-day joys, dilemmas and challenges associated with parenting. So in this sense, Mumsnet can be seen as a public that is motivational (Warner, 2002) and thus political in a personal-political sense. But is Mumsnet political in a way that works with but also moves beyond the personal? I want to explore this question in two ways, first, in terms of the ways it links with formal politics and second, in terms of public mobilisations.

In terms of formal politics, Mumsnet is often visited by politicians who seek to communicate directly with parents about their contemporary parenting experiences. Indeed, in visiting Mumsnet and engaging with Mumsnetters in live web chat forums, politicians position themselves as seeking to learn from 'real' parents about the experiences and conflicts they face. They also – as mentioned above – use their awareness of, and their own discussions on, the website to develop or justify policy positions and developments relating to parenting. This can be seen in live web chats with people such as David Cameron MP, Alan Johnson MP and Harriet Harman MP that are flagged up and accessible to all (not just Mumsnet members) via a link on Mumsnet's home page.

In relation to the growth of the talk-show phenomenon, but with observations that could be extended to other emergent forms of media, Ros Gill has suggested that the media can be seen to be:

> … taking on new roles: they are acting as spokespersons for people to talk back to government and elites; they are offering forums in which politicians can be held directly accountable to the public (for example, when they appear on audience discussion programmes and are questioned about what they are going to do about any particular issue); and they represent a social space for communication amongst the public itself. (Gill, 2007, p 167)

This, she suggests, can be attributed to the broader shift from an authoritarian model of discourse to a more populist and democratic style in which 'ordinary' voices are increasingly made use of in public discussions (Gill, 2007; see also Newman and Clarke, 2009). This could be argued similarly and even more powerfully for interactive websites such as Mumsnet where participants have much more direct control due to a lack of editorial intervention.

In terms of public mobilisations, Mumsnet can also be regarded as a political public as it develops and engages in campaigns about various issues or challenges relating to parenting. One example of this is a 2008 campaign relating to people experiencing miscarriage. From extensive online discussions among people that had experienced miscarriages, Carrie Longton, a Mumsnet founder, began a campaign for more sensitive treatment from health care professionals. She began this by posting the following:

By carriemumsnet on Mon 21 Apr 08 17:40:14 (MNHQ)

> When Alan Johnson came a visiting last week, miscarriage and some of the frankly appalling treatment that Mumsnetters have suffered 🙁
> was one of the talking points. Following on from sfx's comments (and others) this is what AJ had to say: 'it seems to me from all your comments and from talking to the Mumsnet people here that we really should seek to ensure a common set of standards across the country. I think I'm in at the start of a new campaign and it's something I will talk to Ministers about when I return to the Department. Mumsnet have informed me that I will not be allowed to forget this issue!'. So now it's down to us to come up with that common set of standards – guidelines and procedures that we'd like to see implemented across the whole of the UK. I'll happily kick off as a veteran of 2 m/c: but do feel free to disagree with my suggestions/add your improvements: Automatic access to EPU [Early Pregnancy Unit] for anyone with a suspected miscarriage (without having to get a GP referral) and EPUs situated away from regular ante natal clinics/

labour wards and devoid of images of smiling babies – please. Access to all affected to a pamphlet/booklet put together by Mumsnet and full of your tips, advice, empathy and reassurance – describing what might happen and letting folks know they're not alone in this. Over to you ....(Mumsnet, miscarriage section, accessed on 17 December 2008)

Through online interactive discussion, 10 recommendations were subsequently developed and complied in a Code of Practice that was then featured in *The Times* newspaper (*Times Online*, 2008b). This demonstrates the ways in which a public and political campaign was *mobilised* by personal disclosures through online interaction among Mumsnet members and their online discussions with a politician.

Mumsnet campaigning work is not confined to the issue of miscarriage. It also includes discussion about, and involvement in, more well-known issues facing parents, seen, for example, through a campaign called Home Front: Making Like Work, a debate jointly hosted by Mumsnet and Dads Info, and supported by the Equality and Human Rights Commission. This aims to promote awareness of the difficulties and challenges facing parents as they seek to reconcile the demands of paid work with their childcare responsibilities. The message from Mumsnet HQ (the office of the Mumsnet founders and other paid members of staff) is that the campaign aims to compile 'policy suggestions based on your opinions about what's needed to improve parents' work–life balance' (Mumsnet.com home page, accessed 17 December 2008).

In these ways, it is possible to see how personal experiences are being publicly articulated in ways that tap into and seek to shape the public-political agenda. In an analysis of interactive online communication among people with breast cancer, Orgad found this lacking. She argued, drawing on the work of Warner (2002), that this was, in part, because the women she studied failed to recognise themselves as a public 'because they think of their authenticity and their femininity as rooted in necessarily private feelings and domestic (and thus invisible and peripheral) relations' (Orgad, 2005, p 33 online version). In this context, she asked whether interactive websites of this nature could 'constitute more than anonymous therapeutic spaces providing resources for confession, inwardness and self-elaboration?' (Orgad, 2005, p 34 online version). In the case of Mumsnet, it seems, perhaps, that it can; furthermore Mumsnet could be seen to offer something of a feminist public (although not stating or claiming its feminist status) in which it is possible for the personal to be personal *and* political in more public-political ways.

Mumsnet as a privatising public?

It is important to consider, however, that Mumsnet might simultaneously promote more personalised *and privatised* strategies, rather than personalised *and politicised* strategies, for dealing with the parenting challenges and experiences that it discusses and evokes. This invites attention to the political and personal 'risks' such sites can engender.

As suggested by Orgad, Mumsnet does appear to encourage and enable personal disclosure in a way that promotes self-responsibility through an emphasis on personal empowerment and the therapeutic. I am very aware of this through my own personal involvement in the site in the context of miscarriage. In posting and sharing details of my own experiences, as well as responding to others in a similar situation, I have found comfort, support and the strength to deal with my own grief as well as the ability to support others in theirs. The tone or feel of these threads has definitely been one in which people are encouraged to 'go public' with their personal feelings and emotions, albeit in an anonymous and privatised way, which works with and encourages the development of personal strength to keep going in terms of trying to become a parent. Indeed, in these discussions, the personal is so often the focus and much less emphasis is given, for example, to the development or dissemination of the Mumsnet Code of Practice relating to miscarriage that I highlighted earlier.

Mumsnet could be said to work with the 'personal is political' feminist mantra and ethos, in which people are encouraged to talk about the intimate, the private and the everyday in a way that develops understanding and political awareness and recognition for personal experiences. Yet this appears to coexist with a tendency that Gill (2007, p 177) has discussed in which the political is personalised with a reframing of 'every issue in individualistic terms and erasing any sense of the social or political' (see also Gorton, 2007). In the context of interactive online communication, these risks are a central critique made by Orgad in relation to breast cancer websites: that because users mainly discuss the individual and the personal, this encourages self-responsibility for dealing with and overcoming issues and problems they encounter (Orgad, 2005, p 28 online version). This self-responsibility often comes in the form of the encouragement and articulation of a therapeutic, self-empowerment approach that, Orgad argues, somewhat separates rather than integrates problems and concerns from the public-political realm (Orgad, 2005, p 32 online version). Her reading of this is that such sites, while offering a supportive place to 'make public' private and personal experiences, also have a tendency to re-privatise the very issues they speak of.

This can be seen in relation to Mumsnet in terms of miscarriage experiences as well as many other sets of parenting issues discussed on the site. Taking, for example, one of the most popular talk sections of the site, labelled 'Behaviour and development', the threads place much emphasis on the personal reflexive and educative capacities and dispositions expected from, and encouraged by and of, parents. These personalised capacities and dispositions are seen as key for enabling them to be or become 'good' parents who develop and nurture their children into 'happy', 'successful' and 'fulfilled' individuals. This focus, while important, somewhat eclipses discussion of the socio-economic opportunities and constraints that characterise the lives of different parents and their children. This offers an example of a personalised *and somewhat privatised* empowerment strategy rather than a personalised *and political* one.

This analysis resonates, in part, with claims made by Ouellette and Hay (2008) in their discussion of reality TV shows such as Supernanny as well as with Gillies' (2007) argument that New Labour policies focus on parenting skills rather than socio-economic redistributive strategies. Moreover, it works with observations made by Gorton (2007, p 335) in relation to the fate of the second-wave feminist mantra of the personal being political in which 'the personal and its healing became the solution to problems that were largely collective and social'. These processes can be seen, too, in relation to tensions many mothers discuss on Mumsnet and elsewhere about, for example, whether or not or to what extent they should be active in paid work or be present to care for and nurture their child. This is, of course, a publicly political and politicised issue. But a policy discourse of choice is one that plays up personal choice strategies and eclipses and privatises socio-economic or deeply gendered contexts in which such 'choices' are made (Williams, 2005; Lewis and Campbell, 2007; Ben-Galim and Gambles, 2008).

These examples begin, then, to highlight and suggest that the encouragement and articulation of a therapeutic, self-empowerment, deliberative choice approach is *not* as separate from the public-political realm as Orgad has suggested. Rather it may be reflective and productive of a public-political that *actively* works to personalise and privatise social experiences and processes into individual ones through what Nikolas Rose (1999, pp xx, xxiv) has referred to as the 'therapeutic' culture of the self. Rose's suggestion here is that people learn to monitor, supervise and take care of themselves through their own actions, dispositions and choices, which is a way or condition of being that is encouraged by and

> ... perfectly suited to neo-liberal democracies where discourses of structural inequality of power difference are fast disappearing and individuals are exhorted to live their lives through notions of autonomy, self-reinvention and limitless choice. (Gill, 2007, p 171)

This can be seen through the *type* of voice encouraged on Mumsnet: one of a sharing and supportive nature that often works with and emphasises a therapeutic, empowerment, self-help-through-support-and-discussion approach. But as well as considering the type of voice encouraged, it is also important to consider *whose* voice is articulated in the context of exploring the personal and political of Mumsnet. Earlier, I mentioned claims that new forms of media, including interactive websites, are part of a shift from an authoritarian discourse to a more populist and democratic style. The claim for being democratic is made explicitly by Justine Roberts, one of the Mumsnet founders, in a newspaper interview where she claims 'it's modern, it's democratic' (cited in *Times Online*, 2008a). Yet while anyone, in theory, can log on and be a member, Roberts gives a description of the typical Mumsnetter as someone who 'might not be rich, but ... probably is well educated', noting that 73 per cent of Mumsnetters are educated to a degree standard and 20 per cent have gone on to postgraduate study (cited in *Times Online*, 2008a). What is not, of course, stated here is that the typical Mumsnetter is also female and a mother or mother-to-be rather than a *parent* – something, of course, that somewhat disrupts and troubles the claim of the site as being 'by parents, for parents'. This suggests that Mumsnet constitutes and carries a particular voice, both in terms of the ways in which people speak but also in terms of who is speaking. It has implications for what – and whose – personal issues are taken up politically in the context of parenting, and may link to the somewhat eclipsing and privatising of socio-economic and gendered constraints and other sets of issues that face some parents more than others. This invites further questions about whether publics that are personal and political and claim a 'democratic' status are politically representative of the diversity of people to which they – through their public, personal and political status – claim to speak (Davies et al, 2006).

The personal and political of Mumsnet?

This chapter opened with questions of whether web-based, interactive new media could be seen to enable recognition and take-up of people's personal concerns and experiences in public and political contexts or whether it might work to encourage personalised self-empowerment governance strategies that (re)privatise the issues raised. Using the example of Mumsnet, I have highlighted how the very process and content of interactive online communication has the potential to open up personalised and privatised issues or challenges within the public and political agenda. Yet I have also argued that narratives of optimism (see the Introduction to this volume) need to be treated with extreme caution. While the personal might be opened up to the public and political in new and potentially transformative ways, it is important to think of *whose* personal this is, *how* the personal is re-articulated and *what* might be marginalised or silenced in the process.

Mumsnet is a product of its time and both shapes and is shaped by a cultural sensibility, mood and voice relating to the expectations and hopes placed on and expected by parents today. This means that questions about what is at stake go further than a consideration of Mumsnet. They relate, too, to public and political discourses about parenting as well as personal negotiations of parenting that are agonised over by many parents today. I have argued that contemporary public and political action relating to parenting assumes and seeks to develop personalised strategies of learning, reflexivity and evaluation (see also Chapter Seven of this volume). I have also suggested that the focus on personal empowerment can, in turn, work to (re)privatise parental responsibilities even while parenting remains such a public and politicised issue and concern. A structure-of-feeling approach has encouraged me to reflect on these interconnections in the context of Mumsnet as well as parenting more generally, because it assumes and works with the idea of the dialogic co-constitution of public and political sentiments with personal, intimate and *not-so-private* feelings and dispositions. By highlighting the interconnectedness and mutual constitution of the public, political and personal in relation to parenting, the idea and processes through which personal and intimate experiences are deeply shaped by and shaping of the public and political can be kept open for much-needed scrutiny and critical reflection.

References

Ben-Galim, D. and Gambles, R. (2008) 'The "public" and "private" of work–family reconciliation', in M. Seeleib-Kaiser (ed) *Welfare state transformations*, Basingstoke: Palgrave Macmillan, pp 182-94.

Davies, C., Wetherell, M. and Barnett, E. (2006) *Citizens at the centre: Deliberative participation in healthcare decisions*, Bristol: The Policy Press.

DCSF (Department for Children, Schools and Families) (2007) *The Children's Plan*, London: HMSO.

DfES (Department for Education and Skills) (2007) *Every parent matters*, London: HMSO.

Featherstone, B. (2004) *Family life and family support: A feminist analysis*, Basingstoke: Palgrave Macmillan.

Foster, R., Longton, C. and Roberts, J. (2003) *Mums on babies: Trade secrets from the real experts*, London: Cassell Illustrated.

Furedi, F. (2002) *Paranoid parenting: Why ignoring the experts may be best for your child*, Chicago, IL: Chicago Review Press.

Gill, R. (2007) *Gender and the media*, Cambridge: Polity Press.

Gill, R. and Jensen, T. (2008) 'Public intimacies and intimate public: the personal, political and mediated intimacy', Paper presented at the Emergent Publics Seminar Series, 13-14 March, Milton Keynes, organised by the Open University and funded by the Economic and Social Research Council.

Gillies, V. (2005) 'Meeting parents' needs? Discourses of "support" and "inclusion" in family policy', *Critical Social Policy*, 25(1), pp 70-90.

Gillies, V. (2007) *Marginalised mothers: Exploring working-class experiences of parenting*, London: Routledge.

Gorton, K. (2007) 'Theorising emotion and affect: feminist engagements', *Feminist Theory*, 8(3), pp 333-48.

Hardyment, C. (2007) *Dream babies: Childcare advice from John Locke to Gina Ford*, London: Frances Lincoln Ltd.

Home Office (1998) *Supporting families*, London: HMSO.

Lewis, G. and Fink, J. (2004) '"All that heaven allows": the worker-citizen in the post-war welfare state', in G. Lewis (eds) *Citizenship: Personal lives and social policy*, Bristol: The Policy Press, pp 39-83.

Lewis, J. and Campbell, M. (2007) 'Work–family balance policies in the UK since 1997: a new departure?', *Journal of Social Policy*, 36(3), pp 365-81.

Macey, D. (2000) *Dictionary of critical theory*, Harmondsworth: Penguin.

MacLeod, M. (2004) 'The state and the family: can the government get it right?', Paper presented at Rethinking Care Relations, Family Lives and Policies: An International Symposium, School of Sociology and Social Policy, University of Leeds.

Newman, J. and Clarke, J. (2009) *Publics, politics and power: Remaking the public in public services*, London: Sage Publications.

Observer, The (2006) 'Shift parenting hurts families', 26 November, www.guardian. co.uk/politics/2006/nov/26/uk.women.

Orgad, S. (2005) 'The transformative potential of online communication: the case of breast cancer patients' internet spaces', LSE Research Online, originally published in *Feminist Media Research*, 5(2), pp 141-61.

Ouellette, L. and Hay, J. (2008) *Better living through reality TV: Television and post-welfare citizenship*, Oxford: Blackwell Publishing.

Rose, N. (1999) *Governing the soul: The shaping of the private self* (2nd edn), London: Free Association Books.

Telegraph (2007) 'Just give me a little more time', 20 October, www.mumsnet. com/info/press.

Thompson, R. and Kehily, M.J. with Hadfield, L. and Sharpe, S. (2008) *The making of modern motherhood: Memories, representations and practices*, Milton Keynes: Open University.

Times Online (2008a) 'Mumsnet parenting advice expands to books: the single authoritarian voice on parenting is no more. In the world of Mumsnet, everyone's an expert – with a major new book deal to prove it', 15 March.

Times Online (2008b) 'Miscarriage: must doctors make our grief worse?', 20 October.

Warner, M. (2002) *Publics and counterpublics*, London: Zone Books.

Wetherell, M. (1995) 'Social structure, ideology and family dynamics: the case of parenting', in J. Muncie, M. Wetherell, R. Dallos and A. Cochrane (eds) *Understanding the family*, London: Sage Publications, pp 213-56.

Williams, F. (2005) 'New Labour's family policy', in M. Powell, L. Bauld and K. Clarke (eds) *Social Policy Review 17: Analysis and debate in social policy 2005*, Bristol: The Policy Press, pp 289-302.

Williams, R. (1961) *The long revolution*, London: Penguin.

Williams, R. (1977) *Marxism and literature*, Oxford: Oxford University Press.

FOUR

Digitising and visualising: old media, new media and the pursuit of emerging urban publics

Scott Rodgers

Questions of publics and publicness, as the previous two chapters have shown, open up questions of media and mediation. Habermas's (1989) public sphere inextricably links public communication to the practices and institutions of mass media (cf. Garnham, 1992). By contrast, much contemporary debate, both popular and academic, has paid attention to the proliferation of new media technologies and practices that apparently blur long-standing distinctions between the 'mass' and the 'personal' (Lüders, 2008). Unsurprisingly, these radical changes in media and mediation are seen also to entail radically new configurations of publics and publicness (Holmes, 2002), seen as both positive and negative in political terms. Implicitly buried in such accounts is a narrative about the rise and decline of particular *mediums*; the replacement of old with new. A favoured example in this respect is newspapers, a medium usually cast as 'old media' and seen to relate to particular configurations of mass publicness founded in the 19th century, manifesting in many forms throughout the 20th century, and now finally in relative decline (see, for example, Alterman, 2008; Franklin, 2009). Yet in these and other accounts of the relationships of old and new media, and their implications for publicness or public communication, what is actually implied by 'medium' often seems rather opaque.

One of the more notable conceptualisations of 'medium' in media theory is that of Marshall McLuhan (1964), made famous by the dictum that the 'medium is the message'. McLuhan was worried that too much media research fixates on the *content* of media, when the truly important message of a medium is not its content but the change it brings about in the pattern, scale, pace and scope of human affairs. This priority placed on the materiality of mediums is why so much controversy surrounds McLuhan, who is typically problematised as a technological determinist (though for some, not technologically determinist enough – see Kittler, 1999) with little to say about politics. At least on the surface, his demotion, even refusal, of so-called content may sit uncomfortably with a sense of publicness based around discoursing (see, for example, Warner, 2002). A closer reading of McLuhan, however, reveals that the distinction being drawn between medium and content is merely rhetorical, since:

> ... the 'content' of any medium is always another medium. The content
> of writing is speech, just as written word is the content of print, and
> print in the content of the telegraph. If it is asked, 'What is the content
> of speech?', it is necessary to say, 'It is the actual process of thought,
> which is itself nonverbal.' (McLuhan, 1964, p 8)

From such a standpoint, there is no dichotomy between medium and content.
It follows that it is difficult to set apart and identify the newspaper, or indeed
any medium, as fully determining the fortunes of public content (for example,
discourses, affects). It may well be that the printed newspaper as media *technology*
is undergoing radical transformation, and indeed, may even disappear in any
recognisable form in the near future. But it is misleading to couple such
technological transformations together with the multiple practices, settings and
mediums that make up how public communication gets rearticulated through
newspapers as *organisations*.

With this in mind, in this chapter I rethink and problematise distinctions often
made between old and new mediums of publicness, focusing on the ways in
which new media technologies get adopted and adapted through the settings of
ostensibly old media organisations. The organisation in question is the *Toronto Star*,
a major Canadian metropolitan newspaper that was the setting for ethnographic
fieldwork undertaken in 2005 as part of my PhD research. I focus specifically on
the efforts of editors and management to align – in part by using and reacting
to new media technologies – the futures of their newspaper organisation with
those of their imagined public and market. Most *Toronto Star* editors viewed their
newspaper as an institution of public responsibility, public trust and public advocacy
in relation to Toronto; a 'great metropolitan newspaper' serving the city and its
surrounding region for over a century. But much as it was with city newspapers
elsewhere, there was a problem. This urban public was seen to be composed
of rapidly changing patterns of work, family, leisure, lifestyle and ethnicity, all
engaging the public world through a proliferating, mobile and instantaneous media
environment. There were both worries and actualities of declining circulation,
lost advertising, stock devaluations, budget roll-backs and staff lay-offs. So even
as editing was a site of organisational authority and earnestness about its own
public remit, it was also a locus of pervading anxieties about the *Toronto Star* as
organisation, and imperatives to reorient, reorganise and re-equip in the pursuit
of emerging urban publics.

In what follows, I introduce two brief accounts of how new media or mediums
were adopted and adapted into the configurations of urban public address (cf.
Iveson, 2007) in which the *Toronto Star* was entangled. The first was a 'magazine
sensibility' – new forms of layout, design and presentation – through which
editors hoped to attend to the rising visual acumen of audiences. The second was
the presumed inevitability of a digital or online newspaper, and the rupture its
particular qualities of spatial display, temporality and interactivity posed in relation
to the printed newspaper. I then turn more directly to editing, considering the

efforts of editors to integrate these and other technologies into the timing and spacing of the *Toronto Star* through new forms of team organisation and so-called flat management.

I focus on editing work in this chapter to highlight it as a particular milieu of public action that is orientated towards, and at the same time subject to, more extensive public spaces of circulation. In so doing, I will describe editing as a *site*, by which I mean a nexus between, first, the routines, rules and shared senses of purpose that make up editing as practice, and second, the material arrangements of bodies, objects and technologies on which editing as practice inherently depends (Schatzki, 2002). This is a specific style of researching the question of publicness, and in recognition of that, I begin the concluding section by drawing some connections between my methodological choices and the theoretical account provided. In focusing on the interaction between editing as site and public spaces of circulation, I will underline the importance of understanding public action as performed and situated, and therefore fragile. A side effect of this understanding is that media technologies get considered for their uses and effects in particular practical settings, rather than in general or abstract terms. This perspective lays the groundwork, in turn, for me to offer a critical take on claims about the radical novelty of new media in relation to old, and their implications for the making of publics.

Visual publics

Early on a Tuesday morning in March 2005, on Yonge Street in downtown Toronto, a man brandishes what looks like a kitchen knife. He's surrounded by around six members of the Toronto Police Service, guns drawn. He's not backing down, he's shouting, he's waving his knife about. Officers in one of the nearby police cruisers decide to use their car in an attempt to corral him. They move the car forward at low speed, there's an impact, and the man is vaulted on to the hood of the moving vehicle. He soon falls off, but quickly steadies his balance; more shouts, knife in hand, foot officers again back away. Then, the police cruiser moves forward once more and the man is struck, pinned between the car and a metal bicycle stand. His knife drops, the car reverses, and shortly thereafter the man gets to his feet and surrenders.

The events making up this stand-off were captured by nearby closed circuit cameras, recorded and replayed soon after on Toronto-based, 24-hour television news channel CP24. On the overhead monitors in the centre of the *Toronto Star* newsroom at 1 Yonge Street, the footage brings about a lot of interest, a little shock and certainly a buzzing discussion among editors and reporters watching. The interest was not just in the events themselves, of course, but in the fact they had been captured on video. Coincidentally, this all happened on the morning that the weekly features meeting was scheduled, at which editors pitch ideas for, and discuss the status of, special feature articles:

11.47am. The conversation has turned to the video footage of the early morning police takedown, which most of the editors seated around the table seem to have seen. They discuss what seem to be the 'difficulties' of the situation, which was diffused without the use of firearms. Lee Bourrier[1], the City Editor, jumps in: 'I think we should do a big feature graphic, with images, because we got them, and say here's how the cops follow their protocol, like actually dissect it.' A lively discussion ensues. Talk of the stages that made up the stand-off: speculation about whether the use of a cruiser is in fact protocol; the technique involved in using a car for such ends; and who the knife wielding man was. And all along, talk about the materials at hand: on using the video stills; on the necessity of additional graphics; on the likely need for annotations; and that it all needs to makes sense and look coherent. It comes back to Lee Bourrier: 'Okay, anatomy of a takedown, using these images. If we tried to do that for tomorrow, one, we'd need a full page. Colour. And we'd need the Art Department involved.' Wilson Omstead, the Deputy City Editor, adds: 'We could move some ads off page three to accommodate it.' Other editors around the table nod. Some take notes. The discussion turns for a short while to police ethics more generally, its performance in various tense situations, but the chair soon moves the discussion on to other matters. (Observation Diary, 8 March 2005)

In the following day's newspaper, photo stills from CP24 were arranged next to a story of about 600 words. But the larger and more elaborate visual graphic that Lee Bourrier and his editorial peers had discussed did not materialise. Ideas discussed in features meetings sometimes remain fantasies that cannot be translated within a day into arrangements on published page. Nevertheless, the scenario that I have recounted above provides a snapshot of a wider and important disposition that I both observed in the practical work of editing and discussed with editors in interviews. This was their attempt to grapple with what they understood to be an increasingly sophisticated visual acumen among their audiences:

"You know, the younger readers in particular, I think, are much more, have much more of a, uh, magazine sensibility. Their expectations, in terms of design, are very different than people who grew up with older fashion newspapers, where frankly they were a dog's breakfast in terms of they, things were just thrown kind of in there … expectations have changed, and, you know, technology allows us to present in a much more clean way, and effectively, I think. And I think readers are expecting that." (Irwin Connelly, Editor-in-Chief)

Over a number of years, studies had shown that reader eyes were drawn to colour and shape more so than to text. And increasingly, major newspapers were seizing on the visual presentation techniques – photography, graphics and innovative page design – associated with the magazine medium.

At the *Toronto Star*, a rather bold move in this regard was an experimental Sunday edition, introduced in early 2005. Colloquially labelled by editors as a 'magapaper', it combined newspaper format (that is, page size, paper quality) with a magazine-like use of photos, design, layout and longer, well-written stories, across 72 full-colour pages. Since its introduction in 1977, the Sunday edition had been a poor sibling to the flagship weekend paper on Saturday. This latter edition had long been the *Toronto Star*'s platform for weekend features deemed to be truly important, and with very few events classifiable as 'hard news' taking place on Saturdays, Sunday was a comparatively thin edition, with low advertising take-up. This meant, however, that the Sunday edition offered a flexible canvas of page space and opportunities for more advance planning, making it a good 'petri dish' for experimentation, which is how the Sunday Editor pitched the proposal to the normally unadventurous Board of Directors at parent company Torstar. The experimental nature of the magapaper was eventually confirmed when, following a major redesign of *Toronto Star* in late May 2007, the *Sunday Star* reverted to a design template closely mirroring the other editions throughout the week.

But working alongside and multiplying from this experiment were many smaller efforts to enhance the overall visuality of the *Toronto Star*. These included not only new styles and techniques for displaying photographs, but also various innovations in the use of illustrations and graphics. Perhaps most interesting was the increased use of 'infographics', which are graphical diagrams, sometimes quite elaborate, designed to organise complex concepts, processes or events; in other words, to visually order such content as "this, this and then that" (Valorie Zeigler, Head of Graphics). These particular types of graphic design were thus explicitly understood to be ideal for doing the explanatory and factual work of journalism:

> 3.00pm. I arrive, with transportation reporter Manny Ingleston, at the University of Toronto's IntelliCAN Transportation Systems (ITS) Centre. Sitting in a presentation room, facing a large-screen TV surrounded by 20 monitors showing live traffic via closed circuit cameras, we are about to endure a demonstration of a complex highway simulation model. Manny introduces me to Gil from the Graphics Department, who's attending the demonstration to explore the possibility of making a graphic related to the event, and of course, to Manny's article. Without any prompting, Gil assures me: 'You know, we don't just do these things to fill space; I only come into play if a visual graphic is the best way to explain the information.' (Observation Diary, 29 March 2005)

To approach these new presentational techniques and technologies purely through textual or semiotic analyses of newspaper content would fail to apprehend the practical work entailed by such efforts. Editors at the *Toronto Star* were developing new methods to deal with issues of design and graphics as part of their daily discussions and decisions around the overall organisation of the newspaper content:

> "To give you an indication … this morning's meeting, two of the editors were drawing graphics on their [notepads], and I laughed about it, I thought, this is great … it's good because now we've got a shared language…. They're all confident illustrators now which is totally cool … I laugh about it, [but] at a certain point I won't be necessary any more, because they'll all be so aware that they'll be able to communicate directly with the illustrators and the artists." (Valorie Zeigler, Head of Graphics)

But more than simply developing practical competencies vis-à-vis graphic design, editors were making implicit and explicit practical judgements on the reading circumstances of their audiences. For example, they made complex judgements about the possibilities printed imagery provides for readers to absorb and engage detailed information, whereas by comparison television imagery is constrained by viewers' attention within a specific span of time. So, along with the coming together of new visual literacy and new technologies were new repertoires for representing and addressing publics. Increasing attentiveness to photos, graphics, illustrations, layout and colour were taken to be effective and affective registers of feel, style, aesthetics, pattern, attraction and emotion. Yet despite the important shifts implied by such new visual experimentation, simultaneously entering the site of editing was a medium that, to invoke McLuhan, brought forth a rather different 'message' or set of effects and affects: that of internet technology as the incipient platform for an online newspaper.

Digital publics

In the middle of the 1990s, a modest website made its way into the new forms of publicness then quickly emerging through the World Wide Web. A bare-bones, sparse web page, split into two columns, news content to the right, scarcely formatted section hyperlinks and a few small advertisements to the left. Thestar.com was the *Toronto Star*'s response to what was still seen, even at that recent juncture, as a newly surfacing form of online communication. At its genesis, and for much of the decade that followed, thestar.com was a website that more or less straightforwardly reproduced the content from the printed newspaper, and was updated only once a day. As with other North American metropolitan newspapers, its initial intention was largely to be a tentative online barrier, erected to preserve the newspaper's monopoly of public discussion and market share in relation to its urban-regional geography of circulation (Barnhurst, 2002).

Yet by 2005, there was a palpable sense that internet-based technologies would become the inevitable medium of circulation for future newspapers. Indeed, over a mere decade, thestar.com had evolved – through both major redesigns and many smaller but cumulatively significant changes – into a multilayered, complex website based on a 24-hour news cycle. At the point of my own fieldwork at the newspaper, editors, designers and other production staff were working towards a quite radical redesign using completely new web architecture. The new thestar.com, eventually launched in 2006, enabled enhanced use of photos, audio, video and podcasts as well as much more cross-linking between related stories. It also included an inset media player, a powerful search tool, compatibility with RSS feeds and new opportunities for readers to tag content. In working up and working with an online edition, there was hope – if sceptical, qualified, reserved – that somehow the metropolitan newspaper model, or something akin to its specifically urban scale of public and market circulation, might translate to a new digitised medium, with its altered rhythm of circulation:

> "If 20 years from now there is, you know, newspapers really have died
> … and people … are preferring to read, you know, an electronic news
> service several times a day rather than a newspaper once a day, maybe
> the advertisers will have, by that time, have completely migrated over to
> that … some kind of electronic news service that's like a newspaper in a
> lot of the same kind of *intangible* ways…. It's not a bulky paper product
> that's trucked, by gasoline burning vehicles, across a wide geographic
> area. Instead, you put all those same resources, at the editorial side, and
> the advertising side, and the creative side, and design, and puzzles, and
> community information, and listings and all of that stuff is now just
> electronic. You know, as long as they, as long as you can make it work
> on the same scale, that's a good thing." (Erik Yongken, Internet Editor)

Intrinsic to the translation demanded by online media technology were shifts in the ways in which newspaper journalism might communicate and resonate (Ettema, 2005) with its publics. Web *display*, to begin with, was seen as introducing capacities and constraints into the experience and practice of reading news that were different from the printed page. The scale and resolution of most viewing technologies (computer monitors, but also increasingly portable devices) associated with internet-based presentation meant there was a basic tension with the concurrent experiments with enhanced visuality discussed above. But the implications of internet technology were rather more fundamental. Newspaper pages provide a finite – yet relatively flexible and customisable – space for the arrangement of content into a printed milieu of adjacencies and connections: "In the paper you get, you know, maybe more of a layout where everything can sort of come together and, and people can look at it really quickly, then focus on one thing" (Erik Yongken, Internet Editor). As Nerone and Barnhurst (2003) observe, newspaper pages characteristically set out a kind of diorama, presenting readers with a series of represented relationships between content, an intimate sort of social map, which, beyond transmitting or ritualising content (see Carey, 1989), creates a certain kind of ethereal *environment* that affirms the public world to which the newspaper as medium relates. Web display, by contrast, is based on a potentially limitless content space, yet one also organised into relatively fixed design templates and subdivided into pages, requiring news readers to select and make their way through an indexed environment of stories. So arguably, web display 'unveils the plumbing system of the newspaper' (Nerone and Barnhurst, 2003, p 122), disassembling the dioramic presentation so fundamental to the newspaper's distinctive metabolism of collated, printed pages.

The templated nature of content on a site like thestar.com is directly linked to the new *temporal* rhythms implied by the web-based presentation of news. In the early months of 2005, during my observation period, the site of editing was overwhelmingly based on practical routines and a material setting orientated to the *daily* production of the newspaper, from the timing of work shifts and meetings, to the arrangements of workspaces and newsroom technologies. Through the iterative work of assembling a diorama, editors and journalists seemed to reaffirm, in turn, their daily participation in a public discussion, which had certain implications for the sorts of news and commentary thereby valued. Yet on thestar.com, content was being added, changed and removed much more frequently – almost continuously – introducing values somewhat more akin to radio and television:

> "... a local story about a traffic accident, or something like that, might be a much bigger story on the website than it is in the paper.... You see this, the same, similar thing happening on radio and TV. A story that's a top story all day on the radio, if it's a traffic (story), for example ... but by the time it's over, if, if there wasn't major implications for, you know, for transportation in the GTA [Greater Toronto Area] beyond a single day, it's not likely gonna be a big story in a paper. But, it will be a big story on the web because people ... are interested, this is the kind of information that they find useful in the day." (Erik Yongken, Internet Editor)

The newspaper transpiring through an online medium theoretically offers no (or much less) obvious 'punctuation' for public address, because unlike the printed newspaper, it is not an artefact requiring the same type of physical transportation and distribution to its audiences across space (Warner, 2002, pp 97-8). This does not mean an online newspaper cannot connect with a phenomenology of dailiness (cf. Scannell, 1996 on radio and television broadcasting) – and many efforts were dedicated to making thestar.com relevant to the specifically daily routines of readers – but a temporality of daily public address is not an intrinsic feature of circulating news online.

Perhaps above all, however, it is the potential *interactivity* and *flatness* of online circulation that is so often posed as the principal challenge, if not outright threat, to journalistic and editorial authority. New journalistic technologies such as blogging, for example, do not necessarily require infrastructure for or intervention by the various sorts of editing work that exists at a newspaper organisation like the *Toronto Star.*Yet despite these (very often hyperbolic) qualities associated with online communication, *Toronto Star* editors and management hoped for and were dedicated to an adaptation of online communication that was at least partly on their own terms:

> "… at the end of the day, I cannot imagine a society in which quality information, reliable and verified information, and a serious editing role, and informed and trusted commentary, are not things that are all valued. And I would argue in a world of more and more information … in which, to some degree, everybody can be a journalist, and therefore it becomes harder and harder to know … what's true and what isn't, that the true reporting function, and the editing of that, and the editing of this mass of information into some form which is accessible and manageable for people, and informed commentary, … I believe all of that is gonna have as much value, or more value."
> (Osborn Chamberlane, Publisher)

Nevertheless, internet technology, and web browsers in particular, bring about some basic forms of interactivity almost by default. The data trail left through the page views of visitors, for instance, offered editors an unprecedented trace of reader attentiveness to different types of content. Thestar.com was a place where, often, 'quirky' and 'odd' stories would become the most read, and in anticipation of this internet editors were sometimes placing such stories higher up on the main news page hierarchy. So, in effect, with the click of their mouse, online readers were now collectively expressing their own preferences in terms of content and news importance, rupturing a sphere of decision making previously reserved for the professional judgement of editors and journalists (cf. Nerone and Barnhurst, 2001).

Timing and spacing editorial authority

So far I have used efforts at visuality and digitising to elucidate new mediums entering into and disrupting the site of editing. Yet I have said relatively little about the site of editing specifically, and why it is such an important lens for considering the adoption and adaptation of these new media at the *Toronto Star*. I would like to suggest that the site of editing is important because it was a site of authority, not only in relation to the organisational spaces of the *Toronto Star*, but also in relation to its entanglement in a circulatory public. Editing is, of course, more than just an unrelated collection of practices such as proofreading, explaining, emailing, turn taking in meetings and so on. These sorts of dispersed practices are bound together by the teleoaffective structuring (Schatzki, 2002, p 80) of editing: the emotions and normative ends that are expected, accepted and shared in relation to editing practices. Perhaps the most important teleoaffective dimension of editing at the *Toronto Star* was the notion of a reading public, as an explicit end for their work, as well as something with and for which they had implicit trust, responsibility, belonging and attachment. In sharing these sensibilities of acceptability, propriety, expectation and desire, editing had performative coherence and degrees of ascribed normativity and managerial responsibility vis-à-vis other organisational sites, such as reporting. Moreover, the nature of editing as site meant that it was distinctly positioned at a formative moment in which the *Toronto Star* came together as *both* media artefact and organisation. Editing was therefore a site in which the effects of such new technologies as visual and online presentation were particularly noticeable and acute.

For editors, the new timings and spacings of public address brought about by these new media technologies (and others as well) correspondingly necessitated new timings and spacings of organisational work at the *Toronto Star*. During my 2005 fieldwork, a good deal of turbulence had been created in the wake of a study commissioned by senior editors that analysed the ways content ('copy') moved through the work areas of the organisation until eventually reaching the newspaper's suburban press centre. This report seemed, for editors, to have an overall thrust: that work flow was getting more and more complex, certainly in part resulting from the new demands of visual and online presentation, and decisions around the final arrangement and angle of particular stories were being made later and later:

> "I mean you really have, you've been here at a time, well I think you've seen both ends of it, or at least you've seen the old way it was done, and sort of a glimpse of what we're trying to do. And the old way was, you know, like the news desk, the afternoon operation would come in and they would start making decisions, and really key decisions wouldn't be made until the absolute final moment. Um, and that's a … sort of journalist approach to the world, which is holding off, holding off, holding off 'cause something could change, but, uh, well, it doesn't work that way." (Lee Bourrier, City Editor)

The last remark may appear to be an empirical claim, but it was spoken with overtones of normativity. It was for senior and departmental editors – the 'morning operation' – to formulate the main presentation and angle of major news stories, not principally news or copy editors, whose proper focus was meant to be on detailed or technical matters such as the length, grammar, structure and factuality of content. Because of these concerns, the timing, conduct and location of daily news meetings, for one, became a central controversy for editors. But meetings were just part of the equation; important gatherings of important people, yes, but effective only by corresponding with the rhythms of activity elsewhere in the organisation (Boden, 1994, p 83). Simultaneously under way was an experiment with a new team-based (also called 'pod') system in the City Department, in which new editing posts were created to lead on flexible thematic groupings of content (such as 'New Toronto', 'City Features', 'GTA Politics', 'Education' and so on). These new editors were to arrive midday, liaise with city reporters working stories in their thematic area, and at the same time, interact with senior city editors, graphics staff, photographers and others over the day and into the early evening. In the longer term, team editors were to become the primary intermediaries between reporters and senior editors across the organisation, to follow groups of stories as they developed (and also mutated online), and identify various sorts of presentational possibilities for their themed content in the printed newspaper.

It would not be an overstatement to say there were great hopes for these attempts at reorganising, which imitated the experiments of other newspapers. The insertion of team editors was meant to make for new spaces of time and establish new connections between areas and stages of work; in other words to transcend, or otherwise work across, the traditional spatial divisions of newsroom work, and the Fordist-like stages of newspaper production:

> "I mean, and that's just part of the Star evolving away from the strict segmentation of, you know, I make the letters from hot lead, and I take this, this guy over here takes those, turns them into words, and this guy sets those up in type, and this guy, you know, they haven't even started reporting yet. So it's all, kind of, coming together." (Innes Witcar, Team Editor, City Features)

In tandem with other initiatives (notably in retraining), journalists were to become more empowered, more able to be interdisciplinary, able to work their beats more imaginatively, engage with graphical forms of communication and write with distinctive voices online and in print. Many journalists saw things differently, of course. There was more than a hint of correspondence between these initiatives and the management discourses of the business world, on the merits of so-called flat management and overlapping workspaces over rigid hierarchical control and segregated work areas. Academic work has read these as managerial techniques to more subtly regulate and activate the practices and subjectivities of workers (du Gay, 1996; Dale, 2005; Thrift, 2005). In a sense, journalists saw things in a similar way; or at least, they could see the managerial imperatives at play in such initiatives:

> "You know we just introduced this new pod system ... this is the system that's gonna completely alter the way we do business in the city section, and this is gonna save us, and make us ... as *if.* I think it's these guys, all sitting in a room, figuring this all out, you know, it's like a chess game or something, you know, then we're gonna do this, then we're gonna do that, and of course, in the meantime there's the real world, which, you know, has nothing whatsoever to do with their plans." (City Columnist)

Efforts to reorganise the timing and spacing of work were not just attempts to realign the actual physical coordinates and chronological times at which different activities and technologies came together, but to do so in ways that were normatively *well-placed* and *timely* from the standpoint of editorial authority (cf. Czarniawska, 2004).

In focusing on the site of editing, I have tried to point out that even as the materiality of particular media technologies is in interplay with the wider complexities making up *mediums of publicness*, they cannot be regarded as two interchangeable configurations. In my own accounts above, the former are material entanglements helping to constitute what the site of editing inherently was or could be. The latter is perhaps better thought of as the circulatory configuration of public communication in which the site of editing and *Toronto Star* as organisation were entangled as very powerful obligatory points of passage (see Couldry, 2000, p 5, drawing on Callon and Latour, 1981), which affected in turn how such new media technologies were put to use.

Conclusion

At this point, I want to momentarily step back from the substance of this chapter, and reflect on the sort of field research that has led to the discussion so far. After all, attending to the site of editing in the way I have done stems directly from (and required) a certain kind of methodological work: situating myself in the newsroom, observing the performance of different routines, noting down material settings and objects in use, shadowing bodies in action, listening to talk in meetings and elsewhere, carrying on conversations and asking questions. These relatively short-lived experiences were in countless ways exciting and rewarding. Yet on reflection they also imply a certain style of research that is subject to the limitation of radical partiality often ascribed to ethnography as a methodology. For example, I could see that the site of editing was insulated, both practically and normatively, from those sites concerned with the business of the newspaper, such as advertising, marketing, circulation, promotions and syndication. More than a partition wall separated these business and editing workspaces. They were on different floors, part of different divisions of the company. Editorial and business staff crossed paths in places like the cafeteria, or otherwise in meetings arranged for specific purposes, to which I was often not invited, or which, of course, occurred before or after my arrival. Even if my situated observations helped me to piece together some of the ways this insulation was maintained, it would be accurate to say that I barely scratched the surface of cross-fertilisation going on. The pursuit of urban publics by editors seemed to also be, with sometimes precious little distinction, the pursuit of urban markets.

Even if, in response to my own self-worry, I were to affirm that my focus was on the *public* work of editing, rather than its quasi-business rationalities, I nevertheless would have to admit that my research style was radically partial. Indeed, I seemed to be subconsciously aware of it, given my near-relentless anxieties about 'being there'. I frequently worried about my timing and placement; I wanted to see, hear and even feel the various events I considered relevant to the taking place of editing work. Yet on reflection, Law (1994, p 45) seems exceedingly accurate in (only half-jokingly) observing that very often 'where the ethnographer is, the action is not'. And it was more than just being there: I was also worried about remembering to take notice of and record those matters in which I was most interested. To be sure, I used additional methods to mitigate my worries and fill in some of the blanks: I tracked daily newspaper content over six months, read across several documentary sources and, importantly, conducted 58 in-depth interviews. But there were nevertheless multiple dimensions important to editing as a site of public action, and in turn the *Toronto Star* as a configuration of public address, which I quite simply did not and could not get at.

Why reflect on these matters of method? To begin with, I hope they provide an insight into one approach that might be taken in researching the practices and settings of public action. The reason for reflecting on these matters at this point, however, is to underline how the research I undertook leads to the sort of conclusions I can make in this chapter. Partly, this is because ethnography has a propensity for producing the unexpected. In setting out to do my field research, I had not necessarily been interested in the relationships between editing practices and new media technologies, nor had I expected them to be so important. But more importantly, the blind spots I worried about in my research, as well as the ones I have not even recognised (what Law, 2004, calls respectively 'manifest absences' and 'Otherings'), have conversely allowed me to *make present* certain aspects of public action and its related mediums. I will end by focusing on three in particular.

First, this chapter has revisited the notion of mediums of publicness by attending to the performativity and situatedness of public action. This focus has implied, on the one hand, an image of publics as heterogeneous and processual; what Clive Gabay and Simon Hutta both helpfully call 'public becoming' in Chapters Nine and Ten of this volume. On the other hand, focusing on the performativity and situatedness of public action also highlights its fragility, and in my context, puts into question simple assertions of dominance and hegemony common to many accounts of media. Mediums of publicness are often haunted by a conception of media as a quasi-machinic order: *the* media, with power *over* publics and *effective* in relation to subjectivities (Rodgers et al, 2009). In this chapter I have tried to remove some of this mystique, where mainstream media organisations are theorised, yet not very often actually studied, as sites of hegemonic power. Even as the accounts in the chapter have shown editing to be a powerful site of public action, with sanctioned authority and degrees of autonomy over what gets to count as matters of public concern, they have also shown it to be a site at which such matters can never be unilaterally decided. This is because the site of editing is positioned in relation to, and in some ways subjugated by, the public sphere in which it *participates* (cf. Rodgers, forthcoming). Editing is no more in control of its publics than are consumers of media fully attentive to the public world to which they are exposed (Couldry and Markham, 2007). Recognising this is especially important when we conceive of a public sphere as discourses and affects that are reflexively circulated, distributed, strung out over a space of time, and convened through multiple mediums (Warner, 2002; Barnett, 2007).The site of editing enacts its power as a milieu through which much more widely distributed or extensive public spaces of circulation and potential are momentarily crystallised or made coherent (Lee and LiPulma, 2002; Marston et al, 2005, p 426).

Second, this leads to some specific observations on how new media technologies can make a difference to this relationship between editing as a site of momentary crystallisation and wider circulatory spaces of public discourse and affects. We might begin by observing how, in the example in this chapter, these media technologies seemed to *anchor* the work practices and public orientations of editors (Couldry, 2004). Editing was defined not only by participating in discourses of the public, but also by its taking place in and through specific material settings and technologies. In other words, the publics of editing were not only convened in a discursive sense, but also materially assembled or shaped (Carpignano, 1999; Latour, 2005; see also Chapter Eight in this volume).This assembly or shaping made a difference: the more interpersonal nature (Lüders, 2008) of the visual and digital mediums discussed in this chapter compelled editors to engage and enter into (or at least be *seen* to enter into) dialogue with the subjective experiences and perspectives of Toronto's more multiple publics.The increasing appearance of those new media technologies enabled, even demanded, new orientations that de-emphasised addressing the audience as a mass urban public, a well-recognised and long-standing editorial tradition of the *Toronto Star*.All the same, it is important to bear in mind that these material effects did not take place in a vacuum. Editors acted on an understanding of the *Toronto Star* as an important organisation in Toronto's public life over many decades. Editing was also a site of authority in relation to the work of various journalists and production staff, who in turn were connected to various sources of expertise, knowledge and authority in the wider social and political world. For these and other reasons, interplaying with the appearance of new media technologies were practical understandings of editing as, at least to some degree, an adequate and legitimate site of public action. Editors were therefore not only materially positioned to order content and assemble a public representation, but also able to do so in such a way and *claim to be representative* (Saward, 2006) of publics.

Finally, in making the above observations, this chapter has offered a critical antidote to hyperbolic pronouncements about the revolutionary novelty of emerging forms of media. Such hyperbole takes us only so far in understanding actually occurring sites of public action because it tends to speak of new media outside of any situated milieu, while allowing others to make sweeping predictions about how new technologies affect politics, whether positively or negatively. In this chapter, by contrast, we have seen that a so-called old media organisation, the *Toronto Star*, is neither static nor necessarily in competition with an externalised 'new media'. Instead, the vignettes in this chapter underlined that the *Toronto Star*, like all organisations, is constantly in motion and constituted *through* change (Linstead and Thanem, 2007). None of this denies how new media technologies can and do reconfigure patterns of public action or public address.What it does argue against, however, is a strong coupling of specific media technologies with either complex media organisations or the more expansive notion of mediums of publicness. The latter are not always indicated by what seem to be the newest or most unprecedented media technologies; new media technologies must be set into a longer historical perspective, and seen for the ways in which their uses and effects are interwoven with the uneven geographies and temporalities of communication (Boczkowski, 2004; Morley, 2006; Chapters Two and Five in this volume). With these points in mind, we might broaden our imaginations about the scope of possibility for bringing about alternative mediums of publicness.

Note
[1] The names used here – both for human actors mentioned in observation passages and attributions of interview quotes – are pseudonyms.

References
Alterman, E. (2008) 'Out of print: the death and life of the American newspaper', *The New Yorker*, 31 March.

Barnett, C. (2007) 'Convening publics: the parasitical spaces of public action', in K.R. Cox, M. Low and J. Robinson (eds) *The handbook of political geography*, London: Routledge, pp 403-17.

Barnhurst, K.G. (2002) 'News geography and monopoly: the form of reports on US newspaper internet sites', *Journalism Studies*, 3, pp 477-89.

Boczkowski, P.J. (2004) *Digitizing the news: Innovation in online newspapers*, Cambridge, MA: MIT Press.

Boden, D. (1994) *The business of talk: Organizations in action*, Oxford: Blackwell.

Callon, M. and Latour, B. (1981) 'Unscrewing the big Leviathan: how actors macro-structure reality and how sociologists help them do it', in K. Knorr Cetina and A. Cicourel (eds) *Advances in social theory and methodology: Toward an integration of micro- and macro-sociologies*, London: Routledge and Kegan Paul, pp 277-303.

Carey, J. (1989) *Communication as culture: Essays on media and society*, London: Routledge.

Carpignano, P. (1999) 'The shape of the sphere: the public sphere and the materiality of communication', *Constellations*, 6, pp 177-89.

Couldry, N. (2000) *The place of media power: Pilgrims and witnesses of the media age*, New York, NY and London: Routledge.

Couldry, N. (2004) 'Theorising media as practice', *Social Semiotics*, 14, pp 115-32.

Couldry, N. and Markham, T. (2007) *Media consumption and public engagement: Beyond the presumption of attention*, London: Palgrave Macmillan.

Czarniawska, B. (2004) 'On time, space and action nets', *Organization*, 11, pp 773-91.

Dale, K. (2005) 'Building a social materiality: spatial and embodied politics in organizational control'. *Organization*, 12, pp 649-78.

du Gay, P. (1996) *Consumption and identity at work*, London: Sage Publications.

Ettema, J.S. (2005) 'Crafting cultural resonance: imaginative power in everyday journalism', *Journalism: Theory, Practice and Criticism*, 6, pp 131-52.

Franklin, B. (ed) (2009) *The future of newspapers*, London: Routledge.

Garnham, N. (1992) 'The media and the public sphere', in C. Calhoun (ed) *Habermas and the public sphere*, Cambridge, MA: MIT Press, pp 359-76.

Habermas, J. (1989) *The structural transformation of the public sphere*, Cambridge: Polity Press.

Holmes, D. (2002) 'Transformations in the mediation of publicness: communicative interaction in the network society', *Journal of Computer-Mediated Communication*, 7(2), http://jcmc.indiana.edu/vol7/issue2/holmes.html, accessed 5 March 2010.

Iveson, K. (2007) *Publics and the city*, Oxford: Blackwell.

Kittler, F. (1999) *Gramophone, film, typewriter*, Stanford, CA: Stanford University Press.

Latour, B. (2005) 'From Realpolitik to Dingpolitik, or how to make things public', in B. Latour and P. Weibel (eds) *Making things public: Atmospheres of democracy*, Cambridge, MA: MIT Press, pp 14-43.

Law, J. (1994) *Organizing modernity*, Oxford: Blackwell.

Law, J. (2004) *After method: Mess in social science research*, London: Routledge.

Lee, B. and LiPulma, E. (2002) 'Cultures of circulation: the imaginations of modernity', *Public Culture*, 14, pp 191-213.

Linstead, S. and Thanem, T. (2007) 'Multiplicity, virtuality and organization: the contribution of Gilles Deleuze', *Organization Studies*, 29, pp 1483-501.

Lüders, M. (2008) 'Conceptualizing personal media', *New Media and Society*, 10, pp 683-702.

Marston, S., Jones III, J.P. and Woodward, K. (2005) 'Human geography without scale', *Transactions of the Institute of British Geographers*, 30, pp 416-32.

McLuhan, M. (1964) *Understanding media: The extensions of man*, Abingdon: Routledge.

Morley, D. (2006) *Media, modernity and technology: The geography of the new*, London: Routledge.

Nerone, J. and Barnhurst, K.G. (2001) 'Beyond modernism: digital design, Americanization and the future of newspaper form', *New Media and Society*, 3, pp 467-82.

Nerone, J. and Barnhurst, K.G. (2003) 'News form and the media environment: a network of represented relationships', *Media, Culture and Society*, 25, pp 111-24.

Rodgers, S. (forthcoming) 'Mediating new cities of diversity: the *Toronto Star* and Toronto's reading publics', in R. Dennis, C. Morgan and S. Shaw (eds) *The contemporary Canadian metropolis*, London: Institute for the Study of the Americas.

Rodgers, S., Barnett, C. and Cochrane, A. (2009) 'Mediating urban politics', *International Journal of Urban and Regional Research*, 33, pp 246-9.

Saward, M. (2006) 'The representative claim', *Contemporary Political Theory*, 5, pp 297-318.

Scannell, P. (1996) *Radio, television and modern life: A phenomenological approach*, Oxford: Blackwell.

Schatzki, T.R. (2002) *The site of the social: A philosophical account of the constitution of social life and change*, University Park, PA: Penn State University Press.

Thrift, N. (2005) *Knowing capitalism*, Thousand Oaks, CA: Sage Publications.

Warner, M. (2002) *Publics and counterpublics*, New York, NY: Zone Books.

FIVE

Mediating publics in colonial Delhi

Gurpreet Bhasin

> The native newspapers are humble in appearance, yet like the ballads
> of a nation they often act where the law fails and as straws on a current
> they show its direction nowhere else to be found....Whether one looks
> at the stagnation of village life or the need for rousing the native mind
> from the torpor of local selfishness, the importance of the vernacular
> Press is very great.... If government wish correct news to circulate in
> the villages, they must use the vernacular Press as organs for diffusing
> it. The enemies of the English government are not inactive. Already
> ideas are rapidly spreading in various districts that English power is on
> the wane, that the Russians are coming to India and would govern it
> better than the English do .... (Reverend J. Long, cited in Jagannathan,
> 1999, p 18)

In late 19th-century India, the burgeoning of print media and new public
spaces of discourse ushered in distinctive forms of politics as well as new forms
of colonial governmentality. These new media practices politicised public spaces
and they created important links, networks and circuits of discussion – not only
within British and Indian arenas, but also among an emerging global pan-Islamic
movement. This chapter looks at how colonial publics emerged, functioned and
were made effective in late 19th- and early 20th-century Delhi by highlighting
different aspects of public mediation. I emphasise the vital contribution of print
media and other public spaces of discourse to the cultural and political landscape
of colonial Delhi, and draw attention to the various strategies employed by the
British and the Indian elite to shape these spaces.

   I am interested in the late 19th and early 20th century because this era
immediately preceded the shift of the capital of British India from Calcutta to
Delhi, and it was a time when Delhi was becoming increasingly involved in
national and global networks of activities, driven by the growth of print media.
Part of my PhD research was based on the analysis of newspapers, pamphlets and
public meetings as complex public spaces of discourse in which the British and
the Indians participated in order to fulfil diverse cultural and political objectives.
In this chapter, I draw on a post-colonial approach that emphasises the multiple
and differentiated characteristics of colonial public spheres and focuses on their
emergence as a product of the diverse and interacting strategies of Indian elites and
the British colonial government. I begin by describing how post-colonial theories

can be applied to empirical research in order to develop new understandings of how public spaces were mediated and how they functioned in the colonial context. I then briefly discuss how I carried out my research and how I applied a model of discourse analysis to explore the emergence and workings of colonial publics. In discussing the findings of my research, I focus particularly on the impact of print media in fostering the creation of public spheres in the context of local, national and global concerns such as the partition of Bengal and pan-Islamism in response to the First World War. I conclude by highlighting the significance of the politics of mediation.

Post-colonial theories and public spheres

Research in post-colonial theory to date has prioritised the analysis of colonial governmentality. This questions the universalising tendencies of colonial discourses and provokes discussions about the vulnerability of colonial strategies and the recovery of native agency. However, post-colonial geographers and colonial researchers still have some way to go in their efforts to engage empirically and theoretically with the diverse and complex strategies of colonised peoples to create their own spaces and identities. To this end, I propose a more nuanced and, indeed, more accurate, understanding of the roles played by publics, discourse and the print media in defining colonial relations, identities and spaces.

The initial focus of post-colonial theory was on the way that literature by the colonising culture appropriated the realities, distorted the experiences and, as a result, inscribed the inferiority of the colonised populace. Arguably the most influential post-colonial theorist, Edward Said pioneered this field of analysis with the publication of *Orientalism* (1978) and extended and redefined his debates in *Culture and imperialism* (1993). In *Orientalism*, Said describes how the West produced the Orient through a series of discourses, asserting that these discursive constructions of the Orient were a crucial part of the colonisers' strategies to dominate and control the colonised. The originality of Said's contribution is in his use of literary texts and discourses to explain the cultural and political processes of the colonisers. The emphasis on, and use of, discourse theory in Said's work is inspired by Michel Foucault's (1972, 1977, 1978) theorising on power, knowledge, subjectification and bio-politics. Although Foucault's focus is not on colonial studies, his investigations into the operation of power in society and his claims about discourses as crucial to the institutional operation of that power have been developed by post-colonial studies.

Much criticism has rightly been levelled at foundational post-colonial theories for prioritising the analysis of the strategies of the colonisers over those of the colonised and for being built around the concept of 'Otherness', thereby perpetuating binary conceptions of colonial relations. A major criticism of Foucault is that he pays too much attention to the pervasiveness of power and therefore does not allow for investigations into forms of resistance and agency. These critiques have led successive post-colonial theorists to make considerably more nuanced considerations about colonial discourses and colonial power. For example, Homi Bhabha (1991, 1994) shows us that colonial discourses may be permeated and transformed by the discourses of the colonised, thereby paving the way for discussions about the discursive practices of the colonised; whereas Spivak (1994) cautions us to be thoughtful when recovering the agency of the colonised, saying that we must question the modes of representing the colonised as well as the legitimacy of those representations. Post-colonial theory has, therefore, evolved, and no longer prioritises a hierarchical view of colonial relations; rather, it problematises the relationship between the colonisers and the colonised. I would argue that post-colonial theory is now synonymous with discursive analyses that critically examine the operation of colonial governmentality as well as the cultural and political practices of the colonised. In other words, post-colonial theory is concerned with examining the contributions of the colonised and the colonisers to the construction of colonial spaces and societies.

In this chapter, I set out to apply the key concepts of post-colonial theory, that is, the emphasis on the discursive construction of colonial identities and spaces and the problematising of colonial discourses and colonial relations, in order to study the emergence and significance of public spheres in colonial Delhi. I do so by drawing on my investigations in the colonial archives in order to understand how colonial public spaces emerged, how they were mediated and how they functioned. In my research, I looked at public spaces of discourse and communication such as newspapers, pamphlets and even public meetings. These were participatory spaces in which the British and Indians became involved through the attachment of cultural and political values, and through direct action. Jurgen Habermas's theories of the public sphere (1989) have been seminal for our understandings of public spaces of discourse and print culture's contribution to them. Habermas describes the public sphere as a space between the state and civil society that accompanied the transition from representative to more democratic forms of government and he is interested in the social conditions that were necessary to the functioning of this public sphere (Calhoun, 1992). In this sphere, public opinion could form and evolve and the bourgeois press was a critical contributor to its formation. Most significantly, Habermas emphasises the importance of print culture to the development of the public sphere. The public sphere in Delhi, as I discuss in the latter sections of this chapter, was constituted from several public spaces of discourse in which Indians could articulate their cultural and political aspirations and also where the colonial government could design its policies of censorship and control. Print culture was crucial to the development of these public spaces.

Habermas's model of the public sphere is a highly rationalised model of societal integration that is contingent on discourse and communication. He does not explicitly consider varying axes of identity such as race, social class and gender, nor does he consider power as a component of analysis in his discursive model of public space. However, according to Seyla Benhabib (1992), we have the opportunity to expand and enhance Habermas's concepts because the chief virtue of Habermas's discourse model of public space is 'its radical indeterminacy and openness [because] it neither restricts access to public space nor sets the agenda for public debate' (Benhabib, 1992, p 84). Therefore, while I agree that the public sphere was a crucial space for social and political integration and that discourse and print culture were crucial to the functioning of the public sphere, in this chapter I emphasise the view that there were multiple public spheres in Delhi that were constituted by various discourses and for a number of reasons. Sometimes they were highly rationalised, like newspapers and planned public meetings, and at other times they were very spontaneous and highly improvised, like some political pamphlets, spontaneous public meetings and public protests (Warner, 2002). I apply the concepts of post-colonial theory in order to examine the discursive construction of the multiple public spheres in Delhi by the British and the Indians and to demonstrate that, in these spaces, different and often conflicting ambitions and practices manoeuvred for articulation and control.

Understanding Delhi through colonial archives

In order to examine the emergence and growth of public spheres in colonial Delhi, I searched through official colonial records in Delhi and London and also looked at non-state documents such as newspapers and some secondary sources. I read the colonial records in order to understand how the state's political rationale was constructed. As I describe in the following section, the priorities of the state, as far as the management of public spaces of discourse was concerned, adapted in response to the changing political circumstances in Delhi, India and globally and, most importantly, in response to the discourses and practices of the Indians. I also read Indian letters, petitions, pamphlets and newspapers in order to analyse how Indians constructed their own cultural and political understandings. In addition to reading the records *along* their grain, in order to check for patterns and consistencies, I read them *against* the grain in order to question the claims made by the various parties and to check for irregularities and inconsistencies. The archives that I worked in were not merely sites from which I extracted material in order to support my beliefs about processes of colonialism and about the social relations that defined Delhi's colonial spaces. I was always conscious of the social meaning of the archives, as technologies that had been integral to the production of knowledge and power and a part of the apparatus of colonial rule. They were not merely discursive constructs but they also had discursive properties. Inspired by the work of post-colonial theorists, I was keen to uncover the methods by which the British and the Indians mobilised discourses and other resources in order to construct and participate in public spaces, or to disrupt and prevent their construction altogether.

The process of selecting which evidence to use is necessarily complex and does not follow a linear trajectory. Throughout the process of looking for and collecting data, I was guided by intermediaries such as archivists, historians and other academic researchers who also encouraged me to rethink the parameters of my research. Moreover, many colonial records contained only partial files and sometimes files were missing altogether, because they had been misplaced or destroyed by the holding repository. I reworked and adapted my research questions and manoeuvred the direction of my research according to what I found in the archives. Far from being linear, the fieldwork experience was very much a circular process. Archival records are formed of multiple layers of information and knowledge, and the process of reconstructing that knowledge is also necessarily defined by several layers of selection and interpretation.

I used discourse analysis to interpret the data in the archival records. Discourses comprise words and language that construct identities, relations and spaces. Discourse analysts are not primarily interested in distinguishing fact from fiction in discourse; rather, they are interested in the work that discourses do. I examined the productive effects of discourses; for instance, I described how the British produced certain representations about Indians and interpreted their discourses in ways that were designed to exclude them from the public spheres. I also analysed Indian discourses to show how they mediated publics and produced identities and spaces in colonial Delhi. The British and the Indians attempted to mobilise discourses in order to fix or privilege certain meanings over others, so both colonial power and native agency are at stake here and are constantly entangled. I historicised the discourses that I analysed, tracing their changes over time and placing them in their appropriate historical and political contexts. Finally, I looked at how discourses were supported by institutional, cultural and political practices (following Carabine, 2001). In the following sections, I discuss how the British colonial state and the Indians in Delhi contributed to the emergence, mediation, censorship and control of publics in the context of specific events and through a series of discursive and other practices at local, national and global levels.

Print media and emerging publics

Print media emerged as an important medium for the construction and communication of social and political discourses for the Indians after the 1860s. Print culture and technology mediated multiple public spheres and they also shaped relations between the British and the Indians and between Indians in local, national and global spaces in unprecedented ways. Indian-owned newspapers in English and in vernacular languages gradually became important spaces for subjecting society and government to critique. By circulating within and between local, national and international spaces and by carrying news stories from all over the world, often extracted from British and international newspapers, they created important material and symbolic connections between distant spaces. Surveillance of vernacular newspapers by the colonial state began in earnest after the mid-19th century when 'Reports on Native Newspapers' was created, consisting of extracts from vernacular newspapers from all over India (Bayly, 1996, p 341). Following this, the government began a sustained and vigorous campaign to censor and restrict Indian discourses and the public spaces in which they were constructed and circulated, with a combination of press and sedition laws. In 1870, an Act was passed in order to make sedition an offence under the Indian Penal Code. Sedition was described thus:

> Whoever by words, either spoken or intended to be read, or by signs, or by visible representation or otherwise, excites or attempts to excite feelings of disaffection to the Government established by law in British India, shall be punished with transportation for life or for any term, to which fine may be added, or with imprisonment for a term which may be extended to three years, to which fine may be added.... (Cited in Donogh, 1911, p 8)

This deliberately broad and flexible definition of sedition left it entirely to the government's discretion to decide what constituted 'disaffection'. The colonial state awarded itself a rather generous ability to discursively construct the Indians and their words and actions as seditious. It had the lawful authority to interpret the harmful effects of words and language and to prevent their circulation in public spaces. In a further move to bolster the campaign against sedition, the Vernacular Press Act was passed in 1878. In accordance with the Act, Indian newspaper owners had to provide a bond for 10,000 rupees in order to register their papers with the Registrar and they also had to agree not to publish any seditious material (Jagannathan, 1999, p 116). A security deposit was also required for the first time that could be forfeited if the paper were found guilty of publishing seditious material. Indian newspaper owners had no way of legally challenging these requirements or the confiscation of any material. This Act was debated vociferously by the Indian press and at a public meeting, Surendranath Banerjee, creator of the *Bengalee* newspaper in Calcutta, analysed 32 examples of what had been identified by the state as seditious writing and declared the allegations of sedition to be contentious and questionable. Bannerjee showed that, in many cases, certain phrases and parts of articles had been taken out of context (Jagannathan, 1999). In order to restrict the Indians' access to the public sphere, the state had assumed the role of interpreter and armed itself with legislation to enforce its interpretations. What the government had defined as seditious was shown by the Indians to be misinterpreted and false. Indian opposition to the Vernacular Press Act was largely responsible for its repeal in 1881 (Jagannathan, 1999). Soon after the repeal, a colonial officer remarked that the Indian Press was becoming more reckless and he encouraged the passing of even more stringent press legislation because:

> "Language may be tolerated in England which it is unsafe to tolerate in India, because in India it is apt to be transformed into action instead of passing off as harmless gas. In legislating for India we must have regard to Indian conditions, and we must rely mainly on the advice of those who speak under the weight of responsibility and have the

peace and good government of India under their charge." (Cited in
Donogh, 1911, p 64)

The colonial state was emphasising the Indians' differences in order to justify the
creation of laws to restrict the growth of public spaces of discourse. Post-colonial
theorists and colonial researchers have repeatedly shown that the construction
(often ethnographic) of colonised peoples as different was a favoured strategy of
colonial rule (see Chatterjee, 1986, 1993; Metcalf, 1994; Dirks, 2001). The Indian
situation was different, it was argued, and so it required different measures. The
state was mobilising and fixing specific meanings about the Indians that served to
endorse its own role as guardian of Indian public spheres. More restrictive press
legislation would be passed in 1908 and 1910.

In addition to, and in step with, the growth of print spaces of discourse, there was
also an increase in the formation of social and political groups. The formation of
the Indian National Congress represented the first enduring initiative to organise
Indians around nationalist issues and its growing influence in Indian public spheres
became of great concern to the colonial state. Also of considerable concern was
Hindu opposition to the partition of Bengal, in the south of India, into Bengal,
East Bengal and Assam, proposed in October 1905. Among the measures that
Indians adopted to express their opposition were *Swadeshi* (self-sufficiency) and
Swaraj (self-rule). *Swadeshi* was an economic movement that encouraged the
boycott of British products by promoting the consumption of Indian products and
Indian methods of production. All this anti-partition activity was facilitated and
fuelled by the Indian press and public congregation. Indian newspapers in Bengal
promoted *Swadeshi* and anti-partition messages that then got taken up by the press
all over India, including in Delhi. There was an increase in public meetings in
Delhi to share and spread the messages of the Indian National Congress and the
anti-partition activists. The colonial state responded to these events by extending
the legislation against sedition to incorporate public meetings.

According to the Seditious Meetings Act of 1907, the state could determine
which, how many, and indeed whether, people could meet for public political
discussion, and any meetings that were permitted were spied on by colonial officers.
According to this Act, a meeting was 'public' even if it was held at a private place
and any gathering of more than 20 persons was a public meeting. The private
spaces of Indians were politicised and made public and therefore open to state
legislation and control. The state's definition of a 'public' meeting was deliberately
flexible and allowed it to enter into the private lives of Indians and prevent the
construction of spaces of political discourse. With the law of sedition, the various
Press Acts and the Seditious Meetings Act, all obvious spaces of political discourse
were brought under the surveillance of the colonial state.

In spite of and, indeed, because of the state's attempts at censorship and control,
Indians created innovative ways to come together and communicate through the
press and public and private meetings. There was a marked growth in nationalist
activities in Delhi, following the introduction of local self-government, the

creation of the Indian National Congress and the proposed partition of Bengal. Opposition to the measures of censorship and control by the colonial state were increasingly articulated in public forums. In this way, censored discourses were continually brought back into public spheres. Political activists in Delhi expressed their support for anti-partition activists in Bengal with political demonstrations and silent protests and in various print media. In addition to nationalist activities, communal concerns among Hindus and Muslims were manifested in public spheres, through meetings, newspapers and pamphlets. Colonised elites, motivated by communal, nationalist and anti-colonial causes, constructed public spaces of discourse and landscapes of public political practices. Anti-colonial opposition was only one of the motivations for the Indians' participation in public spheres.

When newspapers and printing presses were prosecuted for printing seditious materials, new newspapers and presses sprang up in secret locations. Pamphlets, often coming into Delhi from other parts of India and from exiled political émigrés in Europe and America, became an effective way to circulate political messages all over the city, from railway platforms to school and college campuses. The circulation of newspapers and pamphlets between and within different spaces created symbolic and material connections between them, and their distribution and circulation within multiple spaces in Delhi politicised the urban landscape in unprecedented ways. It is vitally important to analyse the ways in which colonised peoples created discursive connections between colonial spaces because they too were involved in local, national and global exchanges of people, discourses and materials. Research in post-colonial geography has prioritised the analysis of imperial networks created by the European colonisers, but it is essential to recognise that colonised peoples also created and were involved in networks of political practices that informed the policies and contributed to the formation of the colonial state. Colonial spaces and societies were made by these flows and networks of people, discourses and materials at local, national and global levels.

Public spaces of discourse, therefore, were crucial to the expression and communication of the diverse political and cultural ambitions of Indians, and print culture was responsible for the growth of new spaces of discourse such as newspapers and pamphlets. As the political landscapes of India and Delhi became more fluid and volatile, with Indians taking an increasing interest in national and international issues and articulating their ambitions in various public spaces, increasingly through discourse and the print media, the colonial state sought to subject these spaces to surveillance and control. For the colonial state, therefore, public spaces of discourse were integral to the exercise of its authority. However, it always had to negotiate its access to, and control over, public spaces and to contend with Indians who employed a diverse range of discursive and other practices in order to construct and participate in these spaces. The practices of the colonial state, while designed to circumscribe the growth of public spheres in Delhi, often had the opposite effect. It is imperative to acknowledge the emergence and mediation of these new publics as a series of complex processes in response to specific cultural and political imperatives by the British and the Indians.

In the following section, I look at an Indian newspaper in Delhi, the *Comrade*, and at the efforts of its editor, Mohamed Ali, to summon publics in support of the cause of pan-Islamism following the outbreak of the First World War. I look at how Ali mediates publics through discursive practices in the print media and at the efforts of the colonial state to disrupt him, in order to further illustrate the complex processes by which public spaces of discourse emerged and functioned in colonial India.

Pan-Islamism in the public spheres

The colonial state's campaign to disrupt the emergence and mediation of Indian public spheres once again assumed a heightened urgency during the First World War. Immediately prior to the First World War, there were a number of national and international events that especially concerned the large Muslim population in Delhi. In India, the scheme for a Muslim university was rejected and a mosque in Cawnpore (Kanpur) was partially demolished in order to straighten a road. This resulted in a riot in which several Muslims were killed by the colonial authorities. In addition to these domestic events, the Italo-Turkish War in 1911 and the Balkan War in 1912 had a significant impact on Muslims all over India. These attacks by Christian allies of Britain on Muslim populations made many Indian Muslims feel as if the British were not interested in protecting Muslim interests abroad. These events were widely documented and denounced in Muslim-owned newspapers and pamphlets all over India. The state used the Press Act of 1910 to deal with the 'reckless campaign by Muhammadan newspapers against the British Empire, Christianity and Europe' (Delhi State Archives: 54/1918/Home Confidential Files). Sometimes these wars were described as Christian wars against Islam in the Muslim press, but this was not always the case. There were Muslim journalists and newspaper editors who constructed thoughtful commentaries and critiques in response to these events; however, the state insisted on interpreting and portraying even these as anti-colonial and anti-Christian in order to prevent their emergence in public spheres. Support for Muslim causes in the public sphere was responsible for the growth of pan-Islamism, which has been described as a series of efforts by Indian Muslims to choose the ideal of Islamic brotherhood for the articulation of their political aspirations and to organise moral and material support for Muslims all over the world. Mohamed Ali, a Muslim journalist, editor and political activist in Delhi, was instrumental in keeping the government's and the public's attention on domestic and international Muslim causes and events. He encouraged the growth of pan-Islamism by creating networks of communication and support through the medium of his English language newspaper, the *Comrade*. However, Mohamed Ali was not only a Muslim; he was also Indian and a British subject and he used his newspaper to express and negotiate these different aspects of his identity. The colonial state's attention, however, was trained on Ali's pan-Islamic activism.

The *Comrade* was a weekly newspaper that had an extensive readership among the British and the Indian elite. It was a public space of discourse that embodied the diverse and complex cultural and political ambitions of Mohamed Ali and other contributors. At the outset, Ali declared that 'His Majesty's Indian subjects of every class and creed have as much right to give advice in the affairs of the Empire as any resident of the British Isles or of the Colonies, and our voice sooner or later will have a fair hearing' (*Comrade*, 20 September 1913). Mohamed Ali was asserting his identity as a British subject; he was using his newspaper as a medium of communication with the British colonial state, which he believed he was entitled to do as a colonial citizen.

In the *Comrade*, Mohamed Ali wrote and published a number of editorials, articles, humorous anecdotes, short stories and poems, and he featured a number of cartoons on a range of themes, including popular culture, politics and religion. He had a 'Letters To The Editor' section where he received several responses to his articles, primarily from Muslim journalists and community leaders but also from British colonial officials. Ali had created a public space for the communication and exchange of discourses on a range of social issues, from the flippant to the meaningful. Ali's passion, however, was manifested in his dedication to national and international Muslim causes and events (see Jafri, 1965; Hasan, 1979, 1981; Dixit, 1981) and in this way, Ali fostered the creation of connections between Muslims in distant spaces and contributed to the growth of pan-Islamic sentiment and activities. While Ali wrote extensively about Muslim causes and produced deeply reflective articles about Islam, particularly in his later years, he wanted the Muslim community in India to progress. He believed that cooperation with Hindus, and participation in nationalist organisations like the Indian National Congress, would serve the Muslims well (unlike a growing number of Muslims who wanted to separate from India and create an independent state). Therefore, although passionate about Islam, Mohamed Ali was a nationalist who embraced his Indian identity and articulated this in his newspaper.

In the *Comrade*, Ali received letters from fellow Muslim newspaper editors, expressing criticism of the various Press Acts and charges of sedition against certain Muslim newspapers. In this way, Ali created a network of support for his fellow Muslim editors. He himself accused the state of misusing its authority with respect to the Indian press and press legislation and he directly challenged the state's interpretations of 'seditious' discourses. As emphasised above, censored discourses and the state's discursive practices repeatedly became public sites of contestation that pervaded and led to the growth of public spheres all over Delhi and India. Ali saw it as imperative that the publics' and the state's attention remain on the plight of Muslims in India and beyond, using his own newspaper to those ends. However, Mohamed Ali's mediation of publics in these ways conflicted with the colonial state's ambitions for public spaces of discourse and its interpretations of the discourses circulating within them. Ali's commitment was to create a community of concern and support for Muslims in India through discursive practices in the print media which shaped relations, not only between Muslims within India and beyond, but also between different Indian groups and between Indians and the colonial state.

Ali wrote several articles in response to European attacks and invasions of Muslim countries in the Ottoman region, often making passionate expressions of solidarity with Muslims in these regions. He earnestly described the collective sympathy and concern that Muslims felt for each others' suffering. Ali was, however, continually negotiating his loyalties and the various aspects of his identity. He was often keen to emphasise his status as a colonial citizen and British subject. In one article, he declared, 'We can confidently say that the same spirit of loyalty and devotion actuates the Indian Mussalmans to-day' (*Comrade*, 20 September 1913), referring to the British state. In spite of his declarations of loyalty to the colonial state, the Delhi government focused almost exclusively on Ali's pan-Islamic discourses and interpreted them as incitements to disaffection between Muslims and Christian. Ali and his pan-Islamic discourses and activities became the prime locus of the Delhi government's efforts to survey, vilify, manipulate and, indeed, prevent the construction of public opinion in Delhi. Following the outbreak of the First World War, when Turkey entered the war against Britain and the Allies, Ali was torn between his pan-Islamic loyalties to his Muslim brethren in Turkey and his loyalty to the colonial state. He wrote a number of thoughtful editorials about the war that were declared to be seditious and were censored by the state. My own analysis of his articles interpreted them to be deliberative, contemplative and even provocative, but seditious they were not.

The state repeatedly described Muslim public opinion as either for the colonial state or against it, as either favourable or unfavourable. When people like Mohamed Ali constructed thoughtful and complex political narratives in the public sphere that the state admitted were 'within the strict letter of the law', it chose to represent them as harmful and dangerous. Pan-Islamism was not seen as a positive effort to construct a community of support and concern for Muslims; it was always described negatively in the colonial reports as a phenomenon that threatened to undermine the British state. When the state perceived a threat to its authority and credibility in public spaces, it often resorted to negative assumptions about Indians' discourses and identities and it developed harsh and even desperate attempts to manipulate them or exclude them from public spaces altogether. There was a difference between the overtly anti-Christian rhetoric in some Muslim pamphlets and newspapers and the cunning analogies constructed in the *Comrade* by Mohamed Ali. Yet, their effects were interpreted as being equally objectionable and dangerous by the state. Pan-Islamic discourses and activities were not inherently anti-British or anti-Christian; however, the colonial government made concerted efforts to show them as such. This universalising of Indians' perspectives and agendas was designed to reduce complex spaces of discourse to subjects of colonial governmentality. The colonial state shaped its roles in public spaces on the basis of those constructions about Indians' identities and discourses; however, as I have emphasised repeatedly, the state's role in public spaces was always informed by the role that Indians played within those spaces.

Conclusion

As I have shown in this chapter, it is only possible to appreciate the complexity involved in the mediation and workings of colonial public spaces when we engage with the discursive and other strategies of the different people who were involved in them through a dynamic series of relationships. The Indians employed discursive practices, the print media and other mediation exercises such as meetings and demonstrations in order to create and participate in public spaces, and they constructed discursive and material links with people in local, national and global colonial sites that informed the way that public spaces in Delhi were shaped. The British also employed discursive and political practices in their efforts to restrict and shape the growth of public spheres in Delhi, to exclude Indians from them and to construct their roles as guardians of these spaces. As the colonial state shaped its policies and its role in public spaces, it had to do so in response to the Indians who were shaping their own identities and ambitions in these spaces. It is the combination of mediation exercises by the Indians and restrictions on them by the colonial state, or the dynamics of publication and censorship, that determined the emergence of publics of discourse in Delhi. A politics of representation was integral to the strategies of the colonial state, as it was to those of the Indians, with the British representing the Indians and their discourses as different, seditious and dangerous and the Indians publicly articulating their communal, anti-colonial, nationalist and pan-Islamic agendas and identities. Therefore, while colonial discourses and public spaces were sites for colonial power, they were also sites for various manifestations of Indian agency.

My work thus develops post-colonial theories by problematising colonial relations and by analysing the discursive construction of colonial society and spaces through careful archival research that considers the contributions of colonised Indians as well as the British colonisers. It demonstrates, by considering how discourses, print media and publics emerged and functioned, that colonial spaces were complex, multiple and multilayered sites of interaction that were defined by a range of discursive, political, cultural and spatial practices. I have also emphasised that print media was an important innovation that allowed Indians to create and sustain public interest in a range of issues, and I went on to examine the different processes of mediation (through public meetings, the circulating of pamphlets, discursive practices in newspapers) and how they arose very much as responses to specific local, national and global events. However, as much as I have stressed that print media was an important innovation, I have emphasised its significance as a medium or channel of communication that was very much embedded in, and a product of, the larger social and political processes and relations of its time (see Chapter Four in this volume).

This chapter goes some way towards challenging traditional conceptions of the public sphere as a single and highly rationalised entity, showing instead how colonial public spheres comprised multiple and differentiated sites of cultural and political interaction, from the spaces of rational political discussion, such as the *Comrade* newspaper, to the spontaneous public demonstrations and ad hoc meetings that took place in Delhi in response to the partition of Bengal. These were each spaces within which the complex and different aspirations of the colonial state and the Indians manoeuvred for articulation and control. I have also stressed the different motivations of the Indians (nationalist, communal, pan-Islamic, anti-colonial) and the British (interpretation, control, censorship, power) in order to demonstrate that the familiar power–resistance dynamic that pervaded earlier post-colonial theories and analyses is insufficient for analysing colonial spaces. But more than motivations is at stake here. What the analysis offers is a way of engaging with how print media and especially discursive strategies addressed the public and shaped relations and identities in practice. As Chapters Two, Three and Four of this volume have highlighted, it is imperative to engage with different forms of mediation in order to appreciate why and how various publics and forms of politics are constituted and, ultimately, to understand why these publics are such a significant part of our political and cultural landscapes. As I have shown in this chapter, public spheres or public spaces of discourse, mediated by various elements and for a number of reasons, were vital for the British and the Indians. Understanding the politics and different forms of participation involved in mediating these publics is key for appreciating why they are such important arenas for communication and action, how they work and how they can be made more effective.

References

Bayly, C. (1996) *Empire and information: Intelligence gathering and social communication in India 1780-1870*, Cambridge: Cambridge University Press.

Benhabib, S. (1992) 'Models of public space: Hannah Arendt, the liberal tradition, and Jurgen Habermas', in C. Calhoun (ed) *Habermas and the public sphere*, Cambridge, MA and London: MIT Press, pp 73-98.

Bhabha, H. (1991) 'Post-colonial critic: Homi Bhabha interviewed by David Bennett and Terry Collits', *Arena: A Marxist Journal of Criticism and Discussion*, Spring, pp 47-63.

Bhabha, H. (1994) *The location of culture*, London and New York, NY: Routledge.

Calhoun, C. (ed) (1992) *Habermas and the public sphere*, Cambridge, MA and London]: The MIT Press.

Carabine, J. (2001) 'Unmarried motherhood 1830-1990: a genealogical analysis', in M. Wetherell, S. Taylor and S.J. Yates (eds) *Discourse as data: A guide for analysis*, London, Thousand Oaks, CA and New Delhi: Sage Publications, pp 267-307.

Chatterjee, P. (1986) *Nationalist thought and the colonial world: A derivative discourse*, London: Zed Books for the United Nations University.

Chatterjee, P. (1993) *The nation and its fragments: Colonial and post-colonial histories*, Princeton, NJ: Princeton University Press.

Dirks, N.B. (2001) *Castes of mind: Colonialism and the making of modern India*, Princeton, NJ: Princeton University Press.

Dixit, P. (1981) 'Political objectives of the Khilafat Movement in India', in M. Hasan (ed) *Communal and pan-Islamic trends in colonial India*, New Delhi: Manohar Publications, pp 43-65.

Donogh, W.R. (1911) *A treatise on the law of sedition and cognate offences in British India, penal and preventive: With an excerpt of the acts in force relating to the press, the stage, and public meetings*, Calcutta: Thacker, Spink and Co.

Foucault, M. (1972) *The archaeology of knowledge*, London: Tavistock Publications.

Foucault, M. (1977) *Discipline and punish: The birth of the prison*, New York, NY: Pantheon Books.

Foucault, M. (1978) *The history of sexuality, volume 1: An introduction*, London: Random House.

Habermas, J. (1989) *The structural transformation of the public sphere: An enquiry into a category of bourgeois society*, Cambridge, MA: MIT Press.

Hasan, M. (1979) *Nationalism and communal politics in India, 1885-1930*, New Delhi: Manohar Publications.

Hasan, M. (ed) (1981) *Communal and pan-Islamic trends in colonial India*, New Delhi: Manohar Publications.

Jafri, S.R.A. (1965) *Selections from Mohamed Ali's Comrade*, Lahore: Mohamed Ali Academy.

Jagannathan, N.S. (1999) *Independence and the Indian press: Heirs to a great tradition*, New Delhi: Kornak Publishers Pvt Ltd.

Metcalf, T. (1994) *Ideologies of the Raj*, Cambridge: Cambridge University Press.

Said, E. (1978) *Orientalism*, London: Routledge.

Said, E. (1993) *Culture and imperialism*, New York, NY: Knopf.

Spivak, G. (1994) 'Can the subaltern speak?', in L. Chrisman and P. Williams (eds) *Colonial discourse and post-colonial theory: A reader*, New York, NY: Columbia University Press, pp 66-111.

Warner, M. (2002) *Publics and counterpublics*, New York, NY: Zone Books.

SIX

Public and private on the housing estate: small community groups, activism and local officials

Eleanor Jupp

Chapter Five shows how public and private spaces of discourse were contested in colonial Delhi. But a focus on boundaries between public and private has long been associated with feminist struggle, with women working to show how their 'placing' in the private or domestic sphere, as opposed to a masculine public sphere of political and economic activity, has been a key aspect of their oppression and exploitation. Lister (2003a, p 119) talks of 'the historical centrality of the public–private divide to the exclusion of women from citizenship in both theory and practice'. However, this chapter examines these insights within a UK policy context in which citizenship has precisely been seen as increasingly linked to family and community (Rose, 2001), where indeed social policy could be seen as inhabiting the terrain of 'women's work' (Newman, 2009). This context is examined through a focus on the (gendered) lines between private and public lives among small groups of resident-activists, and the local officials with whom they worked on two housing estates in Stoke-on-Trent, UK. The chapter seeks to explore how these women constructed their activism in this policy climate and the 'contact zones' (Pratt, 1992) between officials and citizens in which policies are mediated. A particular focus will be on the work of both the activists and officials with local teenagers and their families. Overall, the chapter will assess how far critical feminist perspectives on the public and the private might need to be reconsidered in the light of this changing context. I will argue that in many respects the feminist critique of such a dichotomy remains salient and important; however, this is now being articulated in a new context that involves reconfigurations of male/female, public/private, and state/citizen categories.

After briefly reviewing relevant literature, I introduce the research setting and some of the overall 'contexts' in which the groups were operating. I then move on to focus on the work of both the groups and the local officials with teenagers. This aspect of local activism and of government intervention is examined as an example of a set of concerns that clearly brings aspects of private and domestic lives into 'public' arenas, and indeed could be seen as involving particular gendered positions, particularly as the activists drew on their experiences of parenting.

The public and the private in theory

The starting point of many feminist critiques has been the suggestion that the public–private distinction is strongly linked to the construction of a patriarchal society, where 'male was to public as female was to private' (Warner, 2002, p 32). Many writers have explored the ongoing construction of this distinction historically (for example, Davidoff and Hall, 1987; Pateman, 1988) and increasingly have drawn attention both to the ways in which such constructions shift over time (for example, Bondi and Domosh, 1998) and to how women have always found spaces in which to assert influence and develop solidarity, even when excluded from 'public' life. For example, Mary Ryan describes how in early 19th-century America, women played a significant role in providing for the poor: 'It was women – excluded, silenced or shouted down in public, democratic and male dominated spaces – who carved out another space in which to invest psychic, social, and political energies' (Ryan, 1992, p 273).

Organising among women, both historically and in a contemporary context, therefore becomes a way of challenging distinctions between public and private, although how this is worked through has been conceived of in a number of different ways. For example, Stall and Stoecker (1998) suggest quite a clear-cut distinction between what they call 'women centred organising' in areas of deprived social housing and a community activism tradition influenced by Saul Alinsky. They see the Alinsky tradition as characterised by 'aggressive public sphere confrontation' (Stall and Stoecker, 1998, p 735) such as demonstrations, mass meetings and highly visible, symbolic forms of protest that seek to shift the balance of power within a particular context. The women–centred model they see as grounded in 'the more relational world of private sphere personal and community development' (Stall and Stoecker, 1998, p 735), beginning with personal transformation, care and 'empowerment', and expanding this in ways that ultimately dissolve boundaries between private and public realms. Stall and Stoecker also link such activism to an 'ethic of care', as opposed to an 'ethic of justice' in which caring and nurturing relationships are extended beyond the home (see also Gilligan, 1982; Day, 2000).

Other analyses suggest that women are more mobile and self-reflexive about their styles of organising (for example, Staeheli, 1996; Fincher and Panelli, 2001). This is linked to broader debates about the nature of gendered identities, and therefore politics. Fincher and Panelli (2001, p 129) propose that women make 'strategic use of spaces, places and various spatial scales' in that they are able to move between spheres and modes conventionally understood as private or public to their advantage. Staeheli (1996) argues that women's collective action can break down boundaries between public and private, but the fact that it is often 'placed' in the private sphere operates to their advantage in giving them 'shelter' to develop strategies that may not be visible. Indeed, Ryan's (1992) analysis of 19th-century women's activities follows a similar argument: 'beyond this flimsy screen of privacy, women met a public need, saved public funds, and behaved as shrewd politicians' (p 279).

Such arguments challenge us to develop new tools of analysis in relation to the public–private divide. Some commentators have used the idea of 'liminal' spaces in which women are actively constructing a new kind of space, between private and public, that will enable them to become 'empowered' as individuals and also in terms of broader political projects (Martin, 2002; Buckingham et al, 2006). Buckingham and colleagues use this term in relation to government-led 'training' spaces for women, spaces that have been set up in order to encourage women into one aspect of 'public' life, formal employment; yet they see them being used by the women in a range of ways that have more to do with socialising and domestic lives. The notion of 'liminality' is therefore seen as a way of understanding the emancipatory potential of such spaces, with the suggestion that a fluidity between public and private might be empowering for women.

However, within the context of my research, such 'liminality' could also be seen more critically as a kind of policy 'tool', in which government interventions are designed to engage with subjects in particular private or domestic settings and to draw them into particular new formations of the public. This would suggest rather different framing of 'empowerment' or 'citizenship', as part of particular government agendas. This resonates with Giddens' (1998) formulation of 'life politics' as part of a climate of the 'third way', and, in a different way, with Foucauldian critiques of new governmentalities of the person. For example, Rose (2001) argues that the economy now needs new kinds of flexible, responsible and autonomous 'citizen-workers' and that this requires policy to be taken into new areas such as family life and the very formation of subjectivities. Indeed, programmes aimed at young children have been criticised (Lister, 2003b) as being shaped by the desire to create 'citizen-workers-in-becoming'.

It would seem, then, that there is a need to challenge the suggestion that there is always a continued and powerful investment in the retention of separate public and private spheres, linked to gendered identities. Much contemporary social policy has developed in ways that link citizenship with family and domestic life, perhaps understood within an extended setting of 'community' (Fink, 2004; Lewis, 2004). For example, programmes such as Sure Start seek to link community and neighbourhood development to spheres of family life and childcare. This challenges arguments that 'social capital' (key within contemporary policy formation) is still understood as based on male-dominated activities such as sports clubs and pub attendance, and a deliberate 'liminality' between public and private is arguably a feature of many spaces in which the state intervenes in everyday lives.

Nonetheless Lister (2003b) also argues that governmental programmes frame spaces that a range of actors may use in different and unexpected ways, while Newman and Clarke (2009) suggest that liminal spaces may not be easily subject to governmental control, becoming sites of instability. Such sites of instability, in which lines between 'state' and 'citizens', as well as between public and private lives, become 'porous and unstable' (Painter, 2006) can also be viewed as 'contact zones' (Pratt, 1992). Pratt developed this concept in relation to colonial encounters, in order to

> ... foreground the interactive, improvisational dimensions of colonial encounters so easily ignored or suppressed by diffusionist accounts of conquest and domination. A 'contact' perspective emphasises how subjects are constituted in and by their relations to each other ... in terms of copresence, interaction, interlocking understandings and practices, often with radically asymmetrical relations of power. (1992, p 7)

I would suggest (following Lendvai and Stubbs, 2007; Newman and Clarke, 2009) that, rather than 'liminality', which perhaps gives less sense of what might actually happen in such 'in-between' spaces, a 'contact zone' analysis foregrounds the active and mutually productive nature of encounters between government and citizens.

Research methods and context

The material presented here is drawn from my PhD project, which involved ethnographic research with two small-scale, resident-led community groups based on the Westfields and Riverlands housing estates in Stoke-on-Trent, UK. These are areas of material deprivation as well as other forms of disadvantage, particularly in terms of health and education. The groups were regarded locally as being highly successful, and undertook a range of social projects as well as physical interventions under broad goals around improving the 'quality of life' for residents in their areas. Both were based in 'community houses', ordinary houses given to the groups on a rent-free basis by the council, and they were supported in various ways by the local state, including particular officials, although they did not have anything like a stable income. Both groups revolved around a committee of volunteers and a wider group of residents who took part in and helped with activities. Ongoing projects were often based around the needs of particular age groups, for example, parent-and-baby sessions, play sessions, youth projects and activities for the elderly.

The focus of the research was on the spaces of the groups' work, one aspect of which was how they intersected with state actors and interventions. I spent around 15 months doing research with the groups. Although I had intended from the start to use ethnography as the central methodology, initial fieldwork visits were structured around interviews and discussion groups, as this somehow felt like what I should be doing in order to 'do research'. However, I quickly found these methods floundering (see Jupp, 2007), failing to grasp the potency of the spaces and practices of the groups, as well as positioning me very firmly as a 'researcher'. As this became apparent, and my own confidence in the settings grew, the project became more fully ethnographic in that I became essentially a 'volunteer', working alongside the women in the groups, playing with children, digging allotments and cooking with teenagers (although continuing to do some interviews with officials). Such an 'embodied ethnography' (Parr, 1998) led me in particular to an analysis of the material and practised aspects of such spaces, as well as the talk that happened within and around them; indeed, as should be apparent in what follows, I came to see these aspects of interactions in the spaces as having particular potency. More broadly, I would suggest that ethnography enables an iterative and pragmatic approach to developing theories of the public, which may be especially helpful given the somewhat abstract theoretical debates in which 'the public' has been a key category.

However, I clearly also needed to place my ethnography of these particular spaces within various kinds of 'context', and one of these was a consideration of a sphere of spaces and discourses that might be called local 'political society' (Corbridge et al, 2005, p 188, following Chatterjee, 2004). This is the wider realm of sites and discourses of power struggles involving elected politicians as well as officials and citizens, and mediating relations between local people and government in more complex ways than framings such as 'civil society' may suggest. I was particularly interested in the gendered aspects of this sphere, and how these relate to notions of 'public' and 'private' activities and spaces, as well as relations between government and citizens. As I shall argue, interactions in this broader sphere often demonstrated the persistence of conventional constructions of public and private, tied to oppressive gender relations in particular. Within this context, the realm of neighbourhood-based state activities and 'contact zones' may be seen as one particular version of the state; however, it is a 'feminised' one. This echoes Sharma's (2006, p 73) analysis of 'empowerment work' among women as marginal compared with 'proper state work as facilitating productive economic growth'.

A particular gendered mode of local politics was apparent at a number of more formal 'public' meetings that I attended, including a series of 'community forum' meetings set up by the local authority, as well as the 'public' meetings set up by the groups themselves, such as their annual general meetings (AGMs). These occasions tended to be dominated by elected officials who were overwhelmingly male. Their presence could sideline the interests and capacities of the community groups. For example, at a meeting on Westfields organised by the community group about a controversial proposed redevelopment of the estate, the local MP made a number of long speeches, referring on occasion to "the good work done by the girls here with families and kids", but effectively allowing them very little voice in the meeting. Despite the fact that the group was actively campaigning around the development plans, the suggestion was that their activism, with its roots in the private, domestic sphere, did not engage with the 'public' politics of economic decision making. Jill, the chair of the community group, later described the MP's style as "oppressive". She also told me that he was just "jumping on the bandwagon" of the issue.

On another occasion, at the Riverlands AGM, it was not just the groups who were referred to in gendered and potentially disempowering ways by local politicians, but also a (female) local official who was working as a 'community facilitator'. The 'community facilitation service' was an experiment that involved seconding certain council officials to act as key points of liaison with residents in particular neighbourhoods. In many ways, it set itself up as a challenge to local councillors as conduits of public opinion, and was certainly experienced by councillors as a threat. Indeed, the scheme was eventually brought to a close because of lack of support from councillors. The meeting in question was nominally chaired by a council official, but was controlled by the local councillor, who began the meeting by introducing the official: "We have a new young girl here tonight, the pretty one there in the middle". The councillor stood up throughout the meeting, sometimes roaming around at the back, interjecting comments and intervening when the conversation became particularly heated. He therefore very much positioned himself as the mediator of local opinions, using a particular gendered and performative mode of politics. It should be noted that on such occasions there were often more interesting discussions over cups of tea before and after the meetings, and Young (2000) has drawn attention to the importance of greetings and small acts of hospitality on the edges of overtly 'political' occasions. Nonetheless, there is an importance attributed to 'public', visible politics; it is notable that the press reported on the Westfields meeting quoting only the MP.

Such a fracturing of modes of politics and indeed of modes of government work could also be seen in discussions with senior council officials, who often contrasted 'community'-based interventions, associated with domestic spheres of family and neighbourhood, with 'strategic' (that is, economic) ones, in ways that could be read as gendered. An official with city-wide responsibility for green spaces spoke to me about the importance of investing in 'strategic' (that is, incoming generating) as opposed to 'local' spaces: "talking to the community isn't the be-all and end-all, we've got to take the wider view ... somebody somewhere has to take a strategic view of the world". The community- and neighbourhood-based work remained part of the state's work, but for the senior officials that I interviewed, based in central council offices, such work was often seen as marginal, feminine and perhaps not part of the important, 'public' work of the council.

By contrast, the officials who featured more regularly in the lives of the community groups tended to be women, who were often based in 'local' offices in or near the neighbourhoods. It is in their contacts with the groups that the boundaries between public and private lives and politics seemed to become more uncertain and unstable. Of course, the fact that this whole sphere can be seen as gendered does not in itself suggest anything about its normative politics; rather, it is a question of seeing that there are multiple forms of government work that bring with them different potentials in relation to the public and the private, and perhaps new forms of 'contact zone'. It also undermines any straightforward account of government social policy and the 'third way'. I will therefore now move on to considering the young people and teenagers in the neighbourhoods, an issue that fell into the realm of concern both for the community groups and for some of the officials in the neighbourhoods.

Young people in Westfields and Riverlands

'Young people' or 'teenagers' were often seen locally, both among officials and some local residents, as the defining *problem* for both neighbourhoods. Sandra, the chair of the Riverlands group, spoke to me about the 'negative light' in which young people were seen, "you know, all youth are useless, they're no good, they cause trouble on the streets". Indeed, it was young people's presence in the outside spaces of the neighbourhoods that was at the centre of discussions and feelings about their behaviour; this clearly generated real fear for other residents, particularly the elderly. For example, one elderly woman told me that she didn't like going outside in the neighbourhood any more, because of "too many 15- and 16-year-olds taking over the streets". Among young people themselves, concerns about other young people's 'gangs' were expressed to me, and there was also suggestion of involvement with drugs, although more often the 'problem' seemed simply to be their presence outside, or low-level 'messing around' (see Valentine, 1996, 1997, 2004 for a more general discussion of young people's presence in outside spaces). Indeed, I sometimes found it hard to get beyond the ongoing discussion and concern about young people in both neighbourhoods to understand what might actually be happening on the streets. My most striking conclusion was that this was a highly contested issue that brought residents into conflict with each other and also framed particular encounters with the local authorities.

Indeed, for the two community groups that were the focus of my study, the issues around young people were one of the motivating factors behind their activism. Both groups consciously distanced themselves from discourses that circulated on the estates positioning young people as a problem, and rather attempted to take a more holistic and sympathetic approach to collective life on the estates. As Sandra said:

> "Riverlands residents didn't come together over one issue, it was the community, what can we do to improve the lives of people round here, rather than we want to shift these youths from outside ... but it was more, we were concerned with the quality of life, social aspect of life round here, the services which weren't being provided that should be provided, so it wasn't just something like that."

The 'like that' I took as a reference to other residents' collective initiatives that focused on a negative approach to young people.

In taking up these views, there was a clear link with the private lives of the activists, who were nearly all parents, or indeed grandparents, and were often related to the young people seen as problematic. There were a number of instances of several generations from one family being involved with the groups, and even if not active as group members, volunteers' children would come along to the groups' activities. Furthermore, in terms of material spaces, the location of both groups in 'community houses' meant that they had very clearly continuities with the domestic realm. At Riverlands, Sandra lived next door to the community house, with Mick, her husband, and three teenage children, all of whom were heavily involved both as volunteers and participants in various activities.

One way of understanding the groups' activities, therefore, and one that has resonances with some of the analysis with which I began this chapter, would be as an extension of family life into the wider public realm. Mick told me that before starting the group, Sandra had always organised activities for local children on an entirely informal basis. Mick said: "Years ago, when our kids were little ... half the kids on the street, she would take them off on 'adventures' ... so we always had lots of kids around." A number of the volunteers were at a stage where their own children were grown-up; in interviews, they often drew on capacities and memories from their own experiences of parenting, or even of being children. Paul, one of the Riverlands committee members, who organised a group of local young lads to work on an allotment, often talked about his own childhood and family life; for example, during one session when we were constructing a shed, he recalled building a shed with his own father. Underlying these engagements was a strong sense of an ongoing and long-term commitment to children and young people within the neighbourhoods. This was articulated to me many times by volunteers; for example, Jill said: "We always stick up for young people round here, nobody else does." The approach was also generally about enabling rather than seeking to control what teenagers did (presumably drawing on their own experiences as parents). Mick told me:

> "We don't want to paint a different picture so that people can look at them in a different way, you know ... we'll ... if we have to supply the paints and the brushes for them to paint a different picture, then that's OK."

Indeed, much of the everyday work with children and young people undertaken by volunteers was rooted in activities associated with the domestic sphere, such as gardening, cooking and small-scale arts and craft projects. Through my ethnography, which involved participation in such activities, I became aware of how the micro-interactions and material engagements involved could draw participants, both young people and adults, into new connections and shared senses of achievement (see Jupp, 2007). As well as organised activities, there were more informal sessions, and for young people at Riverlands the community house provided an important space in which to 'hang out', space for socialising, jokes and conversations. Much of their time was spent in this way and provided a powerful basis for other kinds of engagement for the young people both within the neighbourhoods and beyond. Indeed, a group of young people who came regularly to the house set up a more formal 'youth forum', which enabled them to access funding and resources for local projects including an adventure playground. In this and other ways, the community house could function as a 'contact zone' between informal family and neighbourhood life, and local government policy and resources. However, policy programmes on the estates generally took quite a different approach to teenagers.

Targeting 'problem' families and teenagers

The work of the two community groups clearly brought them into contact with the realm of more 'public' government interventions that attempted to target 'problem' teenagers and indeed wider families. It is to this realm that I now turn, before considering specific sites of contact between the two. These interventions involved discursive categories and policy programmes, and also the embodied actions of officials working on or near the neighbourhoods.

One striking aspect of the discourses around these issues is that the 'problems' tended to be seen in terms of disruptive impact on the rest of a neighbourhood or 'community', rather than in terms of the issues affecting the lives of the young people themselves, with the term 'anti-social behaviour' playing a key role in such framings. 'Anti-social behaviour' is a term associated with government policy and legal interventions; the 1998 Crime and Disorder Act defined it as 'behaviour which causes harassment, alarm or distress to one or more people who are not in the same household as the perpetrator' (Home Office, 2003). This approach clearly chimed with the views of some residents in both areas, with a focus on authoritarian regulation of behaviour and exclusion. Policy tools aimed at disruptive young people included 'acceptable behaviour contracts' and 'anti-social behaviour orders', both aimed at particular individuals, and 'exclusion zones', which focused on particular areas on both estates in which police had powers to break up gatherings of young people. For example, on Westfields, there was an exclusion zone in operation in a central shopping area where young people often gathered in the evenings. Such processes were essentially quasi-legal proceedings. A local housing officer spoke to me about 'gathering evidence' and keeping certain families 'under surveillance', and private detectives and the police, as well as neighbourhood wardens, were involved in these interventions. Neighbourhood wardens had been recently introduced on both the estates, undertaking informal 'patrols', often essentially 'policing' the behaviour of young people. As part of this legal or quasi-legal approach, attempts to deal with the 'problems' of young people were often led by housing officials. Their professional roles appeared to lead them to be more concerned with the overall 'popularity' and feel of a neighbourhood rather than the welfare of individual young people, and this could lead to a focus on the built environment. For example, one housing officer recounted how some housing on a neighbouring estate had been demolished purely in order to evict the families living there, and on Westfields, bus stops and phone boxes had been removed as they were seen as a target for problematic behaviour (see also Lupton, 2003 on such 'selective demolitions'). So within such a framework, the 'problems' of young people were seen as inextricably linked to particular material spaces, rather than connected with local people's lives and experiences more broadly.

Overall, such an approach seems to signify the breakdown of 'welfare-based' approaches to working with young people and their families, and stands in stark contrast to the approaches of the community groups. Certainly there was little or no 'youth work' in evidence on the estates, beyond some short-term, temporary projects. However, other kinds of discourses, perhaps linked to 'community development' and 'youth work', did circulate among officials within the neighbourhoods, at least indicating an awareness of the inadequacy of the existing approach. This entailed more focus on individual resources, networks, 'skills' and 'confidence'. For example, the same housing officer who was involved with demolitions and with serving anti-social behaviour orders on Westfields said that on the estate "many young people lack resources to run their own lives, lack networks of support"; she spoke of her desire to instigate more positive approaches to working with them. A community outreach officer attached to the local secondary school at Riverlands spoke of local young people's 'low aspirations', and "the kind of culture of putting people down in terms of success, not really looking for success". Indeed, the term 'low aspirations' was widely used to describe local people, along with 'low horizons' and 'lack of ambition'. This was generally within the context of encouraging young people into the employment market, and could be seen as part of the kind of discourse of shaping new subjectivities referred to earlier in this chapter However, while these ideas may have been present, there was little action and few resources targeting young people on these terms within the neighbourhoods.

While it may seem that the approaches of the community groups and the local authorities towards young people were very different, in fact they intersected and influenced each other in significant ways. First, the chairs of each group in particular took on the role of mediating between their work and the discourses and practices of the local authorities, and this inevitably led them to narrate their own work in terms that fitted into such frameworks. The term 'anti-social behaviour' was often discussed and questioned by the activists; for example, one of the volunteers at Riverlands told me about a group of young people who were constantly being 'moved on' by neighbourhood wardens: "They've been seen doing terrible things like sitting on a wall and talking". But at other times it was used strategically: Sandra at Riverlands had worked with the police to demonstrate that the establishment of its youth forum had reduced reported incidents of anti-social behaviour. The groups had also learnt to frame their work with young people in ways that resonated with discourses around 'aspirations' and 'ambitions', essentially reframing the informal activities they undertook in terms of 'skills' and 'training' that might eventually lead to employment. Indeed, the group had gained a 'kite mark' for its work with young people, a process that involved auditing and evaluating its work in these kinds of terms. While the chairs of the groups often talked in terms such as 'confidence building', 'skills' and 'raising aspirations', it was acknowledged that the young people themselves would not have viewed their activities in these terms. Rather, they can be considered as a set of embodied and material practices (Jupp, 2008). For example, Sandra talked about one of the young women in the youth forum getting a place on a training scheme:

> "... you know, they just get on with it [involvement in forum], they don't necessarily think about what they're doing, it's not until you sit down and talk about it that they realise what they've gained, all that experience and confidence."

In this way, the 'contact zones' of the community group's activities with teenagers involved ongoing mediations, often between informal socialising and the identification of 'useful' or 'productive' elements that might attract funding or at least recognition from the authorities. For example, both groups received a small amount of money and some support to run projects with young people through a housing association-led project called the Dream Scheme. Through this scheme, young people essentially undertook 'useful work' in the community (such as gardening, litter picking, fundraising) in return for 'points' that could be spent on outings and activities. This was clearly an attempt to reshape the young people's relationships with their neighbourhoods in particular ways, and I was quite surprised to learn that it was popular among young people. However, when I attended some sessions I realised that the scheme was interpreted loosely in practice – 'useful work' was very much defined by the young people themselves and it was not solely those who undertook it who took part in the outings and other ('non-useful') reward activities. The Dream Scheme was seen as an opportunity to access some resources for the young people, and in this and other projects there was an ongoing balancing act between the informal ways that the residents worked together and some degree of intervention and support from local government. As I was leaving the fieldwork site, a new youth club was being set up at Riverlands and there was much discussion over whether it 'belonged' to local people or to the local authority. Sandra described it as a 'community-led youth club' and told me that they didn't actually want new youth workers on the estate: "We want help to grow our own youth workers."

In undertaking such work, the community groups were clearly providing support and resources for young people in exactly the ways that the local authorities failed to do. This was against the background of a recognition from officials that the approach of simply excluding young people from certain spaces did not 'work' even within its own limited goals, and the same spaces (for example, the central shopping area on Westfields) remained a 'problem' as a gathering place for young people. As such, a police officer described the Westfields group to me as 'a godsend' because of its ability to work with 'difficult' young people on the estate. The neighbourhood wardens on Riverlands, who had only recently started working in the area, spent most of their time 'moving on' groups of young people, and they told me that they were aware of the inadequacies of such an approach, yet felt constrained by their role. One of them said: "What was called fun when I was a child is now called 'anti-social behaviour'"; it is interesting to note the use of memories from personal family life in a similar mode to the resident-activists themselves.

Indeed, questioning of the term 'anti-social behaviour' was common among such officials, and, in interviews at least, they often sought to distance themselves from the authoritarian/quasi-legal framework previously discussed. While they often cited the constraints of their role, time and resources, they did say that they were aware of the need to work more positively with young people. Supporting the work of the community groups seemed to give them a way of doing this. One of the community facilitators told me: "Sandra and Mick always give young people a second chance, no matter what", adding, "I don't know how they manage it". There was an implicit contrast here with the authoritarian approach outlined above. One of the officials based at the school in Riverlands told me that many of the young people involved with the group were seen as "very challenging young people ... who don't generally achieve at school". She said that through the work of the forum she had become aware of those young people's "commitment to their community". She commented: "The skills they're getting down there, well, they have acquired skills, but we've got nothing to show for those skills in school." She was suggesting that she wanted their achievements to be 'recognised' within the formal setting of the school, but felt she had no means to do this. There is a sense in her wording here of the inadequacy of the policy discourses around young people, which in itself points to the inadequacy of resources and staff at the neighbourhood level. This is in contrast to Sandra's words about young people recognising what they had achieved.

These feelings among officials did mean that some ongoing alliances were formed between local officials and the community groups that could be beneficial for the community groups in accessing small amounts of money and political support. I also witnessed some surprising moments of identification. For example, on a number of occasions, officials attended neighbourhood events (which were often held on evenings or at weekends) with their own children and families. During a summer party to celebrate the opening of a new adventure playground at Riverlands, one (trainee) community worker told me that she felt more 'at home' and welcomed in the neighbourhood than she did in her own. A more senior housing official had her baby grandson in a pushchair at the same party, and as some of the residents gathered round to talk to him, there was a strong sense of the intermingling of public and private roles, as well as between officials and local people.

Nonetheless, it is important to place what may be moments of identification and connection in the 'contact zones' between officials and residents within the wider context of government work in the neighbourhoods that, overall, appeared to place little importance on the ongoing everyday work of supporting young people in disadvantaged circumstances. It is to an overall assessment of this context that I now turn.

Conclusion

Behind any particular alliances and feelings between officials and local people remained the 'radically asymmetrical relations of power' (Pratt, 1992) of encounters in which resources and discursive framings were ultimately controlled by officials and the policy terms worked through them. Overall, young people within the neighbourhoods only really came into view in terms of the 'problems' they might present for the 'rentability' of a neighbourhood, and were therefore dealt with through ideas such as anti-social behaviour and interventions to remove physical spaces. Although ideas around raising the skills and aspirations of young people were also present, as part of discourses of employability and training, there was little in the way of funding and staffing from the local authorities to develop this agenda on a neighbourhood level. Concerns around young people's everyday lives were still experienced on an individual level among officials, perhaps related to their own experiences as carers, but they struggled to reconcile them with the roles and policy discourses at their disposal. While these areas of concern did provide some opportunities for the community groups to access support and resources around young people, conventional ideas of 'welfare' provision seemed largely absent, in what might be termed the 'do-it-yourself-post-welfare state' (Brin-Hyatt, 2001, p 228).

To return to the gendered lines between public and private, a concern with the everyday lives of young people in the neighbourhoods seemed not to be part the local authorities' 'public' agenda and policies, but was rather relegated to the domestic spheres of family and neighbourhood in which the community groups were seen to operate, and to which a low level of support was given. One senior council official told me he sometimes felt that community groups should spend less time campaigning and more time working with children – in other words, that they should not enter arenas of public discussion. I would argue that this demonstrates a persistence of gendered divisions between public and private spheres, rearticulated in terms of different aspects of government work, with 'feminised' aspects (Sharma, 2006) continuing to be marginalised. Therefore the 'contact zones' between public and private, and between state and citizens, that formed around particular issues and concerns within the neighbourhoods were very much sustained by residents who ultimately had more invested in the issues, rather than by officials.

In some ways, this goes against the governmentality thesis of ever-expanding concerns with the personal and private (cf Chapter Three of this volume), showing instead how government concern with individual private lives can be selective and short term. On Westfields, a teenager, who had been involved with the community group and previously branded as 'difficult' locally, gained a place on a local authority training scheme. Her story was publicised in the regeneration press; however, by the end of my fieldwork she had dropped out of the scheme and was expecting a baby. This is not to suggest that she had not benefited from the training, but rather that lives can move in different directions and young people may need flexible and long-term support rather than seeing entry into employment or training as an end in itself. To undertake the low-level, mundane, everyday work of supporting and caring for vulnerable young people whose behaviour may be difficult or who may not easily move into employment or education, seemed to remain beyond the main concerns of the local authorities in the neighbourhoods. Rather, the approach was simply about excluding difficult individuals from certain spaces and areas, an approach that remained focused on certain aspects of 'public' life in the neighbourhoods. The sphere of 'public' local politics, as briefly indicated in the opening sections of the chapter, remained largely tied to a performative mode of male-dominated politics. Overall, I did not feel that new models of citizenship that spanned conventionally public and private spheres were being 'publicly' recognised within these contexts, even if they were experienced by volunteers and sometimes even by officials (Jupp, 2008).

This chapter has considered a specific spatial context (the two neighbourhoods) and focused on one area of concern (young people). As I was finishing my fieldwork on Westfields, a new children's centre was being developed that promised to provide ongoing resources and support to parents and children under five. Although the government's Children's Centre programme has been seen as another attempt to shape citizens in certain ways (Lister, 2003b), it also represents a sustained engagement with local families' lives with potential to bring them material benefits. However, it may be that the challenge of engaging successfully with problematic teenagers is too difficult and time-consuming for local authorities, as opposed to interventions with under-fives. Therefore what remains as residual and beyond the reach of the authorities within the neighbourhoods is constituted as 'women's , essentially left to local activists to try to hold together, as they find ways of working with and through the local authorities and the policy contexts they mediate.

References

Bondi, L. and Domosh, M. (1998) 'On the contours of public space: a tale of three women', *Antipode*, 30(3), pp 270-89.

Brin-Hyatt, S. (2001) 'From citizen to volunteer: neoliberal governance and the erasure of poverty', in J. Goode and J. Maskovsky (eds) *The New Poverty Studies: The ethnography of power, politics and impoverished people in the United States*, New York, NY: New York University Press, pp 201-35.

Buckingham, S., Marandet, E., Smith, F., Wainwright, E. and Diosi, M. (2006) 'The liminality of training spaces: places of public/private transitions', *Geoforum*, 37(6), pp 895-905.

Chatterjee, P. (2004) *The politics of the governed: Reflections on political society in most of the world*, New York: Columbia University Press.

Corbridge, S., Williams, G., Srivastava, M. and Véron, R. (2005) *Seeing the state: Governance and governmentality in India*, Cambridge: Cambridge University Press.

Day, K. (2000) 'The ethic of care and women's experiences of public space', *Journal of Environmental Psychology*, 20(2), pp 103-24.

Davidoff, L. and Hall, C. (1987) *Family fortunes: Men and women of the English middle class, 1780–1850*, Chicago, IL: University of Chicago Press.

Fincher, R. and Panelli, R. (2001) 'Making space: women's urban and rural activism and the Australian state', *Gender, Place and Culture*, 8(2), pp 129-48.

Fink, J. (ed) (2004) *Care: Personal lives and social policy*, Bristol: The Policy Press.

Giddens, A. (1998) *The third way: Renewal of social democracy*, Cambridge: Polity Press.

Gilligan, C. (1982) *In a different voice*, Cambridge, MA: Harvard University Press.

Home Office (2003) 'A guide to anti-social behaviour orders and acceptable behaviour contracts', available at www.crimereduction.gov.uk.

Jupp, E. (2007) 'Participation, local knowledge and empowerment: researching public spaces with young people', *Environment and Planning A*, 39(12), pp 2832-44.

Jupp, E. (2008) 'The feeling of participation: everyday spaces and urban change', *Geoforum*, 39(1), pp 331-43.

Lendvai, N. and Stubbs, P. (2007) 'Policies as translation' in S. Hodgson and Z. Irving (eds) *Policy reconsidered: Meanings, politics and practices*, Bristol: The Policy Press.

Lewis, G. (ed) (2004) *Citizenship: Personal lives and social policy*, Bristol: The Policy Press.

Lister, R. (2003a) *Citizenship: Feminist perspectives* (2nd edn), Basingstoke: Palgrave Macmillan.

Lister, R. (2003b) 'Investing in the citizen-workers of the future: transformations in citizenship and the state under New Labour', *Social Policy and Administration*, 37(5), pp 427-43.

Lupton, R. (2003) *Poverty Street: The dynamics of neighbourhood decline and renewal*, Bristol: The Policy Press.

Martin, D. (2002) 'Constructing the "neighbourhood sphere": gender and community organising', *Gender, Place and Culture*, 9(4), pp 333-50.

Newman, J. (2009) 'Working the spaces of governance', Paper presented to the Canadian Anthropology Association Conference, Vancouver, May **[date?]**.

Newman, J. and Clarke, J. (2009) *Publics, politics and power: Remaking the public in public services*, London: Sage Publications.

Painter, J. (2006) 'Prosaic geographies of stateness', *Political Geography*, 25(7), pp 752-74.

Parr, H. (1998) 'Mental health, ethnography and the body', *Area*, 30(1), pp 28-37.

Pateman, C. (1988) *The sexual contract*, Cambridge: Polity Press.

Pratt, M. (1992) *Imperial eyes: Studies in travel writing and transculturation*, London: Routledge.

Rose, N. (2001) 'Community, citizenship and the "third way"', in D. Meredyth and J. Minson (eds) *Citizenship and cultural policy*, London: Sage Publications, pp 1-17.

Ryan, M. (1992) 'Gender and public access: women's politics in 19th century America', in C. Calhoun (ed) *Habermas and the public sphere*, Cambridge, MA: MIT Press, pp 259-88.

Sharma, A. (2006) 'Crossbreeding institutions: breeding struggle: women's empowerment, neoliberal governmentality, and state (re)formation in India', *Cultural Anthropology*, 21(1), pp 60-95.

Staeheli, L. (1996) 'Publicity, privacy and women's political action', *Environment and Planning D: Society and Space*, 14(5), pp 601-19.

Stall, S. and Stoecker, R. (1998) 'Community organising or organising community? Gender and the crafts of empowerment', *Gender and Society*, 12(6), pp 729-56.

Valentine, G. (1996) 'Children should be seen and not heard: the production and transgression of adults' public space', *Urban Geography*, 17(3), pp 205-20.

Valentine, G. (1997) '"Oh yes I can." "Oh no you can't": children and parents' understanding of kids' competence to negotiate public space safely', *Antipode*, 29(1), pp 65-89.

Valentine, G. (2004) *Public space and the culture of childhood*, Aldershot: Ashgate.

Warner, M. (2002) *Publics and counterpublics*, New York, NY: Zone Books.

Young, I.M. (2000) *Inclusion and democracy*, Oxford: Oxford University Press.

SEVEN

Whose education? Disentangling publics, persons and citizens

Jessica Pykett

The realm of UK education policy may appear to be an unlikely site for an analysis of the emerging objects, subjects and mediums of publicness, since schools are often characterised as particularly fixed or static spaces that have not changed radically since the inception of mass schooling in the 19th century. However, recent reforms in education policy point towards the emergence of new ways of talking and thinking about the public value of education, new forms of educational governance, and a new settlement between the ideals of the public, person and citizen – both as they are imagined through the education system, and as they are lived in teachers' and young people's everyday experiences of schooling. This chapter considers two such reforms: personalisation and citizenship education, which, when explored side by side, throw light on some of the ambiguities between *pessimistic discourses of decline* and *optimistic discourses of originality* (Newman and Clarke, 2009, ch 1) in academic accounts of publics. These ambiguities tend to remain underplayed by critical analysis of current educational trends in the UK.

Personalisation is currently 'the big idea' in school-level education policy in England (Pollard and James, 2004, p 5), and is part of a wider discourse about the personal that sees education, family, health, social and youth justice policies coalesce around the idea of personally tailored services that involve the individual more actively in the service relationship (and, it is argued, contribute to strategies of 'responsibilisation' of the self: Cutler et al, 2007; Ferguson, 2007). The promotion of 'choice and voice' (Leadbeater, 2004; Miliband, 2006) is thus presented as a challenge to paternalistic approaches in the public services and is associated with an 'enabling' state. This signifies a shift from the state as public service provider to a role as broker of various public, private and voluntary sector services, and education is one sector in which this shift has been particularly marked. However, while personalisation may appear to re-imagine education as a personal goal as opposed to a public 'good', when considered alongside concurrent policy directives such as the introduction of citizenship education in England, its rationale, practices and effects become much less straightforward. Young people in schools are constructed equally as private persons *and* as public citizens, and moreover, their 'reception' of such policies is far from certain, mediated as they are by the spatial practices that constitute young people as citizens and produce particular kinds of social relations.

This chapter therefore draws on documentary evidence on personalisation in education policy, together with interview research on citizenship education, to examine how people in particular socio-spatial contexts often fail to live up to the idealised form of the entrepreneurial and self-governing worker- and consumer-citizen implied by personalisation. Understanding an educational agenda such as personalisation requires us to consider wider 'policy trajectories' (Ball, 2000, p 51) that take into account *simultaneous* policy initiatives such as citizenship education, *struggles* and compromises that characterise the policy-making process itself, and the *mediation* of policy texts in practice. In this way, while personalisation appears to promote a privatised notion of the 'educable' person, citizenship education (another key educational reform of the New Labour era) re-imagines the education of children and young people in much broader, and explicitly public, terms.

The chapter goes on to consider the spatial unevenness of the educational landscape as integral to the mediation of a personalised citizen education. This spatial mediation of educational policy and practice raises political concerns about the way in which public goods are imagined and reworked through public policy. In particular, it is argued that teachers' and policymakers' own 'geography talk' simultaneously disentangles children and their families from their socio-spatial contexts while re-entangling them with what are deemed personal attributes associated with people from particular neighbourhoods.

The chapter focuses on compulsory schooling (rather than adult education, informal education or higher education) as a sphere that is both integral to the formation and development of citizen-subjects by the UK government and as spaces that are primarily locally embedded. Teachers are considered important mediums through which a distinction between an 'educable' and 'uneducable' public are summoned, so the emphasis is on teachers' discourse as opposed to the direct experiences of children and young people themselves. The chapter concludes by outlining how we might better understand the active role of spatiality in shaping educational opportunity. Within an uneven educational terrain, and in the face of initiatives such as personalisation and citizenship education, teachers, students, policymakers and educational non-governmental organisations define the purpose of education *both* in terms of public responsibility *and* personal capabilities, reflecting the apparently paradoxical nature of summoning publics (see also Chapters Two and Ten of this volume).

Personalising the public

'Personalised learning' has gained increased currency in educational debates, particularly in England, where it has been promoted by the think-tank, Demos (Leadbeater, 2004), and former education secretary, David Miliband (2006), as well as many educational non-governmental and quasi-governmental organisations, such as the Innovation Unit, the Specialist Schools and Academies Trust, the National College for School Leadership, the Organisation for Economic

Co-operation and Development and Personalize Education Now. At its heart, personalised learning aims to shape the education system around the 'needs, interests and aspirations' of individual learners (DfES, 2004, p 7). The key principles of personalised learning include 'assessment for learning', 'teaching and learning strategies which build on individual needs', 'curriculum choice which engages and respects students', 'school organisation based around student progress' and 'community, local institutions and social services supporting schools to drive forward progress in the classroom' (Miliband, 2006, p 21). Underpinning these principles is a reframing of educational governance as active and participatory as opposed to a more traditional idea of 'top-down' governance. The personalised learning agenda is about enabling 'users' or 'co-authors' of the educational 'script' (Leadbeater, 2006, p 111) to decide what, how and when they want to learn – drawing on the affordances of new technologies and redesigned 'learning environments'.

If proponents of personalisation tend to rather over-emphasise novelty and innovation in this '21st-century' learning agenda, much critical analysis of personalisation in education (for example, Campbell et al, 2007; Hartley, 2007), and of contemporary educational reforms more generally, perhaps tends too far in the other direction. Critics conclude that compulsory schooling is being deregulated, privatised, marketised and commercialised (Davies and Bansel, 2007) by the forces of global neoliberalism. This agenda, it is claimed, endorses an overly individualistic sense of education as an economic gain and destroys the idea of education as a collective or public good. It is said to replace the ideal of the public with a spurious notion of individual or community responsibility.

Documentary analysis of personalisation as it is imagined, represented and narrated in policy texts can indeed indicate how this educational agenda is steeped in discourses of choice and marketisation, individualism and consumerism. The White Paper, *Higher standards, better schools for all. More choice for parents and pupils* (DfES, 2005, p 51), set out an agenda for personalised learning charged with the intention to 'create an education system that focuses on the needs of the individual child'. This would include targeted interventions to ensure that every child mastered the basics of numeracy and literacy, the provision of extra tuition to help students catch up, the tailoring of educational choices around students, and a focus on tracking the progress of individual learners (DfES, 2005, pp 49–63). This was outlined as much more than a collection of strategies for teaching and learning, and was portrayed as a radical change towards more freedom of choice. It set out reforms in school governance that would pave the way for more foundation schools, trust schools and city academies, and a change in the role of local authorities from 'being a provider of education to being its local commissioner and the champion of parent choice' (DfES, 2005, p 1).

Critics have been concerned with pointing out how an emphasis on flexibility in educational provision and measures to ensure parental choice demonstrate a move towards a marketised education system and a consequent narrowing of the concept of citizenship (Whitty and Power, 2000; Crouch, 2003, p 22). It is said that the privatised supply and subcontracting of educational services – from agency teaching and catering services, to competitive league tables and specialist schools, and the undermining and private take-over of local education authorities – indicated a rupture in the link between the government and the citizen, which has been developing since 1997 (Crouch, 2003, p 39). For some, this signifies the deterioration of public services and of the ideal of education as a common good and a universal right.

Further critiques of recent educational reforms in the UK have focused on what is seen as an increasingly individualistic definition of education, an obsession with achievement and standards, and the repositioning of the pupil and parent as individual consumers (Gerwitz, 2002; Ball, 2003; Tomlinson, 2003). A recurrent theme of much of the personalisation agenda, as has been noted, is the idea of individual talent, needs and aptitudes. The most recent guidance sets out the importance of 'tailoring teaching and learning to individual needs' (DCSF, 2008, p 1). It recommends a 'pedagogy of personalised learning' (DCSF, 2008, p 6), suggesting that it is more of a theory of teaching than a political ideal. The *2020 Vision* report (also known as the Gilbert Review – DfES, 2006), which made some of the initial contributions to this agenda for transforming education, specifies a need for the individual to adapt to a rapidly changing world. The report describes how schools need to respond to ethnic and social change; the increasing use of technology; a knowledge-based economy; demanding employers; increased educational choices; and environmental impacts (DfES, 2006, p 8). These are presented as concerns not just for schools, but for individuals who must compete for jobs, make best use of technologies, develop skills appropriate for employers and global markets, choose their own pathways through education and contribute to the sustainability of communities and the environment.

There is a consequent emphasis on developing students' skills and attitudes (DfES, 2006, p 10), including communication, reliability, punctuality, perseverance, working with others, responsibility, self-management, independence, confidence, resilience, creativity and entrepreneurialism. This could be described as the increasing *governing of competency* and will be seen by many as proof of a shift towards the personalisation or individualisation of risk. It would therefore be easy to argue that a personalised pedagogy of skills is part of a wider rationality of reflexive modernity, by which collective publics and solidarities are disintegrating, and increasing demands and constraints are being placed on individuals as masters of their own lives (Beck and Beck-Gernsheim, 2002, p 2). As such, the science of learning, the technologies of pedagogy, the expertise of educational psychology and the institution of the school are mobilised in order to ensure that persons are constructed as self-governing, self-managing and autonomous subjects. The popularity of learning theories, thinking skills, learning mentors and reflective teaching practice are all testimony to what Nikolas Rose terms 'the role of psy knowledge and practices in constituting human beings in certain ways, making up human subjects with particular competencies and capacities' (Rose, 1999, p xvi).

Critical analysis of personalisation may therefore be justified in regarding current educational reforms in the UK and elsewhere as part of the dismantling of public solidarity and the normalisation of personalised responsibility for both educational talents as well as educational 'failure' (for example, Cutler et al, 2007). The policy discourse of personalisation – through its policy texts, pamphlets aimed at enabling teachers to interpret policies, and guidance on teaching practice, school management and leadership – could hence be presented as a straightforward shift from public to private. In reducing educational value to private achievements – by way of qualifications, competitive schools and the fulfilment of individual talents – the notion of personalisation serves to make up a particular version of the person, which could be termed natural, moral and psychological manifestations of the 21st-century child (Pykett, 2009).

Researching educational publics

However, the reading of policy documentation in this isolated fashion is fraught with methodological pitfalls. Extracting messages from such texts is problematic, particularly in the attempt to read off underlying political rationalities and motivations. In contrast, the approach of grounded theory (Glaser and Strauss, 1967) promotes an iterative routine for simultaneous data collection and analysis, coding textual data, developing and refining theories from the ground up. However, in defending the rigour and validity of this approach, there is still a risk of ignoring the way in which policy texts have a social life of their own, and of how teachers and students themselves understand and respond to policies, texts and the teaching practices that are informed – but not determined – by them. A more reflexive methodological approach recognises that analysing texts is a necessarily unreliable activity, involving 'interpretation, argument and analysis' (MacLure, 2005, p 394). In recognising it as such, we are prompted as researchers to consider not simply what is said or meant in educational policies, but the work that such policies do in making educable publics – not 'what language means, but what language does' (Rose, 1999, p xix).

Hence, policies on personalisation cannot be understood in isolation from other parallel educational reforms, the particular socio-spatial contexts of schools and the everyday talk and experiences of teachers and young people – in other words, policies need to be researched simultaneously as texts, discourses and effects (Ball, 2000, p 44):

> The physical text that pops through the school letterbox, or wherever, does not arrive 'out of the blue', it has an interpretational and representational history, neither does it enter a social or institutional vacuum. (Ball, 2000, p 45)

When we consider ethnographic and interview research alongside the work of analysing texts, we can therefore better understand the more ambiguous role of education policies in constituting not only private persons but also public citizens at the same time. It could be that many teachers, necessarily preoccupied with lesson planning, 'classroom management' and school standards, may be little inclined to read apparently obscure publications on the personalised future of education, or the background political context of education for democracy from Her Majesty's Stationery Office. Instead, they may be much more concerned with national curriculum documentation and teaching guidance materials, continuing professional development courses, teaching resources and teaching community self-help websites. The remainder of the chapter therefore makes use of informal interview data in order to shed light on some of the means through which educable publics are imagined in the complex social contexts of schools and their neighbourhoods. Informal interviews with both primary and secondary school teachers and teacher-trainers were conducted over a period of ethnographic research in schools and teacher-training courses undertaken principally in Bristol, south-west England, between 2004 and 2007.

Making public citizens

In contrast to personalisation, which has been said to describe variously an educational philosophy, a technical approach to learning or a framework for managing institutional change in education, citizenship education was heralded as a more straightforward suite of knowledge, skills and understanding that 'equips young people with the knowledge, skills and understanding to play an effective role in public life' (QCA, 2007, p 41). In this sense, the policy of citizenship education could be understood as a more practicable, powerful text, given its manifestation in statutory curriculum documents outlining 'programmes of study', suggested 'schemes of work', exam board specifications, and a plethora of lesson ideas and text books. This could be contrasted to the more amorphous personalisation *agenda*, which, in Ball's (2000, p 45) terms, could be said to 'generate mass confusion' among the very head teachers, teachers, teacher-trainers, school workers and pupils who must mediate and enact (and potentially undermine) such policies.

Citizenship was introduced as a new and compulsory curriculum subject in secondary schools in England in 2002, and was a direct counter to what were seen as the prevailing apathy and increasingly anti-social behaviour of young people (QCA, 1998, p 15). In this sense, citizenship education can be seen as an explicitly anti-individualistic, anti-consumerist reform, aimed at constructing and maintaining a healthy public sphere, in which important topical issues are brought into the purview of public (and youthful) concern. In the Crick Report (QCA, 1998, p 14), which recommended the introduction of this new subject, for instance, one of its rationales is stated to be a response to the fact that:

> ... 80 percent of British pupils revealed that out of school they engage in very little discussion at all of public issues, including issues important in their own communities. Many reported strong social norms 'never

to talk about religion or politics'.... 'Talk' or discourse is obviously fundamental to active citizenship.

While some teachers saw citizenship education as an extra burden, and while critics lampooned it as badly taught, fluffy psychobabble (O'Hear, 2000), a form of governmental bullying or control (Jenkins, 1999) or, worse still, a cover for institutional racism (Osler, 2000; Gillborn, 2006), many teachers and other educationalists viewed it as an opportunity to expand the range of concerns that could be tackled in the classroom, and to contribute to the formation of less selfish, more publicly minded young citizens. One secondary school geography teacher with responsibilities for teaching citizenship expressed a desire to do her own research in order to counter the prevailing view of education as a set of personal achievements:

> "In relation to education. Is it beneficial, I'd actually focus on a balance between, um, looking at those individuals that get strings and strings of GCSEs and A levels, and I'd say, um, what benefit is that to them?... So I would actually look at those selfish people that kind of, get, and this is really awful, this is really opinionated ... but actually doing a study on those people that are like, really self-indulgent and do loads and loads of shit, and just get, loads of GCSEs and A levels, and make themselves ill doing it, because they just have to be perfect and have to be amazing, in comparison to those who perhaps spent a little bit of time giving something back and not just taking, taking, taking, so I'd do research on that." (Lauren[1], geography teacher)

Citizenship teachers also expressed the view that a good citizen is one who does active work on his or herself to keep informed of public issues, by participating in classroom debates, by watching topical news programmes at home and by developing and challenging notions of the 'common good' – showing students that they "do have power and belong to a greater whole" (Clare, citizenship teacher). This anti-individualistic outlook is matched with a sense of citizenship as a 'humane' subject – not simply for creating particular kinds of persons, but for constructing a strong, global civil society by educational means. As such, the realm of educational governance is imagined predominantly as occupying not only a national, but also a global commons (in contrast to Liza Griffin's analysis of the more specifically material commons of fisheries at a European scale in Chapter Eight of this volume). A citizenship teacher-trainer (Dean, interviewed 16 January 2004) defined citizenship education as "basically about strengthening civil society", and indicated that it was resolutely not about skills of personal debt and credit management, but about developing local community involvement in actions with global significance. His course included involving trainee citizenship teachers in the Jubilee Debt Campaign, which demands the cancellation of the indebtedness of poor countries to the rich world (see www.jubileedebtcampaign.org.uk). The spatial scope of the public imagined here is not a narrow sense of bounded community in which young people must compete to be skilled up for individual or national economic gain, but a notion of an interconnected global public in which young people develop capabilities for challenging injustice and taking responsible action.

At the same time as imagining a more global, collective sense of personhood, citizenship education as part of a national curriculum can also be said to re-imagine the local and national educational landscape as geographically uniform rather than structurally unequal:

> ... citizenship and the teaching of democracy, construed in a broad sense that we will define, is so important both for schools and the life of the nation that there must be a statutory requirement on schools to ensure that it is part of the entitlement of all pupils. It can no longer sensibly be left as uncoordinated local initiatives which vary greatly in number, content and method. This is an inadequate basis for animating the idea of a common citizenship with democratic values. (QCA, 1998, p 7)

So although there is much emphasis in citizenship education policy on understanding cultural diversity and historical change, the public citizen imagined uniformly as 'all pupils' exhibits common and national values.

Personalising citizenship education

As I have shown, while personalisation policies can be considered as re-imagining the public value of education as the fulfilment of personal attributes, citizenship education constructs an idea of education as creating publicly informed, empathetic and active citizens. Both were key reforms in New Labour's education programme and thus highlight the ambiguity involved in attempts to identify the political rationales underpinning educational governance in the UK. However, policies do not arrive in local settings in unmediated form; they are actively mediated by schools. It is within schools that policies on personalisation and citizenship education confront existing discourses and practices of the person that circulate in pedagogic repertoires, especially repertoires of educational failure. And it is notable that such repertoires commonly draw on images of space and spatial disadvantage. This section therefore focuses on teaching practices as opposed to attempting to trace the origins of educational policies in search of a unified agenda. It takes into account the way in which the uneven educational terrain in the UK mediates how young people are constituted as publics, persons and citizens – demonstrating, as in Richenda Gambles' account of parenting (Chapter Three of this volume), that education can be seen 'as simultaneously public, political, personal and private'. Through which mechanisms can teaching in schools be said to mediate publicness? Residential segregation, gentrification, middle-class parental strategies on access to education and the exacerbation of social stratification in education catchment areas (Butler and Hamnett, 2007, pp 1165-6) contribute to a complex 'intersection of space, social structure and social processes' that reproduces social and economic inequalities. What is significant here is not just that social dynamics of class and race operate to reinforce social disadvantage, but also that spatial processes work to produce the social contexts in which educational practices take place. As Hamnett et al (2007, p 1278) demonstrate, school composition, or the social mix of school pupils, affects educational performance, and in this way, space can be described as a medium for the production of social relations and citizen-subjectivities. These contributions highlight the significance of spatiality to issues of distributive justice, social exclusion and economic power in education. What is distinctive about approaching school geographies as a medium of publicness, however, is a focus on how socio-spatial contexts of schooling constitute young people as public citizens and private persons alike. This can be demonstrated by the way in which teachers talk about where their students live in relation to their perceived educability.

When asked about the potential for personalisation initiatives to reduce educational inequalities, one primary school teacher (Caroline) working in a deprived area said that she believed that literacy problems began long before children arrived at school aged four. She suggested that their educational problems began at age two, caused by a general lack of talking, playing and stimulation experienced from a very early age, resulting from their mothers' lack of communication skills. To her, this meant that, as a result of where they lived, they were not 'ready' for education when they arrived in reception class aged four. She stated that as a teacher it was too late to prevent educational disadvantage and that she could only teach who she was presented with, describing some of her pupils as "unteachable". She did not regard it as her responsibility as a teacher to intervene in the home lives of her pupils – this was a 'problem' for social workers to deal with. This teacher regarded the attainable literacy level of children in school as dependent on family background, and that her job was to teach 'what she was given' rather than to seek to intervene in societal processes.

In contrast, a white primary school teacher (Linda, interviewed 16 June 2007) working in an ethnically and socially diverse area interpreted literacy problems as specifically related to ethnicity. She claimed that some problems occurred when the parents were not supportive of the Individual Education Plans (which are personalised plans developed by learning mentors for pupils who have English as a second language). She gave the example of Arabic parents who send their children to Arabic schools in their spare time. She felt that such parents were not helping their children to learn English and that their culture was very different. In contrast to the previous teacher, however, she saw her most difficult task as "educating the parents". Some elision can be seen here between teachers' perceptions of individual pupil ability and the social contexts of their parents. In the midst of school practices, therefore, particular imaginations of educable publics can become reproduced, and public–private attributes are blurred to the potential detriment of pupils from particular social groups.

Similarly, a citizenship coordinator discussing social stratification in his school identified a need for targeted interventions in his school for students from particular areas:

> "You know, this is the most comprehensive school I've ever been in, I think it's a model which is rarely achieved really, where you have the, uh, children from incredibly wealthy, uh, privileged, backgrounds, bringing them to school in their Suzuki jeeps, uh, against, uh, against youngsters who are kicked out by their parents every other week, parents are leading feckless, crazy lives, there's all sorts of drugs issues in the community, and attending school is even an issue for them, we get the, we get the range, I think the difficulty is, it's easy to get kids to great input if dad's the consultant whatever at the [local hospital], you know, the school just has to be basically competent there, *but to save some of the youngsters from really difficult home backgrounds, the school has to be incredibly effective*, you have a whisker of a chance, and the intake to the school has changed in recent years, you know, we get more youngsters who really, uh, will struggle, coming in." (Graham, citizenship coordinator, emphasis added)

When teachers considered the practicalities of approaching personalisation and citizenship education, they therefore constructed certain spatial imaginaries. While young people were disentangled from the structural geographies of disadvantage, they were also curiously re-entangled with personal family 'problems' through discursive practices. Despite the frequent reference to particular areas of towns and cities, and the evocation of 'geography talk' in euphemistic reference to indicators of social disadvantage, it was the personal attributes of children and their families that were identified as the cause of their educational failures.

While some teachers talk of the public value of education in terms of forming citizens and reducing social inequalities, as has been noted, others – faced with the ever-pressing necessity of teaching large groups of diverse students – discuss students from particular neighbourhoods as personally problematic, or in some cases, unteachable. Education policies such as personalisation and citizenship education thus take on particular meanings as they are interpreted in school practices, by different teachers and in different social contexts, as well as having a role in shaping those contexts in which teachers make classroom, curricular and other decisions that have very real impacts on the way in which we conceptualise the purpose of education. As I have shown here, a simple interpretive reading of one or two education White Papers cannot adequately account for the emergence of the curious figure of the personalised public citizen outlined here.

In examining spatialities of education, it is necessary to more adequately conceptualise the child as a situated person. The interpretation of the personal attributes of unemployed parents, 'feckless' families and 'single mums' as causes of educational failures is surprisingly prevalent, and indicates some of the risks of a personalised education system, where social prejudices remain, or an education for citizenship that imagines the educational landscape as spatially even. Indeed, blaming 'illiterate mothers' for their children's educational failures is arguably commonplace in the public imagination, shaping the social contexts in which educational policies play out. Griffith and Smith (2005), for instance, argue that the education system as a whole (in their case, in North America) relies on a close relationship between family and school. It is therefore seen as the mother's responsibility to educate herself in the principles of child development, to give herself over to what Walkerdine and Lucey (1989, cited in Griffith and Smith, 2005, p 38) termed sensitive and enabling 'domestic pedagogy'. Thus, mental health problems, underachievement in school and any deviation from 'normal' school behaviours were attributed to 'faulty mothering' (Griffith and Smith, 2005, p 38).

This point can be followed through with the example of personalised education as it relates to debates on children's literacy, mothers' education and the disputed social role of teaching. If we take seriously the person in a personalised education system, we must understand where persons come from, how they come into being through learning and how this affects their educational and social relationships. To blame 'illiterate mothers' for the illiteracy of their children is to blame the person for their own educational failures. Clearly, the linguistic environment in which children grow up has an effect on their success in the linguistic environment of the school – an environment that prioritises certain forms of literacy and grammar above the diverse literacies of their catchment areas. But we cannot make a simple causal link between the personal attributes of mothers and those of their children. To do so would be to state that the school should only cater for personally suitable children, and to abandon responsibility for the *conditions* of education in which people find themselves, and through which educational policies are mediated.

Rather, I want to argue that a more sustained consideration of the spatialities of schooling could help to demonstrate the complex and manifold reasons why education cannot be separated from notions of spatial justice. This is not simply to say that where you go to school makes a difference in terms of educational attainment, life chances, social mobility and the make-up of (particularly urban) spaces more generally, through residential patterns, neighbourhood development and so on – though there is overwhelming evidence to suggest that this is the case (Byrne et al, 1975; Bondi and Mathews, 1988; Butler and Hamnett, 2007). Instead, it is useful here to outline the distinctive contribution of a 'spatiality of education' and strategic calls for geographers to pursue more 'outward-looking' analyses of education (Hanson Thiem, 2009, p 155). This means understanding education as having a spatially produced and constitutive quality, or identifying space as an agent of social relations. As Hanson Thiem argues, there is a need to consider not just the distributional outcomes of the geography of education or the impact of spatial variations of provision, attainment and social segregation (Hanson Thiem, 2009, p 156), but, most importantly, 'how education "makes space"' (Hanson

Thiem, 2009, p 157), constituting particular cultural, social, political and economic processes that have implications beyond education as a sector.

When schools are understood in these terms, education can be seen to be entangled with an agentic sense of space that affects how people interact and contributes to the production of particular citizen-subjectivities. It is therefore important to ask what kind of spatial imaginaries are produced by the reforms of personalisation and citizenship education, and what consequences these imaginaries have for the politics of publics. Furthermore, it is necessary to consider how particular subject positions are negotiated, reinforced or challenged by citizens in these contexts, and how these everyday practices of education produce particular social, economic, cultural and political spaces in turn. In this way, the particular private, public, citizenly subject positions imagined through personalisation and citizenship education can be said to be contingent on the spatial production of education. And as Hanson Thiem has suggested, attention to both these geographical imaginaries (of curriculum/content) and geographies of schooling (context) (Hanson Thiem, 2009, p 163) can help us to better understand both the cultural and governmental significance of schools as an important realm in which ideas about publics are mediated.

The politics of the public: disentangling publics, persons, citizens

In order to critically analyse the politics of publics imagined within the realm of contemporary schooling, I have argued that it is necessary to consider the spatial imaginaries promoted through both personalisation and citizenship education. For that we need to turn in more detail to teachers' lived experiences in schools and the way in which they imagine publics in talking about the geographies of education. However, I have also shown how the idea of personalisation and citizenship education can obscure the geographies of schooling in towns and cities in England today. In presuming a uniquely personal and psychological nature of the learner as the basis for education, personalisation overlooks the performative function of education itself as a process by which persons 'come into presence' in particular spaces (see Biesta, 2006). Citizenship education as a policy can also presume the educational system to be spatially uniform. But in contrast, teachers in their everyday practices imagine young people themselves to be determined by their social backgrounds, and treat them accordingly. This can serve to eclipse the systematic processes of socio-spatial disadvantage that affect generations of families in specific locations. This double process of disentanglement (from geography) and re-entanglement (with persons) relies on a psychological, rather than philosophical, account of learners as persons.

Disentangling publics, persons and citizens as they are imagined in the educational sphere requires not only analysis of contemporaneous and sometimes conflicting educational policies but also attention to the way in which such policies play out in practice. The individuated, 'psychologised' publics summoned through personalisation can be contrasted to the collectivised and other-regarding publics imagined by citizenship education. But when we consider how these publics are mediated by the uneven educational landscape and teachers' evocations of 'geography talk', we can better understand the processes by which spatial imaginaries of education are reproduced. The implication of this process-based account of subject positioning is that we should take seriously not only the context and conditions in which people become educated publics, but also the performative value of the content of that education.

Note
[1] All names have been changed.

References

Ball, S.J. (2000) 'What is policy? Texts, trajectories and toolboxes', in S.J. Ball (ed) *Education policy and social class: The selected works of Stephen J. Ball*, Abingdon: Routledge, pp 43-53.

Ball, S.J. (2003) *Class strategies and the education market: The middle class and social advantage*, London: RoutledgeFalmer.

Beck, U. and Beck-Gernsheim, E. (2002) *Individualisation: Institutionalised individualism and its social and political consequences*, London: Sage Publications.

Biesta, G. (2005) 'Against learning. Reclaiming a language for education in an age of learning', *Nordisk Pedagogik*, 25(1), pp 54-66.

Biesta, G. (2006) *Beyond learning: Democratic education for a human future*, London: Paradigm Publishers.

Bondi, L. and Matthews, M.H. (eds) (1988) *Education and society: Studies in the politics, sociology and geography of education*, London: Routledge.

Butler, T. and Hamnett, C. (2007) 'The geography of education: introduction', *Urban Studies Special Issue*, 44(7), pp 1161-74.

Byrne, D., Williamson, B. and Fletcher, B. (1975) *The poverty of education. A study in the politics of opportunity*, London: Martin Robertson and Company.

Campbell, R.J., Robinson, W., Neelands, J., Hewston, R. and Mazzoli, L. (2007) 'Personalised learning: ambiguities in theory and practice', *British Journal of Educational Studies*, 55(2), pp 135-54.

Crouch, C. (2003) *Commercialisation or citizenship: Education policy and the future of public services*, London: Fabian Society.

Cutler, T., Waine, B. and Brehony, K. (2007) 'A new epoch of individualisation? Problems with the "personalisation" of public sector services', *Public Administration*, 3, pp 847-55.

Davies, B. and Bansel, P. (2007) 'Neoliberalism and education', *International Journal of Qualitative Studies in Education*, 20(3), pp 247-59.

DCSF (Department for Children, Schools and Families) (2008) *Personalised learning – a practical guide*, Nottingham: DCSF.

DfES (Department for Education and Skills) (2004) *A national conversation about personalised learning*, Nottingham: DfES, available at www.innovation-unit.co.uk/images/stories/files/pdf/PersonalisedLearningBooklet.pdf.

DfES (2005) *Higher standards, better schools for all. More choice for parents and pupils*, Norwich: HMSO.

DfES (2006) *2020 Vision. The report of the Teaching and Learning in 2020 Review Group*, Nottingham: DfES.

Ferguson, I. (2007) 'Increasing user choice or privatising risk? The antinomies of personalisation', *British Journal of Social Work*, 37(3), pp 387-403.

Gewirtz, S. (2002) *The managerial school: Post-welfarism and social justice in education*, London: Routledge.

Gillborn, D. (2006) 'Citizenship education as placebo. "Standards", institutional racism and education policy', *Education, Citizenship and Social Justice*, 1(1), pp 83-104.

Glaser, B.G. and Strauss, A.L. (1967) *The discovery of grounded theory: Strategies for qualitative research*, New York, NY: Hawthorne.

Griffith, A.I. and Smith, D.E. (2005) *Mothering for schooling*, London: RoutledgeFalmer.

Hamnett, C., Ramsden, M. and Butler, T. (2007) 'Social background, ethnicity, school composition and educational attainment in East London', *Urban Studies*, 44(7), pp 1255-80.

Hanson Thiem, C. (2009) 'Thinking through education: the geographies of contemporary educational restructuring', *Progress in Human Geography*, 33(2), pp 154-73.

Hartley, D. (2007) 'Personalisation: the emerging "revised" code of education?', *Oxford Review of Education*, 33(5), pp 629-42.

Jenkins, S. (1999) 'Stop being such a bully, Mr Blunkett', *Evening Standard*, 30 September.

Leadbeater, C. (2004) *Participation through personalisation*, London: Demos, available at www.demos.co.uk.

Leadbeater, C. (2006) 'The future of public services: personalised learning', in Organisation for Economic Co-operation and Development (OECD) *Schooling for tomorrow. Personalising education*, Paris: OECD, pp 101-14.

MacLure, M. (2005) '"Clarity bordering on stupidity": where's the quality in systematic review?', *Journal of Education Policy*, 20(4), pp 393-416.

Miliband, D. (2006) 'Choice and voice in personalised learning', in Organisation for Economic Co-operation and Development (OECD) *Schooling for tomorrow. Personalising education*, Paris: OECD, pp 21-30.

Newman, J. and Clarke, J. (2009) *Publics, politics and power: Remaking the public in public services*, London: Sage Publications.

O'Hear, A. (2000) 'Citizen Blair', *Daily Mail*, 14 December.

Osler, A. (2000) 'The Crick Report: difference, equality and racial justice', *The Curriculum Journal*, 11(1), pp 25-37.

Pollard, A. and James, M. (2004) *Personalised learning. A commentary by the teaching and learning research programme*, London: Economic and Social Research Council.

Pykett, J. (2009) 'Personalisation and de-schooling: uncommon trajectories in contemporary education policy', *Critical Social Policy*, 29(3), pp 374-97.

QCA (Qualifications and Curriculum Authority) (1998) *Education for citizenship and the teaching of democracy in schools. Final report of the Advisory Group on Citizenship*, London: QCA.

QCA (2007) *Citizenship. Programme of study for key stage 4*, London: QCA.

Rose, N. (1999) *Governing the soul. The shaping of the private self* (2nd edn), London: Free Association Books.

Tomlinson, S. (2003) 'New Labour and education', *Children and Society*, 17(3), pp 195-204.

Whitty, G. and Power, S. (2000) 'Marketization and privatization in mass education systems', *International Journal of Educational Development*, 20(2), pp 93-107.

EIGHT

Fishing for the public interest: making and representing publics in North Sea fisheries governance reforms

Liza Griffin

John Dewey (1927) was one of the first to make a case that there is no *a priori* or pre-formed entity called 'the public'. He argued that 'the public', or 'publics' as we will later call them, only comes into being around specific issues. That is to say, publics are spontaneous coalitions of citizens who all have an interest in, or suffer the ill effects of, common problems. As Noortje Marres (2005), drawing on Dewey's work, succinctly puts it, if there is 'no issue, [then there is] no public'. More specifically, Dewey claims that publics are called into being when a group of *individuals* becomes aware of how the incidental effects of human activities affect them *collectively*: 'Indirect, extensive, enduring and serious consequences of conjoint and interacting behaviour call a public into existence having a common interest in controlling these consequences' (Dewey, 1927, p 126).

The case of fisheries governance in the European Union (EU) suggests that, following Dewey, the public is indeed a constituted phenomenon. For, as this chapter will show, in fisheries the 'public interest' is only manifested at times of crisis, that is, when there are issues at stake. Mikalsen and Jentoft (2001, p 282) explain that in the past, when there was:

> ... no apparent or well documented resource crisis, there was relatively little interest in fisheries issues outside the sector itself. However, during the last ten years or so, resource scarcity has made the (hitherto dormant) interests of other groups more obvious and 'intense' – increasing the public awareness of, and interest in, fisheries issues.

While this statement asserts that today's so-called fisheries 'crisis' does indeed arouse public interest, it also suggests that this interest was latent for some time prior to being realised. The vast majority of the environmental politics literature assumes the presence of a single public interest around environmental issues that is *a priori* and fixed through time. However, there have been some exceptions. Michael Mason's work, for instance, describes how different 'affected publics' are produced by different environmental catastrophes (Mason, 2005). Similarly, Noortje Marres' research draws on Dewey to consider the various publics produced by different environmentally controversial technologies (Marres, 2007). Notwithstanding such research, and despite the long-standing and wide-ranging work of scholars on the idea of constituted publics, there has been very little research to date on publics vis-à-vis environmental issues. This is all the more surprising given that environmental problems constitute one of the most widely discussed producers of negative 'indirect consequences', as Dewey puts it. So perhaps now is the time, as the title of this book suggests, to 'rethink the publics' that are brought into being by environmental issues, such as fisheries management.

In this chapter, I begin by demonstrating how fisheries in the EU constitute a public issue. I then go on to argue that the 'good governance' reforms put in place to remedy the problems of fisheries management have altered the EU's political landscape. I show how, while good governance has been instituted in part because of a desire by the EU to safeguard the 'public good' of the marine commons, the actions of stakeholder groups in new EU fora demonstrate that there is no single pre-defined public. Instead, different 'publics' are brought into being by different stakeholders, and their discourses are mobilised in the emerging fisheries management discourse. Furthermore, the changes brought about by good governance have, I argue, led to struggles between different representative claims and enabled fisheries stakeholders to mobilise public interest in new ways to gain political advantage. I conclude by explaining how these recent processes in fisheries relate to and help to illuminate more general theories concerning the constitution of publics.

The empirical data in this chapter are derived from in-depth case study research involving fisheries stakeholders and the EU's North Sea Regional Advisory Council (NSRAC) between 2004 and 2007. The research analysed EU policy documents, press reports and websites and involved some 50 semi-structured interviews with the key players in North Sea fisheries governance, including ministers, politicians, policymakers, fisheries representatives and non-governmental organisations (NGOs). The research also involved attendance at NSRAC meetings during this period.

Fisheries as a public issue

In recent years, issues like biodiversity loss, pollution, waste disposal and climate change have unsurprisingly received a great deal of public attention. Another important environmental concern that has roused the public's attention and demanded its engagement is fisheries. Fisheries management is typically deemed to be a public issue and nowhere is this more so than in the EU where the issue receives a great deal of interest. For instance, the results of public consultation on the EU's new Maritime Policy suggested that 'the public' was deeply concerned about 'the planet's marine ecosystem and felt that insufficient government action was being taken against practices that damage it' (COM, 2007, Article 2.6).

And there are other indicators that fishing is a public issue. Stories concerning rebellious French fishers protesting about draconian EU regulation often fill the pages of newspapers, as does commentary urging consumers to buy the most sustainable species in their weekly shop. While fishing contributes little to Europe's economy as a proportion of its gross national product, fish are an important source of nutrition for most Europeans. Additionally, fishermen, as 'the last of the hunters', still capture a collective imagination that is fed by this intense media interest in fisheries and fishing's quixotic vernacular culture reproduced in popular songs, stories and myths. And according to one Scottish politician interviewed in 2005, fishing is "high up the agenda nationally. There's a lot more public sympathy and public support [for the fishing industry]. All the opinion polls always say that fishing is one of the most important Scottish interests in elections."

But perhaps the central reason why fisheries constitute a public issue is that they are unavoidably part of the earth's 'commons'. Commons are resources like land, air, forests or oceans that are difficult to privatise for either practical or principled reasons. For example, it is practically impossible to fence off mobile or 'fugitive' resources like the codfish, while it is thought unethical (as well as impracticable) to try to privatise the air we breathe. Hence, because they belong to no one in particular, commons tend to be thought of as a public resource. In most global commons, the benefits derived from their exploitation usually accrue to individuals, while the costs resulting from exploitation are almost always shared among the wider community of publics. This process, which may lead to ultimate collapse of the resource, is frequently referred to as the 'tragedy of the commons' (Hardin, 1968). Many environmental commentators (most notably Ostrom, 1990) have deployed the tragedy of the commons model to exemplify how resource exploitation can neglect broader social-environmental responsibilities. The model suggests that negative environmental and social 'externalities' arise because individual self-interest drives economically rational actors to maximise their economic gain. The ultimate, but unforeseen and indirect, result is resource exploitation above carrying capacity levels, where everyone loses. This, following Dewey, produces the conditions for a new public to form around shared concern (see Mitchell, 2008).

This idea that fisheries belong to a commons was embedded in the EU's 1957 founding Treaty of Rome, which declared that its fish stocks are a 'shared resource' that constitute a 'common pond'. For the nascent European Community of the 1950s, food security and cooperation between nations were both high on the political agenda after the depredation of the Second World War. Thus fisheries became symbolic for the European Community, both as a shared resource that was potentially unifying, and as an important source of food that demanded collaboration and needed protection (Griffin, 2008). Europe had suffered from the devastating effects of overfishing before, with the collapse of the Great North Whale fishery in 1880 and of the once booming herring and tuna fisheries in the early 20th century. Building on these concerns, the EU established a *Common Fisheries Policy* (CFP) in 1973 to protect its fishing industry and also to manage stocks that were in potential danger of being overfished.

The CFP was necessary to preserve fish stocks, it was argued, because, as an extractive activity, fishing beyond sustainable yields in some areas can put overall stock levels at risk. Second, there was concern that particular fishing practices, like bottom trawling, might harm the wider marine commons. Finally, 'fugitive' fish resources arguably necessitated a common European policy because they are not fixed in space and habitually traverse national boundaries (Crean, 2000; Mason, 2005). For example, spawning areas and nursery grounds are dynamic features of fish life histories, rarely fixed in one location from year to year (Rogers and Stock, 2001). Thus prudent stewardship by one nation taking great care to manage a vulnerable spawning stock will go unrewarded if the same fish, in their natural cycle, move to another, less regulated. province to feed – whereupon it is promptly fished to oblivion. Consequently, environmental commentators reasoned that the fishes' mobile disposition is best managed by treating them as part of a 'common pool' where political intervention must take the form of common public action to ensure both social unity and environmental sustainability (Ostrom, 1990; Collet, 2002).

Hence we can see how the public nature of fisheries issues implies that their protection is in the public's interest and that interest can be best served by managing them as part of the commons. In fact, this principle has been elaborated under recent EU governance reforms, including reforms to the CFP, which maintain that:

> Fish resources are part of our common heritage.... Fishing and aquaculture are two of the most important uses of the sea. As well as providing a healthy and enjoyable source of food they create much-needed jobs in coastal areas and promote the social and economic well-being of the European Union's fishing regions. Because fish are a natural and mobile resource they are considered as common property. (DGFisheries, 2006)

As a result, perhaps more than ever before, EU fisheries are managed through institutional arrangements specifically designed take this public interest into account.

Good governance and 'the public'

Before CFP reform, controversies surrounding the thorny problem of fisheries management tested the capacity and reach of traditional government institutions. In fact, as Walter Lippmann explained:

> [I]t is in controversies of this kind, the hardest controversies to disentangle, that the public is called in to judge. Where the facts are most obscure, where precedents are lacking, where novelty and confusion pervade everything, the public in all its unfitness is compelled to make its most important decisions. The hardest problems are problems which institutions cannot handle. They are the public's problems. (Lippmann, 2002, p 121)

In essence, Lippmann proposed that opportunities for public involvement in politics open up through the emergence of controversies especially where existing institutions are not sufficiently equipped to deal with them (Marres, 2007). Hence, current increasingly controversial issues are seen to increasingly demand *public* action. However, the prospect of galvanising latent concern into public action is made even more difficult (if it wasn't hard enough already) in an era where the state's power is perceived to have diminished and where the public sector has apparently been impoverished (Newman and Clarke, 2009).

This state of affairs has been associated with the so-called 'turn to governance'. Put simply, 'governance' refers to a 'new process of governing' or 'the new method[s] by which society is [and ought to be] governed' (Rhodes, 2000, p 55). The last few decades have clearly witnessed a proliferation of new governing techniques that exist inside, or parallel to, traditional government institutions (Newman, 2001, 2005). Governance as a process is now said to involve innovative arrangements that might include new stakeholder fora and both state and non-state actors. These actors range from private interest groups and civil society organisations to experts and managers from traditional public institutions (Young, 1994; Rhodes, 1996; Paterson, 1999). As such, the boundaries between public, private and non-profit sectors are said to have become blurred (see Chapters Three and Six of this volume). As part of this blurring, there is now a recognition that 'steering' social systems is not merely the state's responsibility. The increasing role of private actors and the public in governance processes is supposed to signal a change in the state's role, so that now it is no longer the sole interpreter of what is in the public interest (Rhodes, 2000; Kooiman, 2003).

One of the ways that the public interest is being reconsidered is through the relatively recent normative discourse of 'good governance'. Following Lippmann's reasoning (2002), we may interpret the increasing deployment of the good governance discourse as a means of fostering public involvement in tricky problems that exceed the current capacity of governments to remedy them. Good governance carries with it a number of claims and prescriptions about how decisions ought to be made. These vary, and are somewhat contested, but they typically include the ideas that a wide range of stakeholders should participate in decision making, that policies should be coherent and effective and, finally, that the process should be accountable to the public. Indeed, the paradigm of good governance was embraced partly because of perceived accountability failures. Generally, the term 'accountability' implies that all decision-making institutions, including government bodies, the private sector and civil society organisations, must be answerable to a public that is not usually present during decision making. As such, accountability is particularly significant in sectors such as fisheries, where management and exploitation occur largely beyond 'public view'. Additionally, the institution of good governance has gained purchase as a way to improve the legitimacy of EU institutions in the eyes of their publics. Legitimacy is considered imperative since it is generally agreed that the higher the degree of legitimacy a management system has, the greater its chance of achieving its goals. For all these reasons, good governance has never been higher on the EU's agenda, and numerous procedures in pursuit of it have been developed; especially in the environmental sector.

Governance for the public good?

In the 1970s and 1980s, the EU approached fisheries in the same way as it did the steel or agricultural industries: the higher the production – the total catch – the better. This was in line with the CFP's stated objective at that time, which was 'to increase productivity by promoting technical progress' and to ensure 'optimal utilisation of the factors of production' (CFP, Article 7). However, it seems that since then the fishing sector has been a victim of its own success (Porritt, 2005). The strategy of making fisheries more productive has backfired, leading to the over-exploitation of some important stocks. Recent scientific reports have made apocalyptic predictions about the state of the Europe's public fish stocks:

> Images of sterile oceans compete with those of burned-over rainforests in public imaginings of ecological collapse.... This sense of crisis reflects a modern understanding of global unity and the notion of a collective planetary future. (Nadel-Klein, 2003)

However, the fishers' view of what constitutes 'the crisis' very often differs from the views of policymakers and environmental groups. Nadel-Klein's 'collective' public view, fishers argue, fails to engage with the experiences of those who must live with the daily and immediate consequences of any resource depletion. Fishers tend to argue that although there may be a crisis, it does not constitute a generalised problem. For them, it is a very particular problem whose causes lie in inadequate fisheries governance, not their unsustainable fishing practices.

Yet although these fishers regularly contest forecasts of wholesale stock depletion, there is little doubt that many stocks are currently at unsustainable levels. Despite recent signs of recovery, North Sea cod numbers are still well below what are considered to be sustainable. Marine scientists and environmentalists have suggested that the spawning stock is on the verge of collapse, estimating that it has declined by over 80 per cent since the early 1970s. The same scientists have suggested that the North Sea's total stock of fish has dropped from 26 million to 10 million tonnes in just over a century (ICES, 2004).

All this strongly suggests that the CFP's unique fisheries arrangement, designed to secure Europe's common heritage, has safeguarded neither a sustainable fishing industry nor a healthy marine environment. In addition, the fisheries policies emerging from Brussels have been viewed as lacking legitimacy and being unaccountable. Hence, in partial response to these failures, a new paradigm of resource management began to emerge in the late 1990s. Today, the majority of resource commentators and fisheries managers, following this paradigm, believe that problems can be overcome through institutional redesign in order to effect good governance. The principles of good governance are now core values in EU fisheries management (Mikalsen and Jentoft, 2003), and have been incorporated into the 2002 reforms of the CFP. The most important aspect of these reforms was the institution of the Regional Advisory Councils (RACs). There are five RACs covering specific areas of European waters. The most developed of these, the North Sea RAC, launched in 2004, has 24 members, with two thirds drawn from the fishing industry and one third representing 'other' interests comprising environmental, community and consumer organisations. RACs are stakeholder consultation institutions with a brief to directly advise the EU's executive body, the European Commission, on fisheries policy. RACs are designed to fully reflect the opinions of stakeholders, and most of them purport to speak on behalf of a shared public interest. This might include ensuring that the EU's marine resources are exploited sustainably in a way that safeguards the wider commons, meeting the needs of consumers, and maintaining the health of the fishing industry and its communities. Before RACs, public interest group opinions were canvassed only in an *ad hoc* way, and the EU could ignore any opinions or advice that emerged from consultations that had no official status (Holmquist, 2004). What's more, stakeholders complained about having to 'break the door down' (IEEP, 2004). In contrast, RACs are meant to provide a formal pathway to the EU's decision-making institutions.

Under the good governance reforms, the RACs are charged with several functions. They should advise the Commission on fisheries issues, channel information between stakeholders and policymakers, react to proposed policy and create advice proactively rather than through short-term crisis management. RACs embody a form of discursive decision making where stakeholder groups are asked to reach consensus through deliberations with each other on possible policy solutions, without depending on mediation by the EU. The new regime therefore radically departs from previous ones, intending, as it does, to provide a consensual, inclusive and long-term perspective on management that takes the European public's views into account. The RACs remind us that the spaces of public discourse are no longer only *national* and that NGOs have a greater input in 'shaping publicness beyond the nation' (Newman and Clarke, 2009, p 40).

RACs, as good governance structures, resonate with some of the political aspirations outlined in the EU's important governance White Paper (COM, 2001), which argued that governing could be more successful if some participatory processes were conducted 'closer to the citizen', to be more representative of the European public's views (Article 3.1). Although the discourse of good governance is relatively new, concerns over legitimacy are long-standing and still extant. Governing bodies have always derived their moral authority through the justification that they act in the public interest (Mason, 2005). But some authors have recognised that this public interest is often latent and requires some help in being realised. Additionally:

A self-recognising European public would also lend much needed authority to those institutions of European governance, particularly the European Commission, whose legitimacy largely rests upon its claim to serve the (hitherto ill-defined) 'European interest'.... For European officials and Euro-federalists the new Europe must therefore be forged at the level of ideas and images as well as institutions. (Shore, 1997, p 168)

This last tells us that the 'public interest' is often mediated or even forged by government institutions in order to maintain the legitimacy they require to govern. It also suggests that the enthusiasm for engaging 'the public' in EU policy does not merely derive from high principle. Public acceptance of policies can lend support to their implementation and is therefore in practice imperative to a policy's success (COM, 2001, Article 3.1). But it also is hoped that so-called public involvement can be used to question the substance and independence of the expert advice used in policymaking (Article 3.2). However, to what extent this causes experts to lose their grip on politics, and how much publics are genuinely trusted to solve problems, is a moot point.

Governing bodies also appear to use publics to attempt to establish social consensus and common interest. Individuals, associations and governments 'campaign and attempt to persuade others to adopt interests commensurate with those they are pursuing themselves' (Goodie and Wickham, 2002, p 54). The consensus formed via the RACs' processes serves to give stakeholders' claims extra legitimacy and in turn further reinforces their influence in the process.

As part of this drive for legitimacy then, RACs, as 'vehicles for good governance', are being used to improve public participation in decision making (in contrast to previous stakeholder bodies prior to the reforms, RACs are open institutions and any member of the public can theoretically contribute to the debate). This, at least, is ostensibly the case. According to democratic theory, publics are supposed to be able to hold government actors to account for (environmental) management policies through the effective incorporation of the public's interests by those with relevant decision-making authority (Mason, 2005). Accountability is also intended to find expression in fisheries governance through the Commission's commitment to 'clear definition of responsibilities' (DGFisheries, 2002). However, new forms of regulation under good governance are frequently left wanting where accountability is concerned. In fact it is said to be easier to hold traditional government structures to account than new governance arrangements:

In accountable systems, those who make decisions that the public deems to be wrong can be re-called, denied re-election or re-appointment, or otherwise held responsible. [Whereas] multistakeholder regulation and industry self-regulation [arrangements] are unaccountable. The participants are self-selected. The ill-defined 'public' in these cases can hold people accountable only through indirect means, [for instance] by their choices in the market place. (Haufler, 2002, p 243)

Haufler perhaps comes to this conclusion because governance innovations, like those in the fisheries sector, often give rise to fragmented institutional landscapes. For instance, the Commission did not make it clear how RACs would function alongside pre-existing bodies also designed to feed stakeholder views into the policy process. Such fragmentation might better reflect the contingencies and messiness of real world politics, but it makes it difficult to ensure that 'accountability as clarity' is a consistent feature across these new arrangements of public bodies, private institutions, quasi-public agencies, state actors, civil society organisations and private interest groups. Haufler also notably suggests that the public that is present in new governance structures is 'ill-defined'. But he perhaps does not acknowledge that there may be *multiple* and *contingent* publics being assembled by governance reform and the fisheries crisis.

Representing and mobilising publics

The most significant change brought about by the institution of RACs and the fragmentation resulting from good governance processes is that now fishing stakeholders must mobilise in new ways to gain leverage in policymaking. For instance, in the fresh institutional environment of the RACs, particular interest groups have been able to jostle for position in order to dominate agendas (Griffin, 2007). In this altered governing milieu, it appears that one of the most significant ways in which diverse stakeholder groups try to gain influence is through the mobilisation of 'the public' and by claiming to speak on behalf of (that is, to represent) the public interest. In fact, it seems that 'the rhetoric of public interest' is becoming 'the currency of arbitrage between these contesting groups' (Phillips et al, 2002, p 466).

As discussed earlier, this is perhaps because the claim to represent the public (be it self-proclaimed or otherwise) appears to enhance groups' legitimacy. Thus politically strengthened, such groups can gain get better access to decision making in the EU, which is anxious to appeal to 'the public', whoever they are. But not all North Sea RAC stakeholders necessarily mobilise the same 'public'. In making their cases in RAC meetings, environmental groups and the fishing industry each invoke quite different constituencies of publics.

Most fishers have deeply embedded beliefs about their rights to fish, dating back to the first sea laws of the 17th century when fish were thought plentiful and belonged to no one until caught (Couper and Smith, 1997). To justify these beliefs and to generate support from the public, fishermen play on the ideas that we collectively still hold about the wild and dangerous ocean (Collet, 2002): "By a factor of thirteen it's the most dangerous occupation in the UK. So if anyone ever gives me a hard time in the media I always roll that wee statistic out" (Scottish fishermen's representative on NSRAC, 2005).

Another way that fishing industry groups attempt to mobilise the 'general public' is by portraying themselves as representatives of particular 'vulnerable fishing communities' that rely on income from fishing and fish processing. Fishing communities are commonly thought of as being traditional (Couper and Smith, 1997), local and having pre-capitalist, 'natural' identities (St Martin, 2005). This is almost certainly why the prospect of their destruction provokes such a great deal of media attention. And it is perhaps unsurprising in a time when notions of community and place have gained greater significance, amid a nostalgia for 'locality', 'home' and 'roots'. There are few economic sectors in Europe still embedded within the discourse of community, but fishing is one such, and there is a sense emanating from some sources that we should protect fishing communities from being decimated by the policies of faraway governments. This feeling is demonstrated not only by the number of press column inches dedicated to the issue, but also by the exponential growth of fishing heritage centres around the UK and elsewhere.

The anti-CFP organisation, the Cod Crusaders, has actively traded on this nostalgia in its campaigns for public support and in so doing has helped to construct this notion of vulnerable communities devastated by a distant and centralised Eureaucracy:

> For generations, the West family and thousands of other fishermen in the Scottish Fleet have trawled for cod in the North Sea.... Wives in the community, calling themselves the 'Cod Crusaders', besiege EU committee hearings in a last ditch effort to save the industry. (Cod-Crusaders, 2006)

The Cod Crusaders are not members of NSRAC, and they use this outsider status in support of their public campaigning, which has to date made an impact: "I think that the work of the Cod Crusaders has been a tremendous success in raising the awareness of the public" (spokesperson for the Cod Crusaders).

Similar strategies are deployed by those environmental interests that are also non-members of NSRAC, but who speak on fisheries issues in the North Sea. Many environmental NGOs use persuasion and seduction techniques, such as sophisticated marketing campaigns, to attract public support. For instance, marine-focused environmental groups regularly limit their efforts to the plight of a single 'charismatic species' like the blue whale to persuade the public to their cause and lever public backing for campaigns:

> As enigmatic as they are enormous, the animals represent a lot of open questions and mysteries ... there is no better symbol of the need to protect the ocean and all that's in it. Blue whales capture the imagination and mobilise people to action. (Watson, 1996, p 7)

Although much environmental concern lies with the cod in the North Sea, this species has not been similarly promoted, seemingly because it lacks charisma. Yet environmental causes are often about unappealing species, which are just as vulnerable and as ecologically significant as charismatic species. Although cod have received plentiful press coverage, unsurprisingly much sympathy seems to be with species like whales and dolphins, rather than with the unattractive codfish, which most people could only identify in batter. This is quite possibly because 'minds are not easily converted or governments turned by things wet and cold' (Jentoft and Mikalsen, 2001, p 282).

As a consequence of their campaigning, environmental groups are generally thought to be better at mobilising publics than are formal fisherman's groups, like the UK's National Federation of Fishermen's Organisations:

> "[T]he difference between environmentalists and the fishing industry is that [the former] communicate a lot. So they get their message through to the public. And we [the fishing industry] don't. When we write articles it's always exclusively in specialised publications which are read by fishermen and nobody else. [Whereas] they have been writing articles on dolphins. That's the big difference. And they have been presenting the situation as if it was the end of the world.... So when you ask anybody in the street what they think about fishermen today, they will all tell you, 'I think they are criminals emptying the seas'." (Spokesperson for a UK fishermen's organisation, 2005)

Doubtless this view is held because environmental NGOs regularly claim that the levels of fishing activity called for by fishermen are actually likely to contravene the wider public interest, because '... the public good [is] degraded as resources are monopolised by a governing class of self-serving owners' (Phillips et al, 2002, p 459). Because environmental NGOs generally see themselves as untainted by the *vested interests* that characterise the fishing industry, they argue axiomatically that they are in a better position to promote the *public interest*. Indeed, it is common for environmental groups to posit themselves as agents for 'the public' (Goodie and Wickham, 2002):

> We need to get over the notion that fisheries resources are the sole concern of the fishing industry.... At the end of the day, fisheries are a public resource and decision-making must therefore take this public interest into account. (David Butcher, World Wide Fund for Nature, Australia, cited in Mikalsen and Jentoft, 2001, p 281)

So it is perhaps unsurprising that campaigning NGOs like Greenpeace and the Sea Shepherds see themselves as witnesses for the public:

"I am what you call a campaigner on ocean and sea issues. [For us] bearing witness is the key.... Bearing witness for the public, especially out at sea, where the problems are not really clear to the people ... where they cannot see what is happening on the water ... to show them what damage is being done." (Greenpeace interviewee, 2005)

For campaigning groups like Greenpeace, RAC membership would undermine their ability to bear witness. Hence self-exclusion from RACs is a strategic decision about how they want to be represented in the media and wider public sphere.

Greenpeace clearly feels that RAC membership would taint its reputation with supporters, since it would be seen to be 'on side with the industry' (Greenpeace interview, 2005). In good governance, such outsider groups have different strategies of power open to them. While those on the 'inside' of RACs (its formal members) are obligated to 'behave responsibly', outsiders may not be so compelled, not having signed up to the rules of the game. From this outsider status, enhanced via media stunts (see Figure 8.1), they can, paradoxically, frequently have greater scope than insiders for mobilising publics.

Figure 8.1: 'The last cod'

Source: Greenpeace (2006)

Both Greenpeace and Sea Shepherds have played on dolphin entrapment in 'walls of death' (trawling nets) to attract publicity, through which, they maintain, they have successfully provoked widespread disapproval of fishing. They could not have done this as NSRAC members where the terms of the discourse are largely technocratic and rational and where there is less space for emotive argumentation or the public staging of campaigns.

By contrast, environmental NGOs that have joined NSRAC, such as the World Wide Fund for Nature, the Royal Society for the Protection of Birds (RSPB) and

Seas At Risk, have positioned themselves as environmental moderates, operating within the dominant technocratic discourse. The 'insiders' principal role is to provide invaluable information for the Commission and to monitor policy. Such groups are considered legitimate actors (Todd and Ritchie, 2000) and the EU is keen to involve them as the proxy voice of 'organised civil society' (Europa, 2003). Although they generally do not mobilise publics around fisheries issues in the same way as Greenpeace and the Sea Shepherds, they are, by contrast, invited to speak on the public's behalf in formal governance environments, being construed as their official representatives. This is perhaps because they assert that their broad-based membership affords them a 'unique capacity to represent the public concern' (Goodie and Wickham, 2002, p 55). But as well as purporting to represent the public in a narrow sense, many environmental NGOs claim to speak on behalf of a much wider civil society, including unborn populations, who, they say, have a right to inhabit and inherit an unspoiled environment. Since the consequences of overfishing will be felt by future generations, it is no wonder that environmental groups evoke these unborn 'publics'. The RSPB's slogan 'For Birds, For people, Forever', makes it clear that the organisation not only represents birds and civil society but also an unborn civil society that cannot inform the RSPB about what it requires or desires. Neither can such constituents apply for membership; they become involuntary affiliates.

Similarly, the anti-CFP group Save Britain's Fish maintains that it speaks for "all those who believe that control of fishing rights should be repatriated to the nation state" (spokesperson for the group, 2005). Here again, membership of the organisation is not always actively applied for; citizens with a particular, nationalistic, point of view are enrolled by default. Once more, representing such a membership can be problematic. 'Constituents' of the Sea Shepherds and Save Britain's Fish have no recourse if they feel that the organisation insufficiently embodies their views. This may be a truism, but it indicates how even the most populist stakeholders have power over publics, beyond any formal remits; they have presumed authority to speak on behalf of others. In the new governance arrangements, the stakeholder organisations have varying methods of deciding on representation and feeding back to constituencies. But their links with publics could be more tenuous than is often assumed.

Many environmental campaigners assert that as well as representing human publics, they also stand for the entitlements of another constituency, that of non-human nature. For instance, the marine group, the Sea Shepherds, asserts that its 'clients are marine creatures'. Here, the Sea Shepherds are not only 'speaking of' fish, but are also 'speaking for' them (to use Spivak's (1988) distinction). However, it is, of course, arguable whether we can conceive of these latter as a 'public' or, indeed, whether the preservation of nature for non-instrumental reasons is even in the wider public interest. Environmental NGO literature frequently makes claims about representing 'nature', without ever really articulating what this might involve. Interestingly, the Sea Shepherds assert that they represent 'animals', arguing that though protecting creatures would ultimately benefit humanity, it is the protection of animals for their own sake that is important to them (Sea Shepherds interview, 2005). Non-humans cannot, of course, communicate their wish to be involved in the political process, let alone articulate their demands (though it is safe to assume that, if they could, seals would lobby against a proposed cull). If such non-human constituents (publics?) are to be represented meaningfully in governance arrangements, more thought is needed about how they might be spoken for or enfranchised in a way that does not entirely reflect social prejudices (Latour and Weibel, 2005).

This section has shown how several different constituencies of publics are brought into being by stakeholder groups. Hence, the tricky matter of the governance of the commons appears to produce rather uncommon publics. Some are concerned with the decimation of fragile communities, while others are mobilised by the plight of charismatic species. Other invoked publics may comprise rather different constituents, including those of future generations and non-humans. So as Lippmann (2002) explains, there is no single omnipotent 'people' with one will and one point of view. This fact casts doubt on whether the public is a knowable body with fixed membership. For Lippmann, the public is a 'mere phantom', an abstraction (2002, p 77). So we can never fully know its characteristics or the full parameters of its membership: 'A public is always in excess of its known social basis. It must be more than a list of one's friends. It must include strangers' (Warner, 2002, p 4). What's more, while the members of any one public share an identity, coalescing around some common area of concern, the exact numbers of constituents belonging to any public are always in flux: 'When one addresses a public the addressee, intended or otherwise, is actually not there, not yet, not at least as a member of a public' (Barnett, 2007, p 9). It is because we can never know exactly who these publics are that gives groups who claim to speak on their behalf their power. Hence, it is very difficult to contest the assertions of would-be representatives of the public when it is impossible to determine for whom and for how many they speak.

This last point reminds us that the public (whether human or non-human) is rarely present in its own right. It is usually only brought into being with some sort of 'prosthetic support' (Barnett, 2007, p 2). Barnett cites Derrida (1992), who argues that the public does not and cannot speak for itself, it can only ever be represented, and therefore there is scope for it to be misrepresented or for elements of it to be excluded. What is more, any act of representation requires masses of intermediaries (Latour, 2005) and therefore it can be manipulated.

The constitution of (uncommon) publics

But how do publics actually come into being? A number of vernaculars and metaphors are used in social theory to evoke the making and representation of publics. For example, Latour and Marres deploy the language of 'assembly' to describe the process of public formation. An assembled public is a:

... delicate affiliation of a loose assemblage of agents and agencies [that involves alliances formed] not only because one agent is dependent upon another for funds, legitimacy or some other resource which can be used for persuasion or compulsion, but also because one actor comes to convince another that their problems or goals are intrinsically linked, that their interests are consonant. (Goodie and Wickham, 2002, p 57)

So this conception of public formation foregrounds the issues at stake (to use Marres' terminology) or, to put it another way, it is matters that matter in the constitution of publics (Latour, 2005). In the fisheries case, these are matters of common interest in protecting the common good, of over-exploited stocks and of lost jobs and decimated communities.

Furthermore, publics are assembled in the sense that they are *put together* through various combinations of things, mediums and techniques, like persuasion, intrigue or seduction (Goodie and Wickham, 2002, p 57; Latour and Weibel, 2005). Thus assembling publics is an active process that requires effort to forge the (sometimes disparate or conflicting) connections between the individuals and interests that will constitute a public body (Li, 2007). We have seen that non-North Sea RAC members, the Cod Crusaders, Greenpeace and the Sea Shepherds, all rely on a particular set of techniques, mediums and procedures to bring their publics to life. The visceral stunts (such as the 'last cod'), the marches, the petitions and the campaigning boats used to track fishing vessels all appear to suggest that these publics are *assembled*.

In contrast to the idea of assembling, publics theorists Barnett and Warner favour the notion of 'convening'. To convene is first to hail interested citizens, and then to wait for 'a public' to reply. That is to say, the process of convening involves a call and a response. Like Dewey, Michael Warner (2002, p 14) explains that publics are discursively summoned or 'called up'. However, for him, they must actively answer this summons (that is, respond to it) before they can be properly considered as a public. As Warner puts it, publics cannot be simply conjured into being just by the force of one's intent; a relation of attention between the addressor and the addressee must first be established. For Barnett (2007, p 9), this idea helps us appreciate the sense in which 'publics appear through representative acts': that is, being spoken for and being spoken to.

As we have seen above, many official North Sea fisheries groups appear to convene their publics, discursively bringing them into being when they claim to represent them in EU institutions. However, since North Sea RAC members have already had their authority to talk on the publics' behalf bestowed by the EU, they do not need to receive a response from prospective interested citizens when they are hailed. Thus, instead of convening, NSRAC members merely make reference to 'the public' by claiming to represent it, in order to suggest that the NSRAC has broad support for its agenda and to gain legitimacy in the eyes of EU institutions.

This is in contrast to non-NSRAC members, that is, the 'outsiders' of the formal fisheries governance process. With their theatrical media stunts and persuasive campaigns, we might prefer the notion of assemblage to describe their publics' constitution. However, these outsider groups generally *do* rely on a response from their publics. Indeed, the activities and stunts of these outside groups are actively designed to elicit a response. And it is the response of interested citizens to these summons that gives outsider groups their legitimacy to represent matters of concern on their publics' behalf. We might therefore say that for these groups an element of convening as well as assembling publics is in effect. For outsiders, publics are not simply put together around issues at stake; publics must have first responded to a call.

We have seen that North Sea RAC members – the insiders – appear to be convening publics (that is, deploying discursive techniques to hail them). However, a crucial part of the process is missing – that of an active response. This raises doubts as to whether the publics that these groups claim to represent are really publics at all. Crucially, because of these doubts we might want to argue that outsider groups have a more credible set of publics than insiders. If this were the case, it would be surprising, given that insider groups (NSRAC members) are the ones bestowed with the formal legitimacy to represent 'the public' and give credibility to new governance regimes.

In this way, we see that the processes of convening and assembling publics are not, as one might have imagined, mutually exclusive. For instance, it is clear that outsider groups in North Sea fisheries governance form publics using both discursive and material strategies, both convening *and* assembling them. Of course, assembling, putting together, convening and calling together have similar etymological roots. However, it is perhaps fair to say that the acts of representation involved for each are different. This might be explained using Latour's (2005) two meanings of representation in democratic practices. The first 'designates the ways to gather the legitimate people around a matter of concerns', while the second, presents or rather '*represents* what is the object of concern to the eyes and ears of those [publics] who have been assembled around it' (Latour, 2005, p 6, emphasis added). It appears that the acts of representation occurring outside of formal fisheries governance involve *re*presentations of issues to citizens who have a real stake in fishing for the public interest, while those processes going on inside RACs relate most strongly to the first sense of representation – that of acquiring legitimacy.

And yet, while insiders possess the legitimacy to represent the public interest, we also see that NSRAC stakeholders are in fact *manufacturers* of the public interest; they not only hope to represent it, but they also help to define, manipulate and promote it. When we hear talk about 'the national interest' we have become accustomed to being sceptical, and this research suggests that we should be just as vigilant with claims to represent the 'public interest' and the 'common good', no matter how legitimate they appear. As Barnett explains:

Some of the worst excesses of our times have been made in the name of populist movements who claim to embody the singular will of a unified people against the inauthentic, divisive impostures of parties, experts, elites, or other representatives. So, one reason to embrace the mediated appearance of publics is to cultivate a healthy scepticism about any given claim to embody 'the' public will or interest. (Barnett, 2007, p 2)

It is clear that publics in fisheries management can be misrepresented, excluded and manipulated. This isn't a problem in itself. As we have seen earlier, publics are always mediated, as they are brought into being or represented (see also Chapters Two and Four of this volume). But when we hear stakeholder groups talking about their claim to protect the common good and wider public values, we should always be circumspect. While we may never know how many they speak on behalf of, we can ask ourselves what *particular* interests are at stake, who or what is being excluded in their accounts, and how the publics are actively responding to interpellations.

References

Barnett, C. (2007) 'Convening publics: the parasitical spaces of public action', in K. Cox, M. Low and J. Robinson (eds) *Handbook of political geography*, London: Sage Publications, pp 403–18.

Cod Crusaders (2006) Homepage, www.cod-crusaders.org.uk.

Collet, S. (2002) 'Appropriation of marine resources: from management to an ethical approach to fisheries governance', *Social Science Information Sur Les Sciences Sociales*, 41(4), pp 531–53.

COM (2001) *European Governance White Paper*, COM (2001) 428 final, Brussels.

COM (2007) 'Conclusions from the consultation on a European Maritime Policy', *Official Journal of the European Communities* L 574 final, Brussels.

Couper, A.D. and Smith, H.D. (1997) 'The development of fishermen-based policies', *Marine Policy*, 21(2), pp 111–19.

Crean, K. (2000) 'The influence of boundaries and the management of fisheries resources in the European Union: case studies from the UK', *Geoforum*, 31(3), pp 315–28.

Derrida, J. (1992) *The other heading*, Bloomington, IN: Indiana University Press.

Dewey, J. (1927) *The public and its problems*, New York, NY: Henry Holt and Company.

DGFisheries (2002) 'Reforming the Common Fisheries Policy – Q and A', available at http://ec.europa.eu/comm/fisheries/reform/q&a_en.htm.

DGFisheries (2006) 'Managing a common resource', available at http://ec.europa. eu/fisheries/cfp_en.htm.

Europa (2003) 'Commission keen to draw more on organized civil society', *European Union Online*, www.globalpolicy.org/ngos/int/eu/2002/1211civsoc. htm.

Goodie, J. and Wickham, G. (2002) 'Calculating "public interest": common law and legal governance of the environment', *Social & Legal Studies*, 11(1), pp 37-60.

Greenpeace (2006) www.greenpeace.org.uk.

Griffin, L. (2007) 'All aboard: power, participation and governance in the North Sea Regional Advisory Council', *International Journal of Green Economics*, 1(3/4), pp 478-93.

Griffin, L. (2008) 'Food security and the fisheries crisis', in H.F. Munck and. R. Munck (eds) *Globalisation and security: An encyclopaedia*, California: Praeger Press, pp 120-36.

Hardin, G. (1968) 'The tragedy of the commons', *Science*, 162, pp 1243-8.

Haufler, V. (2002) 'New forms of governance: certification regimes as social regulations of the global market', in E. Meidinger, C. Elliott and G. Oesten *Social and political dimensions of forest certification*, Remagen-Oberwinter: Verlag.

Holmquist, J. (2004) Speech to the North Sea Regional Advisory Council General Assembly, Edinburgh, February.

ICES (International Council for the Exploration of the Oceans) (2004) 'International Council for the Exploration of the Oceans: introduction', www.ices.dk, accessed July 2005.

IEEP (Institute for European Environmental Policy) (2004) *Analysis of EU fisheries policy reform proposals and communications*, London: IEEP.

Jentoft, S. and Mikalsen, K. (2001) 'From user-groups to stakeholders? The public interest in fisheries management', *Marine Policy*, 25, pp 281-92.

Kooiman, J. (2003) *Governing as governance*, London: Sage Publications.

Latour, B. (2005) 'From Realpolitik to Dingpolitik, or how to make things public', in B. Latour and P. Weibel (eds) *Making things public: Atmospheres of democracy*, Cambridge, MA: MIT Press.

Latour, B. and Weibel, P. (2005) *Making things public: Atmospheres of democracy*, Cambridge, MA: MIT Press.

Li, T.M. (2007) 'Practices of assemblage and community forest management', *Economy and Society*, 36(2), pp 263-93.

Lippmann, W. (2002) *The phantom public*, London: Transaction Publishers, first published 1927.

Marres, N. (2005) 'No issue, no public: democratic deficits after the displacement of politics', Unpublished doctoral dissertation, University of Amsterdam.

Marres, N. (2007) 'The issues deserve more credit: pragmatist contributions to the study of public involvement in controversy', *Social Studies of Science*, 37(5), pp 759-80.

Mason, M. (2005) *The new accountability: Environmental responsibility across borders*, London: Earthscan.

Mikalsen, K.H. and Jentoft, S. (2001) 'From user-groups to stakeholders? The public interest in fisheries management', *Marine Policy*, 25(4), pp 281-92.

Mikalsen, K.H. and Jentoft, S. (2003) 'Limits to participation? On the history, structure and reform of Norwegian fisheries management', *Marine Policy*, 27(5), pp 397-407.

Mitchell, J. (2008) 'What public presence? Access, commons and property rights', *Social & Legal Studies*, 3(17), pp 351-67.

Nadel-Klein, J. (2003) *Fishing for heritage*, Oxford: Berg.

Newman, J. (2001) *Modernising government: New Labour, policy and society*, London: Sage Publications.

Newman, J. (ed) (2005) *Remaking governance: Peoples, politics and the public sphere*, Bristol: The Policy Press.

Newman, J. and Clarke, J. (2009) *Publics, politics and power: Remaking the public in public services*, London: Sage Publications.

Ostrom, E. (1990) *Governing the commons: Illustrating the evolution of institutions for collective active action*, Cambridge: Cambridge University Press.

Paterson, M. (1999) 'Interpreting trends in global environmental governance', *International Affairs*, 75(4), pp 793-802.

Phillips, G., Kriwoken, L. and Hay, P. (2002) 'Private property and public interest in fisheries management: the Tasmanian rock lobster fishery', *Marine Policy*, 26(6), pp 459-69.

Porritt, J. (2005) *Fishing for good*, London: Forum for the Future.

Rhodes, R. (1996) 'The new governance: governing without government', *Political Studies*, 44, pp 652-67.

Rhodes, R.A.W. (2000) *Transforming British government*, Basingstoke: Macmillan.

Rogers, S. and Stock, R. (2001) *Technical report produced for strategic environmental assessment: North Sea fish and fisheries*, London: Centre for Environment, Fisheries and Aquaculture Science.

Shore, C. (1997) 'Governing Europe: European Union audiovisual policy and the politics of identity', in C. Shore and S. Wright (eds) *Anthropology of policy: Critical perspectives on governance and power*, London: Routledge, pp 126-49.

Spivak, G. (1988) 'Can the subaltern speak?', in C. Nelson and L. Grossberg (eds) *Marxism and the interpretation of culture*, London: Macmillan, pp 217-313.

St Martin, K. (2005) 'Disrupting enclosure', *Capitalism, Nature, Socialism*, 16(1), pp 63-80.

Todd, E. and Ritchie, E. (2000) 'Environmental non-governmental organizations and the common fisheries policy', *Aquatic Conservation: Marine and Freshwater Ecosystems*, 10(2), pp 141-9.

Warner, M. (2002) *Publics and counterpublics*, New York, NY: Zone Books.

Watson, J. (1996) 'Charisma! – charisma in animals', *International Wildlife*, Jan-Feb.

Young, O.R. (1994) *International governance: Protecting the environment in a stateless society*, London: Cornell University Press.

NINE

De-naming the beast: the Global Call to Action against Poverty and its multiple forms of publicness

Clive Gabay

The naming of publics is an important political and ontological process. Several chapters of this volume (for example, Chapters Three, Eight and Ten) speak to the processual nature of publics; the idea that publics do not pre-exist the process of their becoming, and are not a substantive 'thing'. Naming is part of this processual becoming, but naming is also the moment that complexity, contingency and contradictions are flattened, or as Law (2003) would argue, 'othered'. This chapter will therefore address the attempted 'names' (categorisations) that have been developed in the post-Cold War era to fix the processual becoming of global publics. I want to show how the act of naming is not only an epistemological act, providing us with an increasing number of perspectives from which to understand the same processual reality, but also an ontological act, closing down the possibility of understanding publics in their fully contradictory and multiple realities. This is important for any politics of the public in that the act of naming can itself close down other possible becomings, open up silences and mask the relationalities of power, space and legitimacy through which publics are summoned. This matters for how participants in such publics understand their own agency, and for how much transformative potential those who study such publics invest in them.

This chapter will address the publics that have been variously labelled global civil society, the global justice movement, and the movement of movements (see Table 9.1). It is, of course, important not to reify these terms, not to turn them into 'straw publics'. As will be explained, while these concepts contain contradictions, they also offer partial insights. Many of them speak to each other, explaining theoretical or empirical offshoots of global publicness. How, methodologically, do we negotiate this mess? While they are at times interchangeable, these terms all describe something particular about the process of global public formation, and understanding how and when to deploy them is vital if we are to avoid confusing the normative and the explicatory in our research.

This chapter draws on my own research on the Global Call to Action against Poverty (GCAP). GCAP consists of a secretariat (recently moved from South Africa to the Netherlands) supporting a Global Governing Council (elected by a Global Assembly) that decides all global policy (that is, all policy without an explicitly national dimension). When deciding where to study GCAP, it was on the national coalitions, and not the global body they temporarily constitute, that I decided to focus. My research illustrates how GCAP is a multiplicity of publics, structures and agencies, and objects and subjects, much of the time simultaneous. Indeed, in 'naming' itself outside of these labels (a global 'call'), GCAP also mobilises, in practice, a public unique to itself. This reinforces the notion of global publicness as contingent and unfixed. I will also pose questions concerning the legitimacy performed by these different public formations, and the kind of power that they exhibit and that sustains them. Implicit as we go along will be the challenges that confront the study of multiple messiness.

Introducing GCAP

Born out of discussions between several international non-governmental organisations (NGOs) in late 2003, GCAP was negotiated into existence at a series of international conferences between 2003 and 2007, attended by a large range of northern and southern NGOs. During this time, GCAP acted as a campaign hub, coordinating the campaigns for trade justice, fair trade and international aid held across the globe in 2005 around the time of the G8 summit in Gleneagles, Scotland. GCAP provided the global umbrella for initiatives such as Make Poverty History in the UK and the One Campaign in the US. After 2005, GCAP grew to encompass over 100 national campaigning coalitions. By 2008, GCAP was focusing its activities around broad themes and events such as World Poverty Day and the United Nations Millennium Development Goals (MDGs).

It is time, however, to own up. As the author, I am in a privileged position. I have just presented to you a short description of GCAP. I have, in John Law's (2003) words, made GCAP 'present'. But this is only a particular kind of presence – my kind of presence – and, in making GCAP present, I have inevitably made other things absent. As Law argues: 'The problem is not exclusion as such…. Rather it is about the denial of that exclusion. The refusal to acknowledge that this is going on' (2003, p 7). It is what is *not* going on in the above description that provides the basis for the rest of this chapter; by addressing the variety of names that have been applied to actors like GCAP, it will become clear that the fixity that they all implicitly aim for in their categorisations actually conceals multiple realities that involve concurrent processes of subject and object formation, and the creation of mediums of publicness.

Before going into more detail on GCAP's multiplicities, I want to introduce some of the concepts that have been developed over the past 10 to 15 years and have attempted to develop a common vernacular around the forces of global justice, human rights, environmentalism and peace. The following is a very brief typology of the three main and overlapping theorisations that have predominated this thinking and the forms of publicness they each in turn imply. This will serve to provide some context to my subsequent use of these concepts and begin to illustrate how they are at once interrelated and also unique. The process of affirming their relevance to some expressions of global publicness will also involve problematising their universalistic explanatory power, and therefore the veracity of some of their claims. Following Table 9.1 is a discussion of how GCAP is all and none of these concepts, thus disturbing efforts to name and fix actors similar to it.

Table 9.1: Categorisations of global publics

Category	Features of publicness	Problematic assumptions of publicness
Global civil society (Keane, 2001; Kaldor, 2003)	Civil society is an inherently progressive public space The global is a separate, pre-existing and equally accessible site of public contestation with the state Global civil society represents a medium of plurality, where power is dissipated among public actors in order to hold states to account	Too binary: cannot account for counter-progressive forces Assumes pre-existing and non-power-differentiated public mediums
Global justice movement/alter-globalisation movement (Reitan, 2007)	Recognises global civil society as a terrain (a non-smooth medium) rather than a normative force Global justice movement is a progressive actor on that global terrain Aims include alternative visions of globalisation	The global justice movement is considered to be a bounded and fixed public medium This creates conceptual and real tensions between the actors within this movement (that is, NGOs, activists, states and so on, some of whom constitute subjects and others objects of public concern)
Movement of movements (Della Porta and Tarrow, 2005)	Adds empirical support to Hardt and Negri's notion of the multitude (2004), an always-becoming and everywhere-existing public Views difference between individuals and groups as a strength Contains multiple but tolerant identities – an 'evangelical search for dialogue' (Della Porta and Tarrow, 2005, p 186) Subsumes local difference into global unity	Ignores the difference between tolerance (closed, negative, reflective of impersonal relationship to other subjects) and understanding (open-ended commitment to other subjects) and thus retains the difficulty of differentiating subjects from objects apparent within the global justice movement Cannot account for insurmountable difference; that is, what happens at the end of tolerance (for a more detailed discussion, see Gabay, 2008)

I want to illustrate how some of these concepts have been over-extended from identifying one manifestation of publicness to offer totalising definitions of publicness. I will go on to draw on research data from my own study of GCAP to illustrate how aspects of these concepts can be retained, but only in extremely contingent ways. I argue that it is important to investigate the degree to which the concepts above are able to adequately capture the processes of GCAP, the publics it summons and how GCAP itself might be summoned as a form of public. This is important because of the normative claims made by and about GCAP (and its constituent campaigns such as Make Poverty History) that it is a force for global justice (Saunders and Rootes, 2006) and that it is constituted by civil society (www.whiteband.org), a common definition of which implies a multiplicity of un-coerced and autonomous actors (LSE, 2004). These claims suggest that GCAP is accessed by, speaks for or somehow represents a global community. But this global community is variously named a global civil society, a global justice movement and a movement of movements, all of which, as we have seen, involve different and sometimes contradictory modes of subjectivity.

Here I want to take issue with the work of one author in particular, John Keane, who has attempted to conceptualise actors like GCAP, and whose most recent work was trailed at one of the seminars around which this book was formed. Keane is interesting in that he developed some of the earlier work in this area (2001) as well as some of the most recent (2008). His earlier work posited that global civil society was a space analogous to a living biosphere: 'These ecosystems of Global Civil Society … are interconnected. And they are more or less intricately balanced through continuous flows and recycling of efforts among … populations of individuals of the same species' (Keane, 2001, p 24). This notion is, however, highly contestable, not so much for what it says, but for what it does not say. Massey (2005) argues that what we traditionally define as being global is relationally constructed through the daily practices of people and institutions in different places (themselves relationally constructed). As such, Massey contends that:

> [D]ifferent places will stand in contrasting relations to the global. They are differentially located within the wider power-geometries. Mali and Chad, most certainly, may be understood as occupying positions of relative powerlessness. But London, or the USA, or the UK? These are the places in and through which globalisation is *produced*. (2005, p 101)

This challenges Keane's notion of a finely balanced global civil society – different spatial arrangements incubate differentiated power relations, which means that one cannot create relationships with other places without taking account of one's own actions in constructing them. So, while Keane's conception of global civil society takes a relational perspective, it implicitly flattens or smoothes the processes by which spaces are constructed. In so doing, it ignores the power crucial to these constructions and fails to address how power circulates differentially, empowering some more than others. This is important for my analysis (or any analysis of actors like GCAP) because translating GCAP into a notion of global civil society leaves us with an uncritical and fixed assessment of it. It ignores how GCAP is constructed as a public object via a differentiated and relational process, as well for whom GCAP speaks.

However, it is Keane's more recent work on monitory democracy (Keane, 2008) that elucidates further the *a priori* normative values with which he invests his supposedly analytical categories. He argues that since 1945 there has been a proliferation of non-traditional democratic forms, noting over 100 alternative models (for example, participatory budgeting, truth and reconciliation commissions, social forums and so on) whose common function appears to be their monitory capacity, that is, their capacity to monitor traditional (the state) and newer (multinational corporations) sites of power. Keane argues that democracy has always been based on representation, and that these new monitory institutions embody forms of representation. The multiplication of sites of representativeness to monitor the exercise of power is therefore positive. This argument leads him to posit the need to defend these institutions. It should be noted that Keane's monitory democracy continues the essentially liberal intellectual tradition of global civil society theory, adding a sharper focus on the organisations that writers such as Keane invest with the ability to 'speak to power' on behalf of various publics (see, for example, Falk, 1999; Kaldor, 2003).

There are a number of methodological approaches one could adopt here. From a Foucauldian perspective, one could query whether the multiplication of sites of monitory institutions merely represents a form of advanced governmentality. This is something I will develop shortly in relation to my research data. However, at this point, I want to draw attention to power *between* organisational forms, rather than within them. As Clegg (1989) pointed out, organisational forms are fluid, in a constant state of contestation as forces within fight (sometimes literally) to fix its representativeness. Monitory institutions therefore do not simply monitor, but take on a whole range of other, sometimes contradictory, roles revolving around power relations. Keane (2008) argues that when monitory institutions work well they contest and break down power, but while this may indeed be the case, it offers only a partial picture, one that ignores entirely the potential creation and recreation of new elites and oligarchies. In a discussion of the public role of such institutions, this means they are being worked through by other actors (such as the state) as well as working on them. This has implications for the kind of potential for social change we invest in what are, in reality, normative concepts like global civil society or monitory democracy. We need to treat these concepts as normative processes, rather than fixed descriptions.

Keane flattens the actors he is attempting to categorise, erasing problems of power and agency. This a feature common to all of the different theorisations of these actors mentioned previously. For instance, global justice performs the same normative trick as monitory democracy. And where Reitan claims that the ideal global activists are '… those who are immediately suffering firsthand the structural violences of neoliberalism … more and more becoming transnational agents themselves …' (2007, p 52), Routledge et al (2007) have shown how in many cases it will not be the victims of structural violence who control the formation of a particular movement, but rather those who are resourced to imagine the network – its forms, potentials and representations – who will often be NGO professionals.

What I have tried to do here is significantly disturb some of the terms we use when we describe and explain struggles, protests, campaigns and other expressions of activism that appear to contain a global dimension. Indeed, while I would not argue that the global can somehow be removed from formations of the local, and vice versa, there is a kind of unthinking globality that infuses some of these theorisations and closes down any kind of relational and processual analysis. This form of analysis seems flawed, as it can only depict public processes as singularities. When these processes are broken down, however, it is easier to appreciate that different kinds of publics are being summoned, with different kinds of legitimacy and different ontologies. To illustrate this further, the next section draws on empirical data that hopefully provides pointers for studying similar phenomena.

De-naming to re-name ... contingently

The following interview responses and group observations come from a PhD research project conducted with GCAP national coalition members in India and Malawi. Questions posed to respondents were an attempt to elicit responses that would shed light on the various relationships involved in building their particular network. While bearing in mind that all were nominally part of the same global network, different participants stood in different relational positions to each other. These relational differences are spatial; however, they cannot be only reduced to nationality and geographical position, but reflect the type of organisation participants belonged to (and their subsequent perspectives on the appropriate scales of public action), the degree to which they travelled outside their country and thus constituted what Townsend (1998) has named a 'transnational NGO community', and their relative positions in urban centres, national-regional and global-regional areas. Questions therefore focused on what respondents felt was the purpose of their national network, what they thought GCAP was, and which actors they conceived of as being important to the network. I also observed network meetings and conducted some ethnographic interviewing with key members of the national networks.

GCAP as global civil society and monitory public

Keane's notion of a developing monitory force certainly resonates with how many members of the GCAP national coalitions in this study view their own roles, and should not therefore be discounted. Indeed, in a survey of all GCAP national coalitions, the top two priorities they identified for their campaigns were public engagement followed closely by (and arguably implicated in) government engagement (GCAP, 2008). In response to questions concerning the purpose of their coalition's activities, nearly every participant gave answers such as:

> "That great aim is I think to remind government leaders of their commitment." (Interview 5)

"Mobilising people so that they can persuade the parliament and the leaders to stick to their words." (Interview 8)

Such responses show how GCAP provides an object of public concern: the performance of governments against their commitments under national programmes and under international agreements around the MDGs. They also suggest that publics must be summoned and engaged in MDG discourses in order to galvanise their support to such a governance accountability programme – what many participants called 'sensitisation'. The GCAP national coalitions provide the means by which the global GCAP body seeks to achieve this, both through the dissemination of educational materials and campaign ideas, and through the global coordination around the Stand Up against Poverty events that take place annually on World Poverty Day.[1]

So far, so monitory. Indeed, further support can be given to Keane's hypothesis in the form of the actual results of this monitory activity. In both case study countries, governments have been forced at least in part by GCAP-galvanised public action to honour pledges and implement policies as a result of the national coalitions' actions. However, Latour's instruction to 'follow the actors' (2005) in participant responses and GCAP documents reveals the very partial ontology of GCAP as a monitory actor or set of actors, speaking for a pre-existing monitory public. A very important actor that problematised GCAP's monitory ontology, the MDGs, only became apparent to me because of the epistemic hold it appeared to wield over the particular spatial configurations of power I found in Malawi.

The Millennium Development Goals

The MDGs have guided development agendas around the world since they were endorsed by the UN General Assembly in 2001. They bind governments and international agencies to a set of shared aspirational goals, under which sit lists of numerically defined targets to be met by 2015 (see, for example, www.undp.org/mdg/goal4.shtml). Efforts to harmonise development agency and government approaches at national level have further enhanced the political legitimacy granted to the MDGs. It is not surprising therefore that, for civil society campaigns seeking to hold governments to account on development priorities, the MDGs should form a central plank of their analysis.

However, this linear reading of the history of the MDGs belies a more complex process of creation. Once again, it is important that we do not take names for granted, and the 'development' label has certainly been a historically contested one (see Bello, 2004; Broad and Kavanagh, 2008). David Hulme (2007) has provided an extensive account of how the role of state actors, particularly the Organisation of Economic Co-operation and Development (OECD), was important in the development of the MDGs as an intellectual and policy paradigm. Particularly influential were the International Development Targets (IDTs), the OECD's forerunner to the MDGs, which were subsequently merged with the UN's efforts to form the MDGs (Bradford, 2006). Colin Bradford, US representative to the Development Assistance Committee in the 1990s, relates that finding an alternative ideological narrative with which to 'sell' development in the aftermath of the Cold War was a major motivation in the drafting of the IDTs (2006, p 2). One can already detect issues of contention here for actors that may have different notions of development to that of the OECD.

Some have argued that the MDGs represent a 'valid attempt to define the purpose of work by both international development agencies and national governments' (White and Black, 2004, p 22). However, others have seen in the MDGs an attempt by powerful actors to extend their economic hegemony (Amin, 2006; Cammack, 2006). What will become clear from the following analysis, however, is that whether the MDGs are simply 'good' or 'bad' (most likely a mixture), in the context of this chapter their presence in GCAP significantly problematises the degree to which it can be considered uncritically as a pre-existing monitory public. Rather, in certain important respects (and places), GCAP is summoned by the MDGs as a monitory public that legitimises this particular development framework. One can also view this from a Foucauldian perspective, whereby what participants imagine is possible when they talk about 'development' is conditioned by both assemblages of knowledge and individual agents of that knowledge. This is what I will try to illustrate here.

The MDGs play a major part in how the coalition members, particularly in Malawi, conceive of their campaigns. The campaigns were to be:

> "… a watchdog of the international community in pursuing the Millennium Development Goals." (Interview 2)

This poses the following question:

> "Are the stakeholders, our government, really doing something to achieve these MDGs, that's the most important, I think."(Interview 2)

Indeed, many of the participants referred directly to the MDGs, with no prompting, as soon as our conversations began. One participant, in response to an email I had sent inviting him to take part in this research, responded in great detail about exactly which MDGs his organisation matched. Another respondent told me that the achievement of the MDGs in his country, Malawi, would be like heaven. Another claimed that:

> "… for Malawi, a third-world country, I mean, that would cure everything." (Interview 11)

The MDGs' pledge is to reduce extreme poverty by 50%, yet Malawi is a country where, according to the United Nations Development Programme, 65.4% of people live below the nationally defined poverty line (UNDP, 2008). Even halving this figure would still leave a third of the population living in extreme poverty. The MDGs, it seems, must exert a powerful hold to make this scenario appear 'heavenly'.

Malawian civil society is relatively young in the sense of government recognition, formal institutions and mass-movement organising. Government critics were not tolerated during the period of dictatorship pre-1994 (Kadzamira and Kunje, 2002). It has been noted by others that Malawian civil society coalitions and networks are thus very susceptible to hierarchical forms of organising, with certain organisations taking lead roles, attracting and centralising resources and thus reinforcing the hierarchical nature of their coalitions and networks (Tembo, 2003; James and Malunga, 2006). It is within this particular space–power dynamic therefore, that the MDGs have taken an epistemic hold of definitions of poverty and its solution. For example, the role of the Malawian GCAP coalition was, according to one participant:

> "... to support the [civil society] networks in coordinating their activities around the MDGs, because some of them do not have a guide, you know?" (Ethnographic interview 1)

Another claimed that:

> "... the taskforce is a forum, is a platform, where the various stakeholders, the stakeholders of the MDGs, meet and discuss and share." (Interview 7)

What, I thought, about those people and organisations whose concerns were not encapsulated by the MDGs? What about those organisations working on social exclusion or racism, or those organisations that advocate radical social or economic agendas?

The MDGs can be viewed as an epistemic actor constructing the anti-poverty network of Malawian civil society (much in the same way that Law (2007) describes networks as mini-epistemes, in this case discursively and physically ordering the network's actions and responses to poverty in Malawi). So, while GCAP has enabled a monitory space to be opened up in Malawi, this is a space that is heavily ordered, and indeed monitored, by the presence of the MDGs, leading to a very particular process of public formation. And it is monitored in a very ontological manner. At a national coalition meeting held at the offices of the Malawi United Nations Development Programme (UNDP), UNDP representatives claimed that not enough members of the government bureaucracy were aware of the MDGs; coalition members admonished themselves for not attending enough government consultations; other UN representatives called for more formal interaction with the government on their MDG commitments (Observation of Malawian GCAP Coalition Meeting), explicitly de-legitimising outsider tactics of political activism, ruled out as a form of public mediation.

Indeed, this was also an explicit process of public subjectification, a prescription of what types of public action, and thus what types of public*ness* were deemed both acceptable and necessary to further the object of public concern that had been identified – government accountability.

As we have seen, the Malawian coalition's monitory function resulted in new realities for the beneficiaries of policy changes by the Malawian government, so, just as GCAP as monitory does not tell the whole story, neither does GCAP as monitored. And so, once again, we are forced to hold back from the act of fixing by naming. Indeed, the epistemic power of the MDGs described here was only enabled because of the particular space–power dynamic I encountered in Malawi, one that included a weak civil society and a heavy donor presence. In India, where my other case study was conducted, the MDGs played a very different role, providing an oppositional force for a civil society that had a long history of self-empowerment and oppositional politics. Indeed, many of the Indian participants of this study showed considerable disregard for the MDGs, one labelling them the *Minimum* Development Goals (Ethnographic interview 2). This reinforces the problem of translating such disparate space–power dynamics into totalising categorical constructs. However, this does not mean that we do not sometimes come across such categories playing out in practice; the challenge is to retain their contingent nature.

GCAP as global justice movement

Advocates of the term global justice movement do so in part 'because it is inclusive, and because it does least violence to the open, inclusive and global goals of the movement' (Saunders and Rootes, 2006, p 2). The term itself, however open the movement is, nonetheless suggests a public that is broadly cohesive around the aims of global justice, which 'represents nothing more, yet nothing less than a set of emancipatory possibilities rising out of the ashes of the last century' (Kurasawa, 2007, p 2). Can evidence of such a movement be found in the ontologies of GCAP, and to what extent can GCAP be 'named' by such a term?

> "We are saying this is global, it's not just a call to the politicians, it's a call to everybody.... It's actually for everybody to say let us move and do something." (Interview 15)

> "This is a platform where the various players from various countries do meet to deliver a unified message."(Interview 2)

> "... the simple way to put it is, kind of, joining hands together." (Interview 18)

All of these statements assert a notion of unification with distant others (and came from participants in both Indian and Malawi), and a sense of global responsibility for issues that are assumed to affect most people on the planet. Indeed, the global Stand Up against Poverty events that GCAP organises via its national coalition affiliates seem to add credence to this sense of movement on a large scale, with, according to GCAP, nearly two per cent of the world's population 'standing up' on World Poverty Day 2008 (www.whiteband.org/Action/take-action/gcap-mobilisation-2008/). Indeed, several coalition members did profess to experience a sense of global belonging in their activities. Simultaneous with this was the fact that other coalition members had to check their diaries when asked what GCAP was, associating it only with the Stand Up days, thus suggesting an ontology that was rather less global. There are two possible explanations for this. One is that the UN seeks to present a global discourse on the MDGs, and thus problematises the priorities and activities of GCAP coalitions accordingly, often to such an extreme degree that all some coalition members knew about GCAP was the annual Stand Up days in which the UN plays an active role in funding and organising. The other explanation is that people are exposed to GCAP in different ways. While in both India and Malawi some coalition members only experienced GCAP in their respective countries, other people I spoke to had travelled to Japan, Washington and London to experience GCAP as a global articulation of public identity. They thus experienced different ontologies. If there is some sense of a global movement among their more place-bound colleagues, it is because there are 'imagineers' (Routledge et al, 2007) of the network to which they belong in their midst. Neither possibility suggests that the term 'global justice movement' brings us any closer to a complete understanding of GCAP and actors like it. Furthermore, the term 'global justice movement', as illustrated in Table 9.1, smoothes the relationships between the different actors involved in such a movement, and thus occludes the process of negotiation that constitutes the articulation of a global justice public. One GCAP participant involved with GCAP's global secretariat illustrated the difficulty with which one can use a term like global justice movement to delineate a boundary within which only progressive actors exist, thus excluding contentious formative processes:

> "... in Indonesia of course there's huge problems with government, you've got the Ministry of Education standing up, making promises on education which have never been met, and, and this is a civil society who are screaming against the Ministry of Education and for them suddenly to get his space and say 'well we're doing what we can', it's devastating for them, it's awful." (Interview 23)

In India, however, such tensions appear to play a more realised and productive role. Many of the NGO members of the Indian GCAP coalition did not share this explicitly global sense of justice and movement. I will now move on therefore to unfold one of GCAP's other ontologies – that of being a 'movement of movements'. This again will illustrate the problems involved with trying to 'name' global public processes.

GCAP as a 'movement of movements'

According to Della Porta and Tarrow, the movement of movements is a singular yet divergent movement populated by activists and organisations embedded in multiple identities, and positive not only despite this feature, but also perhaps because of it. Because these multiplications occur at the level of the individual, and are thus internally tolerant, they are also externally tolerant, allowing for the movement of movements to include within its coverage a wider range of ideological positions than one would have found in progressive movements previously (Della Porta and Tarrow, 2005, p 237). To what extent, then, can GCAP be described as internally tolerant, as a movement characterised by internal divergence and what Melucci calls a '... composite phenomena of collective action comprising a multiplicity of analytical dimensions' (1996, p 31)?

GCAP as a movement of movements may not be something that one necessarily witnesses in GCAP's global representation of itself. It is therefore not in an epistemological sense that GCAP is or is not a movement of movements, but in particular expressions, or ontologies of GCAP, that we can see it. I now want to draw on one particular example from the Indian coalition that illustrates this point and enacted the Indian coalition as representing, and being, GCAP as a movement of movements. In 2005, at the time of the Make Poverty History events in the UK, several northern NGOs based in India felt that there should be a rock concert to coincide with Make Poverty History. According to the Indian campaign convenor, however:

> "Many groups were very critical of what was happening – how can you have a rock show?... There was a larger political disagreement with celebrity endorsement, the idea of taking it in a very modern kind of direction ... and I think it was a good time for us, good that the rock concert happened ... we became very clear that it had to be a very Indian coalition...." (Interview 19)

This suggests a certain degree of agency on behalf of the publics that GCAP attempts to speak for. The northern NGOs' (many of whom dominate GCAP's agenda in the North) problematisation of GCAP's role did not succeed in India, and created a resistance to it that helped to shape the Indian coalition's tactics and strategy. It might appear, then, that we do not here have a movement of movements, but simply different movements. However, the Indian coalition came to believe that a 'global movement' required southern leadership, and so Indian NGOs came to play an active role within GCAP's global structures. In my study, I showed how they exhibited a fundamental understanding of the importance of GCAP globally, even if that importance was sometimes questioned in the domestic (space–power) context. Indeed, in this way, GCAP appears to be an ontological articulation of Melucci's (1996) description of collective identity formation, characterised by ongoing internal discussion and divergence processes, with no one representation of it ever being more than a contingent and unstable one.

Many publics, many politics

We are left with a variety of partial, contingent and often clumsily deployed names. Beyond the methodological, why is any of this important? To start with, I think that there has been a tendency in research and commentary of post-Cold War global activism to (as one prominent commentator I witnessed at a conference put it) drink the Kool Aid[2] when assessing the possibilities of what at times appears to be a global movement for progressive change. But as we have seen, as soon as this statement of universal stability is made, we are faced with the messy realities of which these movements consist. I came into academia motivated by the desire to understand how activist movements could achieve substantial and long-lasting socio-economic change – in other words, how could they change the world? This was, I subsequently discovered, an empty and far too big a question. After all, whose world was I talking about? Whose change? And what did I mean by 'global', 'activist' and 'movement'? What did this mean for the normativity I sought to bring into, and out of, my work? It was only when I turned some of these questions outwards, on to the subject of my research, that I began to understand the normative implications of this reflexive kind of perspective for our understanding of 'global' publics. Refraining from naming, far from closing down the potential of such articulations of activism and advocacy, actually opens up the always potential becomings of such moments of publicity. In GCAP's multiple ontologies, we can see that its political potential is also multiple, more multiple even than the ontologies it enacts, for by enacting one type of ontology there are always other possibilities left un-enacted. So, many publics, and many more politics. The act of not naming means we always retain the possibilities of all (or at least many) of these politics in our analysis. And it also means we can never write off (like, for example, Chandler, 2004) the potential of actors like GCAP. By focusing on the processes of public becoming, rather than taking them as given, we can recognise that for every articulation of GCAP where it is caught in the epistemic web of state power, there will be other articulations where it has created spaces of contingent emancipation.

Conclusion

As I hope I have shown throughout this chapter, GCAP is a contingent and overlapping collection of ontological *out-thereness*, which can only be partially and subjectively understood by a corresponding set of self-acknowledgingly contingent and overlapping conceptual constructs. The idea here has been to unfold, to explicate, rather than explain. Indeed, to reiterate the point, it is in explaining that we tend to fix things down, something that I have argued is unhelpful in the study of global publics.

In that spirit, then, I would argue that the initial reticence with which I held back from describing or naming GCAP should be retained in the study of actors of this kind. This chapter has argued that the problem with all the conceptual constructs that attempt to explain (rather than explicate) articulations of post-Cold War, internet-age activism is that they overlook the importance of power and space, of relationality, which in turn closes down the processes by which publics of this kind are summoned and public concerns objectified. A relational analysis of these articulations, in this case of the coalition behind some of the biggest public mobilisations ever seen, reveals their ontological multiplicity and the difficulty with which it is possible to nail down exactly what they are. Such an understanding is important methodologically and normatively. Many of us engaged in this field share a broad normative commitment to the ideals of global justice, human rights, environmentalism and peace. However, as we have seen, in an attempt to translate what we study into a larger prescriptive project for progressive social change, we run the risk of ignoring the problems that such large-scale public mobilisations inevitably entail (problems of power, problems of access, problems of legitimacy and representivity), and of silencing voices and realities that are vital if any such project is to succeed in all its divergent, heterogeneous messiness.

Notes

[1] Stand Up against Poverty is the centrepiece of GCAP's programme at the global level. Events are held around the world, organised by GCAP's national coalitions with the support of the United Nations Millennium Campaign. In 2008, 116 million stood up (www.whiteband.org/newslinks/newslink.2008-10-22.5194062447/?searchterm=stand%20up%202008?searchterm=stand%20up%202008).

[2] A sugary drink available predominantly in North America. The association being made here is the uncritical hyperactivity that Kool Aid and events such as the World Social Forum both produce.

References

Amin, S. (2006) 'The Millennium Development Goals: a critique from the South', *Monthly Review*, March 2006, available at www.monthlyreview.org/0306amin. htm.

Bello, W. (2004) *Deglobalization: Ideas for a new world economy* (2nd edn), London and New York, NY: Zed Books.

Bradford, C. (2006) *History of the MDGs: A personal reflection*, Mimeo, Washington DC: Brookings Institution.

Broad, R. and Cavanagh, J. (2008) *Development redefined: How the market met its match*, Boulder, CO: Paradigm.

Cammack, P. (2006) 'UN imperialism: unleashing entrepreneurship in the developing world', in C. Mooers (ed) *The new imperialists: Ideologies of empire*, Oxford: Oneworld Publications.

Chandler, D. (2004) 'Building global civil society "From Below"?', *Millennium: Journal of International Studies*, 33(2), pp 313-39.

Clegg, S.R. (1989) *Frameworks of power*, London, Newbury Park and New Delhi: Sage Publications.

Della Porta, D. and Tarrow, S. (2005) *Transnational protest and global activism*, Boulder, CO: Rowman and Littlefield.

Falk, R. (1999) *Predatory globalization: A critique*, Cambridge: Polity Press.

Gabay, C. (2008) 'Anarcho-cosmopolitanism: the universalization of the equal exchange', *Global Society*, 22(2), pp 197-216.

GCAP (Global Call to Action against Poverty) (2008) *Stand Up and Take Action Survey*, Durban: GCAP Learning and Evaluation Group.

Hardt, M. and Negri, A. (2004) *Multitude*, New York, NY: Penguin Press.

Hulme, D. (2007) 'The making of the Millennium Development Goals: human development meets results-based management in an imperfect world', Brooks World Poverty Institute Working Paper 16, Manchester: Brooks World Poverty Institute, University of Manchester.

James, R. and Malunga, C. (2006) 'Organisational challenges facing civil society networks in Malawi', *Knowledge Management for Development*, 2(2), pp 48-63.

Kadzamira, E.C. and Kunje, D. (2002) *The changing roles of non-governmental organisations in education in Malawi*, Zomba: Centre for Educational Research and Training, University of Malawi.

Kaldor, M. (2003) *Global civil society: An answer to war*, Cambridge: Polity Press.

Keane, J. (2001) 'Global civil society?', in H. Anheier, M. Glasius and M. Kaldor (eds) *Global civil society 2001*, Oxford: Oxford University Press, pp 23-47.

Keane, J. (2008) 'Monitory democracy?', Paper presented at Emergent Publics, Economic and Social Research Council seminar series, Milton Keynes, 13 and 14 March.

Kurasawa, F. (2007) *The work of global justice: Human rights as practices*, Cambridge: Cambridge University Press.

Latour, B. (2005) *Reassembling the social: An introduction to actor network theory*, Oxford: Oxford University Press.

Law, J. (2003) 'Making a mess with method', available at www.lancs.ac.uk/fass/sociology/papers/law-making-a-mess-with-method.pdf.

Law, J. (2007) 'Actor network theory and material semiotics', available at www.heterogeneities.net/publications/Law-ANTandMaterialSemiotics.pdf.

LSE (London School of Economics) (2004) 'Definition of civil society', available at www.lse.ac.uk/collections/CCS/introduction.htm.

Massey, D. (2005) *For space*, London, Thousand Oaks, CA and New Delhi: Sage Publications.

Melucci, A. (1996) *Challenging codes: Collective action in the information age*, Cambridge: Cambridge University Press.

Reitan, R. (2007) *Global activism*, London: Routledge.

Routledge, P., Cumbers, A. and Nativel, C. (2007) 'Grassrooting network imaginaries: relationality, power, and mutual solidarity in global justice networks', *Environment and Planning A*, 39, pp 2575-92.

Saunders, C. and Rootes, C. (2006) 'The "movement of movements" as a "network of networks": the global justice movement and the "Make Poverty History" march', Paper prepared for Capital and Social Movements, Economic and Social Research Council Social seminar series, University of Nottingham, 8 December.

Tembo, F. (2003) *Participation, negotiation and poverty: Encountering the power of images*, Aldershot: Ashgate.

Townsend, J.G. (1998) 'Are non-governmental organizations working in development a transnational community?', *Journal of International Development*, 11(4), pp 613-23.

UNDP (United Nations Development Programme) (2008) *Human Development Report 2008*, New York, NY: United Nations.

White, H. and Black, R. (2004) 'Millennium Development Goals: a drop in the ocean?', in R. Black and H. White (eds) *Targeting development: Critical perspectives on the Millennium Development Goals*, London and New York, NY: Routledge, pp 1-25.

TEN

Paradoxical publicness: becoming-imperceptible with the Brazilian lesbian, gay, bisexual and transgender movement

J. Simon Hutta

> The force of paradoxes is that they are not contradictory; they rather allow us to be present at the genesis of the contradiction. (Gilles Deleuze, 2004 [1969], p 86)

Along with several other texts in this volume (for example, Chapters Two, Eight and Nine), this chapter[1] explores the processual character of publicness. More specifically, it is concerned with the question of heterogeneity and how potentials for change can unfold through interactions of heterogeneous actors and kinds of engagement. My focus is on the dynamics of becoming that unfold underneath and within the antagonistic oppositions and contradictions making up perceivable positions of difference. Such becomings, I argue, are capable of assembling positions of difference in new ways, thereby creating ever-new paradoxical surfaces on which antagonisms, contradictions and new worldings take shape. It is, then, precisely the emergence of paradoxes and paradoxical constellations that may indicate intensely generative dynamics underpinning what Gabay (in Chapter Nine) calls 'public becoming'.

In developing this argument around paradoxical publicness, the chapter picks up discussions by writers such as Brouwer (2001), Fraser (1992, 1997), Warner (2002) and Young (1990, 2001) that have developed further, and moved beyond, Jürgen Habermas's (1989) conception of the 'bourgeois public sphere'. These authors are concerned with the possibilities of political world making, in particular that of marginalised actors. They ask how it is possible to think publics and their potential for social change beyond the limited notion of an exclusive bourgeois sphere governed by the ideal of rational deliberation alone, which renders masculinist, heteronormative and class-related domination transparent. Nancy Fraser (1997), for example, argues that Habermas fails to consider the functionality the bourgeois public sphere has had in establishing gender- and class-related hierarchies (see also Young, 1990). Furthermore, she calls attention to 'other, nonliberal, nonbourgeois, competing public spheres', suggesting a notion of 'counterpublics' (Fraser, 1997, p 74). In a similar vein, Michael Warner (2002) contends that dominant publics that gain agency in relation to the state by means of rational deliberative discourse have been contested by counterpublics that mobilise a range of disobedient, affective and queer forms of engagement.

In these discussions around publics, the question of heterogeneity has been raised in novel ways. On the one hand, differences between (dominant versus marginalised) subjectivities have been tackled and, on the other, attention has been called to enactments that go beyond rational discursive deliberation, such as 'activist' (Young, 2001) or queer, affective and dissident ones (for example, Warner, 2002). The trope of domination versus resistance has guided this debate, which is particularly pronounced in the distinction between 'dominant publics' and 'counterpublics'. While such an attention to different actors and kinds of enactment seems vital for pushing the debate beyond a narrow conception of 'the public sphere' in the singular, a binary between hegemonic publics that exercise domination and counterpublics that are resistant tends to elide, it seems to me, some of the most interesting dynamics at play in public becomings. Change, in such a scheme, ensues from struggles between political subjectivities that are antagonistically positioned as dominant versus resistant. My intention is not to deny the relevance of such struggles, but rather to make the picture more complex and to call attention to the paradoxical dynamics that enable such struggles to unfold in the first place – and that may also render them redundant. Various enactments such as rational deliberation, disruptive confrontation or affective bonding coexist in many cases and are pursued at once by the same actors; the paradoxical constellations such heterogeneous engagements and actors summon up may furthermore announce becomings that bear a potential for change running right across – and potentially un- or re-making – perceived categories of the dominant and the resistant. These paradoxical processes of becoming thus necessarily unfold within registers of what Deleuze and Guattari (2004 [1980]) call the 'imperceptible', as will be further explained later. The power of paradoxicality in such becomings is that it evocatively affirms unexpected constellations and coexistences, thus in itself eliciting new possibilities for political world making. I am using the term 'paradoxical publicness', then, to call attention to the becomings-imperceptible that unfold through the juxtaposition, interaction and re-making of heterogeneous actors and engagements.

Several authors have pointed out the significance of paradoxes in relation to publics and politics. Mahony (2008, and Chapter Two of this volume) uses a notion of 'paradoxical publics', analysing how different publics get constituted through dynamic and paradoxical relations of continuity and change. As Antke Engel (2009) shows, however, paradoxical constellations have in many other cases been conceived merely as a problem ensuing from contemporary societal transformations that needs to be warded off. Axel Honneth and the Frankfurt Institute for Social Research, for instance, call for a transposition of paradoxes into a normative politics of oppositions and contradictions (see Engel, 2009, p 125). Critiquing such an approach, Engel asks instead 'to what extent paradox holds a potential for liberating the political from identitarian and normative constrictions' (p 126).[2] With writers such as Deleuze and Guattari we can push Engel's argument a bit further and tackle the intensely generative dynamics they may announce.

In order to explore in more detail the dynamics of paradoxical publicness, I will discuss some of the publics convened and engaged by the Brazilian lesbian, gay, bisexual and transgender (LGBT) movement. I will draw on historical accounts of the movement as well as research conducted for my PhD thesis. The Brazilian LGBT movement provides an interesting example for discussing paradoxical publicness for several reasons. When it emerged in the late 1970s, the military dictatorship was still in power, and a public that would approximate the ideal of bourgeois stateness seemed even further away than in the western European and US American contexts addressed by writers like Habermas, Fraser or Warner. Easy binaries between (bourgeois) dominant publics and alternative counterpublics seem thus misplaced from the start. Instead, the enactments of LGBT activists have early on comprised attempts to both radically queer life and re-make the democratic state, thereby invoking a particular series of generative paradoxes. Today, activists' positions have partly shifted as a consequence of a number of developments, including the increasing institutionalisation of the movement according to a non-governmental organisation (NGO) model. And yet, a variety of strategies, articulations and enactments are kept dynamically present across a range of levels, from street protests and direct action to public policy conferences. In fact, the liveliness of this dynamic, again paradoxical, coexistence of diverse engagements is what has sparked my interest in, and fascination with, the Brazilian LGBT movement. The movement has as yet not disintegrated into an elite policy lobby that is disconnected from its various social bases, a process that seems to have happened in the case of other movements (for instance, the German gay movement, at least according to Stedefeldt's (1998) account – although this account could also be complicated by an attention to paradoxes). Engaging with this paradoxical liveliness in my research also made me discover new sensibilities for practical possibilities of change and political world making. The practical philosophy of 'becoming-with' elaborated by Donna Haraway (2008) has been useful for me in gaining a better understanding of what is at stake in my own implication within these affective processes of becoming. 'Becoming-with' for Haraway is about the enactment of respectful encounters with difference, it is about *autre-mondialisation*, a response-able kind of worlding or globalisation that asks researchers (among others) to approach the world, not from an apparently transparent position, but with curiosity, diffracting their finite and situated existence into the process of research and joint worlding. This chapter, then, calls attention to possibilities of 'becoming-with' the Brazilian LGBT movement, a 'becoming-imperceptible-with', if I may rejoin Haraway with Deleuze and Guattari in this way.

Heterogeneous enactments in the gay movement's 'first wave'

When the first wave of a Brazilian gay movement (*movimento homossexual brasileiro*)[3] emerged in the late 1970s, it did not merely constitute a belated echo of western post-Stonewall movements. As a number of writers have shown (MacRae, 1990; Green, 1994; Zanatta, 1996/1997; Simões and Facchini, 2005), the broader struggles against the weakening military dictatorship that ruled the country between 1964 and 1985 formed an important social and discursive backdrop to the emerging minority movements and in many ways shaped the kinds of publicness they were able to invoke. These kinds of publicness were in themselves quite heterogeneous and summoned up antagonisms that were, however, situated within paradoxical scenarios.

The relationship between the gay movement on the one hand and students', labour and other leftist anti-dictatorship movements on the other is of particular relevance for a consideration of how such heterogeneity was played out. During the gay movement's first wave between 1978 and 1980, some saw a need to articulate the struggle against the discrimination of gays with a broader vision of socialist transformation. The intention was both to broaden the movement by reaching the 'popular bases' and to integrate the struggle of gays into what was considered the more fundamental struggle of class (MacRae, 1990; Zanatta, 1996/1997). There was, then, an attempt to articulate the emergent queer public with the broader leftist public directed against the military regime and at the overturn of capitalism. Some remarkable events resulted from this impetus, such as the formation of a Gay Faction within the Trotskyist organisation, Socialist Conversion (see Green, 1994, p 47). It was probably in relation to the partial connections established between the homosexual and the labour movements that strike leader Lula da Silva (who later became Brazil's president) in 1981 at the National Convention of the Workers' Party made a plea for not pathologising or criminalising homosexuality and instead defending gay people's respect (Green, 1994; Fry and MacRae, 1991 [1983], p 32). A wider transversal counterpublic got interrupted, however, as parts of the leftist movements denied any legitimacy for discussions of homophobia and sexism, claiming a unified and strict agenda of class struggle to render such discussions – which were said to divide the working class – superfluous. The most polemical debates that harshly disrupted attempts of articulation took place in the context of the Second and Third Congress of São Paulo Women in 1980 and 1981, where feminists, and especially lesbians who called attention to specific forms of oppression, became the scapegoats in the leftist critique of minority politics (MacRae, 1990; Zanatta, 1996/1997, pp 200-2).

Simultaneous with the socialist call for unified class struggle, an opposed, autonomous, impetus became manifest both within the feminist and the gay movement, partly in response to the mentioned denial of legitimacy on the part of the left. Somos of São Paulo, Brazil's first activist gay organisation, was one of the places in which these tensions between autonomous and leftist activists got played out. In the early days of the group, the emphasis was on various forms of consciousness raising. According to João Trevisan (1986), the aim was to establish a political space 'full of tenderness' that enabled gay men to become more conscious about their own bodies and sexuality. They insisted on 'the sexual act as political act', making group sex and cruising 'legitimate components of these meetings' (Trevisan, 1986, p 137). When later on members of the Socialist Conversion (some of which had been members of Somos from the start) began pushing for transversal articulations of the gay movement in particular with the working-class movement, an opposed voice emphasising autonomous gay sociability and organisation got raised. The 'autonomists' feared that the movement was being co-opted by socialist parties and deprived of its critical force, getting subjugated to the socialists' wish to extend their constituencies. This aggravating dispute led up to an open clash at the First National Meeting of Gays in São Paulo in April of 1980. At this meeting, leftist activists from the Socialist Conversion and autonomists fell out in particular over the question of whether the movement should participate in the upcoming May Day March in solidarity of striking workers. This clash anticipated the split of Somos in May, which occurred after a group of activists had participated in the march while others had opted for a picnic in a park celebrating their 'right to laziness and disobedience' (Trevisan, 1986, p 147). Autonomous gay men left Somos and formed their own group, as did lesbians on this occasion (although for different reasons relating to their wish to address their specific demands). Interestingly, this dispute got carried into historiographies of the movement. Two of the most prominent writers, James Green (1994) and João Trevisan (1986), identify with the opposed leftist (Green) and autonomous (Trevisan) wings of Somos and accordingly narrate the events quite differently. A further, and very detailed, account of Somos and the movement's first wave is provided by anthropologist Edward MacRae (1990).

What comes to light in an engagement with the early gay movement is the uneasy coexistence of differently positioned kinds of engagement and articulation – protest, dissidence and party political organisation as well as 'leftist' versus 'autonomous' orientations. (I will clarify my use of the terms 'engagement' and 'articulation' in the next section.) Further tensions ensued from the ambivalent positioning of lesbians as well as blacks within the gay, feminist and black movements. In Somos, for example, lesbians early on lamented forms of male domination and saw the lack of a space for engaging with the specificities of their oppression (Trevisan, 1986, p 140; MacRae, 1990, pp 245-55; regarding the positioning of blacks, see MacRae, 1990, pp 271-3). The positioning of *travestis*[4] was also precarious. While *travesti* show or carnival stars early on became emblematic figures of the movement, it was only around 1980/81 when *travesti* sex work rapidly developed that their specific demands and problems became a prominent topic for the movement, as Carsten Balzer (2007, pp 323-5) shows with reference to the early activist journal *Lampião da Esquina*. The First Brazilian Meeting of Gays (*I Encontro Brasileiro de Homossexuais*) in 1980 included the item '*travestis* and oppression' in its agenda (Zanatta, 1996/1997, p 203), although only few *travestis* participated (see Balzer, 2007, pp 325-6).

The different enactments of the movement entered in many cases into conflict and confrontation with one another. At other moments, however, heterogeneous engagements and articulations coexisted paradoxically and productively. So while in the spring of 1980 serious cracks opened within the Brazilian gay movement around the questions of autonomy versus transversality as well as male domination, in June of the same year forces were joined in an historical march to protest against police violence towards *travestis*, sex workers, lesbians, gays and other marginalised groups in the São Paulo's city centre (Trevisan, 1986, p 149; MacRae, 1990, pp 222-8; Green, 1994, p 49). This protest was also the last public manifestation of the movement's common voice before the first wave abated and its groups fragmented. It seems that the positive effect it is reported to have had regarding the denounced police activities (at least in the short term) was directly related to the somewhat unexpected coexistence of different engagements, articulations and positions. MacRae (1990) thus notes: 'Paradoxically, it was during its biggest crisis that Somos, or better its fragments, succeeded in bringing about the best proof of its presence and acting' (p 222). Paradoxes such as this one may in turn give an indication of intensive dynamics running across heterogeneous engagements and underneath contradictions and confrontations, thus calling for an extension of the analysis beyond such antagonisms. Let me pursue this line of argument and its implications for the study of publics further.

Challenging binary frameworks

Paradoxical publics emerge when heterogeneous engagements and articulations dynamically coexist. What are such 'engagements' and 'articulations', then, and what makes them different? I understand 'engagement', as well as 'enactment' as a 'way of doing', also comprising orientations, desires and imaginings. 'Articulation' refers to the expressive aspects of such engagements or enactments, the particular voicings taking place. These notions of 'engagement', 'enactment' and 'articulation' may complicate an easy conflation of intentions and effects, which sometimes happens when particular aesthetic forms and political enactments are identified with domination or subversion per se. Concepts like 'tactics' and 'strategies' sometimes sustain such a conflation, since they emphasise instrumental relations of actions chosen for particular ends. Notions like 'engagement' and 'articulation' may shift the focus to the immanence of such actions rather than their instrumental relations, taking manifold and paradoxical effects into account as much as what might make up the intended 'strategy'.

A recurrent distinction regarding kinds of public engagement and articulation has been between, on the one hand, rational-deliberative ones that are based on the state and, on the other, ones that maintain a critical distance from the sphere of rational discourse by staging dissident acts, developing affective relations, and creating alternative spaces and media of engagement (see, for example, Young,

1990, 2001; Fraser, 1992, 1997; Warner, 2002). Fraser and Warner put particular emphasis on struggles and contestations between a dominant bourgeois public and alternative counterpublics. For Warner, counterpublics are characterised by an awareness of their subordinate status and mobilise 'poetic-expressive' means against dominant discourse (Warner, 2002, p 86). In so doing, they 'fashion their own subjectivities' (p 87), expanding their own world and publicness into the spaces of the dominant public, where this counterpublicness encounters resistance. Warner's paradigmatic example is queer cultures (he talks in particular about an 18th-century women's group called She-Romps), where 'embodied sociability, affect, and play have a more defining role than they do in the opinion-transposing frame of rational-critical dialogue' (Warner, 2002, p 88).

In their effort to challenge the ideal of the bourgeois public, these writers make two analytic moves. On the one hand, they distinguish between differential kinds of enactment, asking how public becomings happen not only on the basis of rational deliberation, but also through alternative, more embodied, processes. On the other hand, they relate these kinds of enactment to different types of actors (in the case of Young's 2001 distinction between the 'deliberative democrat' and the 'activist') and to positions of dominance versus resistance that enter into struggles with one another (in the case of Fraser, 1992, 1997; Warner, 2002; and Young, 1990). While the challenge to the ideal of the bourgeois public ensuing from such an analytic framework seems vital – and perhaps particularly so with respect to the North Atlantic context – there is a danger of reifying the opposition of 'dominant publics' versus 'counterpublics' and limiting the understanding of how public becoming and change come about. With the focus on counterpublics challenging dominant publics – Fraser (1997, p 85) calls this 'interpublic contestation' – the analysis starts out from distinctive publics that are separated from one another and fixed in relation to political subjectivities. Such an approach needs to elide complexities ensuing from the coexistence of heterogeneous engagements, articulations and actors within a public. Iris Marion Young (1990) moves towards a more complex understanding when she argues for a need of a 'heterogeneous public' (pp 116-21), within which challenges and contestations take place. However, Young does not account for the actual intersections and effects summoned up by such coexistence of heterogeneity, tending instead towards a mere affirmation of difference or, as Fraser (1997, p 190) puts it, a 'wholesale endorsement of the politics of difference'. These approaches, it thus seems, begin and end the analysis of public becoming with the identification, and simultaneous fixation, of distinctive subjectivities and engagements. Daniel Brouwer's (2001) notion of 'oscillation' provides a further example. While his elaboration on how actors oscillate between different strategies goes some way towards complexifying binaries between publics and counterpublics, it still keeps different strategies apart rather than taking into account the effects of intersection or layering.

When heterogeneous enactments are kept apart they also get easily identified with the dominant or the resistant per se, as Anna Schober (2009) points out. Schober critiques Warner (2002) for straightforwardly attributing 'subversive' effects to the articulations and engagements of queer and transgender groups, arguing that – contrary to what Warner seems to assume – political relevance and affirmative or subversive effects of articulations can only ever be decided in relation to the particular context in which they unfold (see Schober, 2009, p 256). If we open the analysis towards the coexistence of heterogeneity within publics as well as the complex effects ensuing from differential engagements and articulations, we may begin to apprehend intense dynamics subsisting within publics that inspire change, precisely because they go beyond binaries of the dominant versus resistant.

Let us return to the example of the Brazilian gay movement, then. Trevisan's description of the early Somos with its disobedient and affective forms of engagement resonates with Warner's characterisation of counterpublics. Furthermore, Trevisan's denunciation of more institutionalised forms has similarities with critiques of the ideal sphere of (supposedly) rational deliberation, which Warner labels 'dominant publics'. According to Trevisan (1986), Somos' autonomous wing was opposed to 'hysterical and sterile political discussions' and 'parliamentary-style representation and all forms of leadership' (p 137). However, a part of this would-be 'dominant' public in relation to which the discourse of resistance and disobedience was formulated staged itself as a revolutionary movement directed at the overthrow of the dictatorship government, thus maintaining a thorough, if differently positioned, counterpublic discourse. To be sure, the dogmatisms and rigidities within the leftist movements betrayed some of their own revolutionary aspirations. Nonetheless, the more institutionalising approaches enacted there forcefully pushed towards profound change, opening up new spaces of articulation – not least for queers, as Green's (1994) much more sympathetic account of the leftist wing of Somos shows. Meanwhile, the 'counterpublicness' of Somos' autonomous wing was undermined by the exercise of male domination, which provoked new resistances from within and made lesbians eventually split off from the group. The easy opposition Trevisan discursively stages between sex-radical disobedience on the one hand and 'hysterical and sterile political discussions' thus gets complicated when a closer look at the political conjuncture is taken. The anthropologist MacRae's (1990) account of consciousness-raising practices suggests that what happened during the early meetings of Somos was not as genuinely subversive as Trevisan would have it, namely the construction and consolidation of the identity of the gay activist. Such meetings, while opening up new political possibilities, also instituted new sexual and gendered norms.

If we were to start from an analytical framework focusing on struggles between dominant publics and counterpublics, the question is then raised about what would run 'counter' to what. I want to suggest, therefore, a shift of focus away from such binaries towards the conditions of emergence of change. Rather than locating a potential for change in blatantly 'resistant' enactments per se that are attributed to given political subjectivities, I suggest taking into account the paradoxes that ensue from the dynamic coexistence of heterogeneous positions and engagements.

Paradoxical becomings

In 1982, when strike leader Lula da Silva and the PT (Workers' Party) had just started an extensive electoral campaign, French activist intellectual Félix Guattari made a trip across Brazil. Having been invited by the Brazilian cultural critic and fellow psychoanalyst Suely Rolnik, Guattari, instead of giving a series of academic lectures, held discussions with social movement activists, political parties, intellectuals – and even with Lula. The collage of texts *Micropolítica: Cartografias do desejo*, which was translated into English under the title *Molecular revolution in Brazil* (Guattari and Rolnik, 2008), ensued from Guattari's travel (see also Nunes et al, 2009, who map out some of the book's key issues in relation to possibilities for contemporary world making). What inspired Guattari to make this trip was his excitement about the vibrant potential he sensed for social change, a potential that ranged from the transformation of bodily and intersubjective relations to the socio-political system (cf. Genosko, 2003). Guattari's understanding of this 'molecular revolution', as he calls it, troubles binary distinctions between publics and counterpublics: '[W]e have to stop thinking about the relation between autonomy and large-scale social struggles in terms of a dualist logic,' says Guattari on his way back to Europe in conversation with Rolnik (Guattari and Rolnik, 2008, p 428). The PT had a special appeal for Guattari, since, as Rolnik summarises, he saw it as:

> ... a vibrating surface of the paradox between the readiness to organize in terms of parties, to struggle under macropolitical banners like 'overthrowing the dictatorship', and, on the other hand, the willingness to allow oneself to be captured by a sensibility for the molecular, by a sensibility for destabilization and the creation of forms of sociability, subjectivity, etc, just as, yet differently essential. (Guattari and Rolnik, 2008, p 457)

With his notion of the 'molecular', Guattari addresses processes that cannot easily be apprehended in terms of political programmes or militant strategies, but that are nonetheless capable of deterritorialising the whole of the social organisation (see also Guattari and Rolnik, 2008, pp 61-9, 179-96). The desire for new affective forms of subjectivity and sociability constitutes a molecular vector for change, as it were, which runs right across apparently opposed formations of the macro and the micro, or of publics and counterpublics. In Deleuze and Guattari's (2004 [1980]) now famous conception, such molecular vectors emerge from a series of 'becomings', in which one is carried away by intensities of something beyond one's formed, 'molar', make-up – becoming-woman, becoming-child, becoming-animal, becoming-imperceptible. *Molecular revolution in Brazil* is replete with discussions of possibilities of such becomings in early 1980s Brazil – a series of vectors that could conjoin in a process of new subjective and political world making. Becoming-imperceptible plays a key role regarding all other becomings, since all becomings entail an undoing of the markers of difference that fix perceived forms and identities. Such a fixing is at work, for instance, in debates that identify particular kinds of engagement with the 'dominant' or the 'subversive' per se. Becoming-imperceptible means reconnecting with the world on levels below our common thresholds of perception, letting us be affected by intensities that run underneath and often right across identitarian markers of difference. This entails the development and opening up to new sensibilities in the way Rolnik describes and by which Guattari himself became affected. Becoming-imperceptible is thus a process where different becomings can conjoin. It is the condition of possibility for new worldings to happen, or, as Deleuze and Guattari (2004 [1980]) put it, 'the immanent end of becoming, its cosmic formula' (p 308; see also Papadopoulos and colleagues' 2008 discussion of 'imperceptible politics'). With Haraway, we can further specify that such worlding is necessarily a 'becoming-with', a collective and respectful process, or else it stages yet another 'sublime' regime of identities (which Haraway, 2008, pp 27-35, senses in some of Deleuze and Guattari's own work).

While the molecular vector for change that Guattari senses in Brazil springs from a desire for new affective forms of subjectivity and sociability, for a new worlding or becoming-imperceptible where different becomings conjoin, the 'molar' level of state politics targeted by the PT creates novel possibilities for this vector to unfold. This crossing of the molecular and the molar, of affective and institutionalising processes, evokes the effect of paradoxicality addressed by Rolnik. In the process of joint worlding, established differences are undone and conjoined in novel, unexpected ways. This paradoxical scenario stages a 'vibrating surface', as Rolnik puts it, on which social change becomes possible. What paradoxicality announces here is thus neither a contradiction striving towards resolution nor a dead end implying atrophy. While the notion of 'contradiction', as Engel (2009, p 118) points out, suggests oppositions that 'cannot exist simultaneously, but occupy clearly separate positionings', demanding either-or decisions, paradoxes announce divergent or incompatible elements that 'nonetheless stay unavoidably linked with one another'. Becoming-imperceptible is thus paradoxical but without contradictions (see also Deleuze and Guattari, 2004 [1980], p 294). In making productive use of the tensions between the divergent elements they keep together, paradoxes may effectuate the lively spilling over and cross-fertilisation of heterogeneous intentions, desires and articulations on different – 'molar' and 'molecular', 'micro' and 'macro' – levels. Contradictions and antagonisms, say between dominant publics and counterpublics, can only take shape as a dynamic of fixing molecular becomings into molar, mutually exclusive, identities of either-or. Elaborating on this relation between paradoxes and contradictions Deleuze (2004 [1980]) thus notes that paradoxes are not contradictory, but instead 'allow us to be present at the genesis of the contradiction' (p 86). The point here is not to claim paradoxes as good or contradictions as bad, but rather to extend the analysis beyond a focus on antagonistic struggles, even if these may also be important.

It is also possible, then, that apparently conflicting tendencies in the early gay movement, such as those between the 'autonomists' and the 'leftists', on another, imperceptible, level conspired to create possibilities for novel kinds of worlding – new affective relations and forms of institutionalisation, new kinds of publicness, new inter/subjectivities. A fuller discussion of this question would, however, entail an examination of the concrete interactions and affective processes that unfolded within the publics invoked and engaged by the movement. While previous historiographies have often started from an account of opposed positions, it would need to be explored to what extent it was precisely the paradoxical constellations ensuing from the simultaneity of heterogeneous articulations and engagements that enabled new worldings. While the sex-radical enactments in the early meetings of Somos had the capacity of fostering new pleasures and intimate relations, the leftist discourse enabled – to an extent – transversal alliances between class- and sex-related struggles against the dictatorship. Lesbians brought up alternative visions to practices of male domination and stirred up discussions around specific oppressions. Both leftists and autonomists may thus have conjoined to a greater extent in embodied becomings – becoming-gay, becoming-democracy, becoming-imperceptible – than some of their discourses staging identitarian positions ('the gay militant' versus 'the proletariat', for instance) would admit. Likewise, *travestis* and lesbians may have played a greater role in instigating vectors for such becomings than more masculinist representations of the 'gay movement' would have it. Furthermore, it needs to be remembered that the movement's first wave coincided with the formation of the Unified Black Movement (*Movimento Negro Unificado*) as well as the blossoming of the feminist movement, all of which were in turn linked to other movements around the globe (see MacRae, 1990 for a discussion of the gay movement's links with the feminist and black movements). Guattari's notion of a 'molecular revolution' points to the manifold intersections of these diverse struggles and articulations, which seem difficult to address within the notion of a subversive counterpublic expanding its world.

The possibilities for change of the publics invoked by the gay movement, then, were premised on a number of imperceptible dynamics that provoked a vibrating surface of paradoxical constellations. It was only on the dynamic surface of such paradoxes, it seems, that a common voice emerged and, under the identitarian banner of 'the gay movement', was able to articulate and denounce an experience of stigmatisation, violence and oppression. While it is not possible here to explore in any detail the concrete affective and paradoxical dynamics at stake, the aforementioned protest against police violence in São Paulo, which resulted from a campaign initiated by a police officer called José Richetti, provides an evocative example of this common voice of the marginalised. While before the event there had been disagreements over where to hold it, lesbians, *travestis* and gay men, marching banner holders and ludic protest dancers ended up moving through the city centre together up to the steps of the Municipal Theatre, bringing forth a counterpublic articulation that was striking precisely because of its inherent paradoxicality. Some of the watchwords that resounded were '*Amor, paixão, abaixo o camburão*' ('Love, passion, down with the police van'), which is a variation of the anti-dictatorship slogan, '*Arroz, feijão, abaixo a repressão*'

('Rice, beans, down with repression'); *'Richetti é louca, ela dorme de touca'* ('Richetti is crazy, she sleeps with a bonnet'); *'O gay unido jamais será vencido'* ('United gays will never be defeated'), which plays on the workers' slogan *'O povo unido jamais será vencido'*; and *'Au, au, au, nós queremos muito pau'* ('Ick, ick, ick, we want a lot of dick') (MacRae, 1990, p 227).

The question of becoming–imperceptible then, turns the analysis of publics and counterpublics upside down and, instead of starting from struggles between antagonistic actors, asks about the conditions of emergence of such antagonisms as well as the dynamics that elude them. This means, however, that the analysis cannot start (and neither end) with given forms and identities. Instead, it needs to be attentive to paradoxes that indicate moments and spaces where heterogeneous engagements and articulations enter into indeterminate constellations and create novel potentials for worlding.

Advocates, dissidents, protagonists ... and more paradoxes

The 1980s saw not only a waning of the recently emerged gay movement in quantitative terms, but also a transformation of the modes of organising, articulation and publicness. Regina Facchini (2005) outlines how activism got reconfigured according to an NGO model of organisation, which gained momentum with the establishment of the democratic system and HIV/AIDS activism during the 1980s and 1990s. Activists thus got increasingly positioned as advocates of rights and social recognition within the emerging publics of civil society. Today, such a new positioning is very pronounced. Toni Reis, at the time of my interview the president of the Brazilian LGBT Association (ABGLT), summarises:

> "[T]oday, we have the concept of 'advocacy' [English word used in the original], the concept that we have to propose public policies, that we have to monitor, participate, criticise ... right. So the concept of the movement changed. We don't work with the politics of confrontation. This is not our practice, and we have realised that we have constantly increased the number of partners." (Interview, 11 December 2007)

Following this new 'concept of the movement' – an advocacy model of public engagement – intervention tended to take place from within the established polity. Today's enactments, then, invoke a different kind of publicness than, say, the protest against police violence of 1981, which manifests in a change of political slogans. As Facchini (2005, p 58) evocatively summarises: 'Watchwords like "*o sexo anal derruba o capital*" ["anal sex knocks down capital"] gave way, in the everyday of activism, to slogans like "*é legal ser homosexual*" ["it's legal/nice to be gay"]'. Activists are increasingly positioned as political advocates rather than protesters and campaigners from the margins.

The paradigm of advocacy aims, instead of disrupting the established system, to promote social and civil rights and the formal representation within the state and its fields, such as health, education, safety and the economy. And yet, the new forms of public engagement are not without their paradoxes. Something of the radical and dissident forms of intervention and worlding enacted by groups like the early Somos runs alongside, and within, the deliberative and diplomatic engagements. Likewise, calls for transversal alliances have not fully waned, and struggles of lesbians, blacks and *travestis* – and more recently transsexuals – within the movement go on. In the remainder of this chapter, I want to consider how institutionalising practice and molecular 'vectors for change' intersect in a new paradoxical scenario of collective agency. This discussion also troubles accounts of both 'new social movements' and NGOs that diagnose an absorption of activism into the vortex of neoliberalism, of its full subscription to late capitalist social relations.

An interesting site for discussing the new situation of queer activism in Brazil is provided by service centres for victims of homophobic violence that have been set up across the country since 1999. These centres, most commonly called *centros de referência* ('reference centres'), register and report cases of homophobic violence in order to enable better crime prevention and offer legal, social and psychological support for victims, also in collaboration with LGBT NGOs. The politics of safety, which are proactively engaged here and are currently playing a prominent role in Brazilian LGBT activism, are discussed in detail in my doctoral thesis and cannot be addressed here. Instead, I want to concentrate on how heterogeneous engagements and articulations intersect in the work of activists in the centres.

While governments in many cities and states have formally supported the establishment of reference centres, funding has frequently been sparse and inconsistent. Thus, LGBT activists and organisations have often carried out the registration of data and provision of services on a voluntary or semi-voluntary basis, becoming responsibilised in new ways and partially professionalised. In producing statistical knowledge and collaborating with state institutions from the social welfare office and local governments to the police, they have acquired a new position within, or on the margins of, the governmental system. Several authors have problematised such tendencies of professionalisation and responsibilisation (for example, Kamat, 2004; Grundy and Smith, 2007). However, if such processes get framed in terms of a straightforward neoliberalisation and depoliticisation, new political possibilities as well as more complex intersections of, say, managerial and dissident or consciousness-raising engagements get elided. Such a more paradoxical scenario is what seems to get played out in contemporary Brazilian LGBT activism.[5]

My interviews indicate that the governmental positioning of activists does not necessarily lead them to eliminate a critical distance with respect to the state. One of my interviewees, whom I call Marcos and who works in a reference centre in Porto Alegre, says: "So sometimes activism turns into a bureaucratic activism. And people accomplish projects and so on … sure, it's important, but there is little time for them to be on the street. And the role of a social movement is to be on the street." This statement indeed indicates the problematic tendencies of a bureaucratisation of activism. Yet, at the same time, Marcos' statement indicates that a self-understanding of activism as grassroots mobilisation, a desire to act, organise and socialise in alternative ways, persists in the more institutionalised setting. In a similar vein, Yone, the coordinator of a reference centre in Rio de Janeiro, talks about activism in terms of '*ir à luta*' or 'going to [the] struggle'. A sense of misfit with respect to governmental practice and even of danger of co-option gets repeatedly expressed in the interview. These statements seem paradoxical, given that they are voiced by those working within these (apparently) managerialised settings. However, this paradoxical coexistence of managerial and dissident articulations and engagement opens up possibilities for a queered practice.

In the following passage, Yone points out the importance of reference centres being run by LGBT activists, who according to her have other capacities than state officials to create a simultaneously open and intimate atmosphere:

> "And the government doesn't have this sensitivity. You can see that a man in T-shirt, Bermudas, and thongs, women in thongs, cannot enter a government building. When it's even a *travesti* ... well, they pick up on it – it's cruel because they start mocking.... People from favelas – guys go in Bermudas because it is their normal clothing – Bermudas, thongs and T-shirt. They won't take it off just because they are going to be attended. That's the social action of the government." (Interview, 10 May 2007)

Yone critiques the class-related and heteronormative ('transphobic') codes and regulations of state institutions, showing solidarity with people from favelas or *travestis* and raising the stigmatisation of their bodies and clothes as a political issue. In a similar vein, Cris, a lesbian activist, lawyer and colleague of Yone's, notes that people who come to the reference centre are aware they "are not talking to a team that doesn't understand the language".

The attendance of victims gets staged here as an embodied practice that locates the ones who attend and the attendees within a comfortable space where different bodies are welcomed and a common language exists. A further passage following on from Yone's above statement brings out the importance of this embodied, queer, practice. Cris points out the meaning that performing one's body can have, giving the example of a *travesti* who has modified her body:

> Cris: "So – sure, 'Wanna take your clothes off and show your breasts? Take off your clothes, show your breasts!... You want to show me your ass? To show me the nice silicone that you had just put in? Show me!'"
>
> Yone: "'Show me, you're at home. You have the right to".'

Cris: "We work a lot like this. Right? We try to – make the person feel really comfortable [*à vontade*]." (Interview, 10 May 2007)

Plastic surgery and other body-modifying technologies – and also showing their bodies in particular cases – form part of *travesti* 'body politics'.[6] The frequent stigmatisation of *travestis* in state institutions has been pointed out in Yone's statement quoted earlier. Here, both women enact a different attitude, aiming to create a comfortable atmosphere that affectively relates them to their attendees. Simultaneously, they enable people to stage such gender-queer performances in a semi-public, partly state-funded environment, reinventing the institutional space itself.

Interestingly, Brazilian LGBT activists themselves often appropriate or invade institutional spaces in dissident or gender-queer ways, pushing the boundaries of dress codes for governmental events or infiltrating formal discourse with queer slang and camp style. What in the ABGLT president's depiction of the shift towards advocacy politics might appear to be the wholesale assimilation of activism into the rationalist-deliberative discourse of the 'dominant public' in many cases turns out to be a paradoxical folding of heterogeneous enactments. Diplomatic advocacy and managerial NGO work are layered with street activism, dissidence and social bonding, as indicated in Cris's, Marcos' or Yone's narratives. It is the very paradoxical nature of such constellations that may allow vectors for change to conjoin in new becomings underneath identitarian categories. Such becomings may also lead to the formation of new discursive positions, an example of which is the increasing public staging of LGBT activists, not as managerial advocates, but as new protagonists in the democratisation of Brazil. Slogans such as 'We are making history!' have echoed throughout a range of political events I attended in my research. Far from disappearing as political subjects in the meshes of neoliberalism, then, LGBT activists are re-enacting a scenario of collective agency from the middle of a new, and again vibrating, paradoxical surface.

Conclusion

This chapter has discussed two series of paradoxes or two kinds of paradoxical publicness that have become apparent at different moments in the trajectory of the Brazilian LGBT movement. While the first one is related to the uneasy coexistence of 'autonomous' and 'leftist' engagements (which together made the most prominent public appearance when the movement seemed most in crisis), the second one concerns the simultaneity of neoliberal reform and social movement activism. In both cases, vectors for change have emerged from the middle of these paradoxical constellations, pushing for the reassembling of established differences. The ways in which such generative paradoxes are taken forward – along with the new contradictions they evoke – are always contingent.

In 2002, 20 years after Guattari made the trip to Brazil mentioned earlier, Lula won the national elections. His PT has now sedimented within the political mainstream, and yet, some of the molecular forces Guattari sensed in the early 1980s got transposed into the present. In June 2007, Lula opened Brazil's First National LGBT Conference in Brasília. What I expected to be a boring celebration of political correctness turns out to be a collective, flamboyant outpouring of hope, excitement, pleasure and rage that queers the formal space of political representation. LGBT activists from all over the country chant on the chairs as Lula enters, some carry a banner with pictures of murdered and mutilated *travestis* in front of the panel, and Fernanda Benvenutty, president of the Brazilian Articulation of Transgenders (ANTRA), decorates Lula with a rainbow cap. While many within his own party, especially evangelical conservatives, vehemently reject a serious engagement with anything to do with homosexuality or transgender, Lula celebrates his own insertion into this queer scenario. In the speeches from the panel, voices of professional politics intermingle with forms of claim-making that mobilise queer slang, black, trans and camp bodies. To be sure, Lula's recent embrace of LGBT politics stands in tension with critiques that denounce his government for limiting support to the symbolic level. It is also true that 'the rules of the game' now established do not stimulate the same hopes of fundamental change pervading the early 1980s. However, prejudging the outcomes of an actually highly dynamic conjuncture would be self-defeating.

Guattari's enactments can teach us an attentiveness to the becomings running through paradoxical publics and the world we engage with as a whole: 'That's molecular revolution,' he states, 'it isn't a slogan or a program, it's something that I feel, that I live, in meetings, in institutions, in affects, and also through reflections' (Guattari and Rolnik, 2008, p 457). Guattari indicates here that the intense dynamics unfolding through registers of the imperceptible simultaneously generate becomings that cannot *but* be perceived. 'There is no contradiction in this,' explain Deleuze and Guattari (2004 [1980], p 310), '... not only are becomings–woman, becomings–animal, becomings–molecular, becomings–imperceptible conjugated, but the imperceptible itself becomes necessarily perceived at the same time as perception becomes necessarily molecular' (p 311). Through our own becomings–imperceptible, the becomings–molecular of our perception, we can engage with the world in novel ways. My experiences at the LGBT conference in Brasília and elsewhere have changed my sensibility towards affective articulations of hope, rage and pleasure that subsist within the current political conjuncture. In becoming bodily and affectively implicated in my sites of study, new response-abilities, new possibilities of becoming-with the various others I am entangled with in my research arise. Such possibilities of becoming-with are not restricted to ethnographic work in 'the field'. Through listening again to interview recordings, daydreaming about events and chatting with friends and colleagues, my own paradoxical entanglements make themselves forcefully perceptible and indicate new ways of becoming-public/democracy/activist/.../imperceptible-with.

Notes

[1] My special thanks go to the Brazilian activists who inspired me to write this chapter. I also wish to thank Davina Cooper, the other authors of this volume, and the editors for their comments on earlier versions.

[2] Translations of the German and Portuguese works cited, as well as of the interview passages, are mine.

[3] While during the movements' first wave some people identified as 'gays', '*lésbicas*' or '*homossexuais*', others rejected these words, attempting instead to subversively appropriate local terms like '*bicha*' (meaning something like 'fag') or insisting on a localised '*guei*' instead of the Anglo-American 'gay'. My use of the terms 'gay' and 'lesbian' in this chapter needs to be read with these dynamics of identification, disidentification and subversive appropriation in mind. From the early 1990s onwards, the generic term '*homossexuais*' used in '*movimento homossexual brasileiro*' gets progressively substituted by acronyms, most recently, '*movimento LGBT – movimento de lésbicas, gays, bissexuais, travestis e transexuais*' (see Facchini, 2005).

[4] '*Travesti*' is a term used in Latin America and other regions for 'male-to-female' trans people who enact performative practices and body-modifying technologies, such as cross-dressing and plastic surgery, without attempting a full assumption of the female sex and gender. In Brazil, they have often been subsumed under the generic category of '*homossexuais*'.

[5] For a discussion in a western European context of how paradoxical demands summoned by neoliberalism can be creatively rearticulated in queer practices, see Engel (2009, ch 3). For a discussion of the complex relations between LGBT activism and state politics in the UK context (on the municipal level), see Cooper (1994, 2006).

[6] Especially when *travestis* do sex work, the shape of their body gains a critical, economically valued, importance. As Balzer (2007) shows, however, there is a great variety in the professions, body performances and experiences of *travestis*.

References

Balzer, C. (2007) *Gender-outlaw-triptychon: Eine ethnologische Studie zu Selbstbildern und Formen der Selbstorganisation in den Transgender-Subkulturen Rio de Janeiros, New Yorks und Berlins*, Berlin: Fachbereich Politik- und Sozialwissenschaften, Free University Berlin, available at www.diss.fu-berlin.de.

Brouwer, D.C. (2001) 'ACT-ing up in congressional hearings', in R. Asen and D.C. Brouwer (eds), *Counterpublics and the state*, Albany, NY: SUNY.

Cooper, D. (1994) *Sexing the city: Lesbian and gay politics within the activist state*, London: Rivers Oram Press.

Cooper, D. (2006) 'Active citizenship and the governmentality of local lesbian and gay politics', *Political Geography*, 25, pp 921-43.

Deleuze, G. (2004 [1969]) *The logic of sense*, London: Athlone.

Deleuze, G. and Guattari, F. (2004 [1980]) *A thousand plateaus: Capitalism and schizophrenia*, London: Athlone.

Engel, A. (2009) *Bilder von Sexualität und Ökonomie: Queere kulturelle Politiken im Neoliberalismus*, Bielefeld: Transcript.

Facchini, R. (2005) *Sopa de letrinhas? Movimento homossexual e produção de identidades coletivas nos anos 90*, Rio de Janeiro: Garamond.

Fraser, N. (1992) 'Rethinking the public sphere: a contribution to the critique of actually existing democracy', in C.J. Calhoun (ed) *Habermas and the public sphere*, Cambridge, MA: MIT Press, pp 109-42.

Fraser, N. (1997) *Justice interruptus: Critical reflections on the 'postsocialist' condition*, New York, NY: Routledge.

Fry, P. and MacRae, E. (1983/1991) *O que é homossexualidade*, São Paulo: Brasiliense.

Genosko, G. (2003) *The party without bosses: Lessons on anti-capitalism from Félix Guattari and Luis Inácio 'Lula' da Silva*, Winnipeg: Arbeiter Ring.

Green, J.N. (1994) 'The emergence of the Brazilian gay liberation movement, 1977-1981', *Latin American Perspectives*, 80(21), pp 38-55.

Grundy, J. and Smith, M. (2007) 'Activist knowledges in queer politics', *Economy and Society*, 36(2), pp 294-317.

Guattari, F. and Rolnik, S. (2008) *Molecular revolution in Brazil*, Los Angeles, CA: Semiotext(e).

Habermas, J. (1989) *The structural transformation of the public sphere: An inquiry into a category of bourgeois society*, Cambridge, MA: MIT Press.

Haraway, D.J. (2008) *When species meet*, Minneapolis, MN: University of Minnesota Press.

Kamat, S. (2004) 'The privatization of public interest: theorizing NGO discourse in a neoliberal era', *Review of International Political Economy*, 11(1), pp 155-76.

MacRae, E. (1990) *A construção da igualdade: Identidade sexual e política no Brasil da abertura*, Campinas: Unicamp.

Mahony, N. (2008) 'Spectacular political experiments: the constitution, mediation and performance of large-scale public participation exercises', Unpublished doctoral thesis, Department of Social Policy and Criminology, Open University.

Nunes, R. and Trott, B. with F. Guattari (2009) '"There is no scope for futurology; history will decide": Félix Guattari on molecular revolution', *Turbulence*, 4, pp 38-47, available at http://turbulence.org.uk/turbulence-4/there-is-no-scope-for-futurology.

Papadopoulos, D., Stephenson, N. and Tsianos, V. (2008) *Escape routes: Control and subversion in the twenty-first century*, London: Pluto.

Schober, A. (2009) *Ironie, Montage, Verfremdung: Ästhetische Taktiten und die politische Gestalt der Demokratie*, Paderborn: Fink.

Simões, J.A. and Facchini, R. (2009) *Na Trilha do Arco-Íris: Do Movimento Homossexual ao LGBT*, São Paulo: Editora Fundação Perseu Abramo.

Stedefeldt, E. (1998) *Schwule Macht, oder die Emanzipation von der Emanzipation*, Berlin: Elefanten Press.

Trevisan, J.S. (1986) *Perverts in paradise*, London: Gay Men's Press.

Warner, M. (2002) 'Publics and counterpublics'. *Public Culture*, 14(1), pp 49-90.

Young, I.M. (1990) *Justice and the politics of difference*, Princeton, NJ: Princeton University Press.

Young, I.M. (2001) 'Activist challenges to deliberative democracy', *Political Theory*, 29(5), pp 670-90.

Zanatta, E.M. (1996/1997) 'Documento e identidade: o movimento homossexual no Brasil na década de 80', *Cadernos AEL*, 5/6, pp 193-220.

ELEVEN

Conclusion: emergent publics

Nick Mahony, Janet Newman and Clive Barnett

The chapters in this collection demonstrate the multiplicity of ways in which the project of 'rethinking' the public is proceeding. It is not our purpose here to summarise them, but to highlight key issues this volume presents for future analysis of the processes of public formation. We do so by returning to the four themes set out in the introduction.

First, we reiterate the paradoxes inherent in contemporary slippages between notions of the public, personal and political. Such slippages slide into the narratives of both decline and proliferation, with the 'personal' offering new voicings and practices of publicness, while also opening up the personal to governmental interest and intervention. In the first section below, 'Personalising publics', we assess how the contributions to this volume engage with these processes, challenging simple narratives of change by tracing ways in which these paradoxes are experienced, played out and negotiated in different sites. Such paradoxes, several chapters suggest, open up as well as close down the possibilities of agency and it is through such agency that the meaning of politics itself may be rewritten.

Second, the volume offers a contribution to contemporary debates about how publics are given voice, represented and spoken for; the deliberative ideals on which notions of a rational public sphere are based are reconfigured by proliferation of new voices, registers and modes of political engagement arising from emergent publics. Understanding these changes in modes of public address is important in grappling with the seeming paradox that representations of publics are proliferating at the same time as forms of public engagement seem to be more and more individualised and personalised. The contributors trace ways in which such claims-making processes interact with, rather than displace, formal politics and representative practices. But we also challenge dominant approaches to understanding representation, tracing ways in which embodied practices of representation combine both expressive claims of authenticity with authoritative claims of agency, delegation and trusteeship. We discuss this further in the second section below, 'Representing publics'.

Third, in challenging the narrative of the decline of publics and publicness (in the face of neoliberal and individualising trends) while also being sceptical of narratives of proliferation (which express excitement about the new possibilities opened up by new media, the web, new global and local spaces of agency, environmental politics and other innovations), we have asserted the importance of thinking seriously about the role of practices of mediation in the formation of publics. If we have emphasised the idea that publics are formed through processes of address, articulation and summoning, this needs to be placed within an understanding that these processes are differentiated by the modes, materialities, times and spaces through which publics are assembled as more or less fleeting or durable, more or less extended or circumscribed, more or less open or selective. We develop this theme further in the third section below, 'Mediating publics'.

Finally, throughout the book we have emphasised the theme of emergence: the emergence of subjects of public action (such as those formed around global mobilisation); objects of public concern (from environmental concerns to community cohesion, national belonging and 'good' parenting); and mediums of public communication (including the web and 'vox pop' experiments by established media or reality TV shows). In the midst of excitement about the possibilities that new developments may offer, or dismay about how they may fragment and further dilute an already threatened domain of public identity and action, we offer an empirically grounded analysis of these processes. This enables us to trace ways in which the 'new' confronts existing institutions and sedimented cultural practices, and to highlight the historical and spatial specificities that shape public formation and action. We develop this theme of processes of becoming in the fourth section, 'Emergent publics'.

Throughout we want to underline the value of this collection as *research led*. Our contributors have offered different possible methodologies and analytical frameworks for researching publics and publicness, but we think that a research-led collection offers something rather more significant. As we noted in the Introduction, work on publicness and publics tends to be long on normative claims and short on empirical substance. It is only through the detailed, theoretically informed empirical work of the kind presented in this volume that it becomes possible to properly frame the normative issues at stake in the analysis of public formation, not least by giving due credit to the ways in which different public values are enacted in practice.

Personalising publics

Feminist scholars have long challenged the notion of a clearly bounded public sphere in which the personal and the affective have no place (see Chapter Six of this volume). The argument that 'the personal is political' has been subject to multiple reinterpretations, and chapters in this volume emphasise how, as Richenda Gambles sets out, notions of public, political, personal and private are deeply interwoven and produced and understood through each other. The reworking of these categories has a generative potential, offering new spaces of mobilisation, for example, in relation to campaigns for government action on miscarriage (Chapter Three) or in neighbourhood organising for and with young people (Chapter Six). The inclusion of issues previously considered personal as proper issues for public dialogue and debate, and the recognition given to forms of expression that enable experiences and desires previously unacknowledged to be voiced, both open up the public sphere to marginalised and excluded actors (Young, 1990; Lister, 2003). These reorientations challenge the idealised norms inscribed in democratic institutions in many nation states, especially norms of rational deliberation and norms of representation (Phillips, 1993; Mansbridge, 2003).

Such issues have been taken up and their analysis extended in this volume. Richenda Gambles' (Chapter Three) analysis of the web as a site of public, private, personal and political identities and encounters challenges the notion of the public domain as a sphere of rational deliberation among public actors, while also highlighting the ongoing significance of formal, representative politics. In Chapter Six, Eleanor Jupp engages critically with feminist literature on 'liminality' in order to theorise the ambiguously public and personal spaces of 'community' activism, while in Chapter Two, Nick Mahony engages with the valorisation of lay expertise and knowledge, linked to the turn to more populist forms of discourse as personal voices are elicited by both governmental actors and media organisations. But he also highlights the overlaying of new voices and forms of expression with older formations of the public. In Chapter Four, Scott Rodgers addresses the place of 'new' media that apparently blur the distinction between the 'mass' and the 'personal'. Rather than a turn from the deliberative to the affective, we have shown the importance of engaging with how these are overlaid on and slide into each other in particular sites, and how this shifts the terrains and practices of 'politics'.

The valorisation of 'the personal' throws into relief the ambivalent relationship between feminist and identity-based challenges to traditional notions of the public realm and the increasing governmental focus on personal lives and personal responsibility. Feminist claims and social movement activity have undoubtedly opened up new domains and sites of governmental activity concerned with personal lives – that is the objective of a great deal of this sort of public action. This leads to the concern that the institutionalisation of feminist politics as state policy, for example, can slide uneasily into neoliberal rationalities of governance (Fraser, 2009; Newman, 2009; Newman and Tonkens, forthcoming). Many governments have become increasingly focused on the inculcation of responsible citizens and the 'empowerment' of communities, taking on tasks previously the province of state agencies. This relies on new pedagogies of personal lives that seek to constitute new forms of citizen-subject (Pykett, forthcoming). But at the same time, Jupp argues, governmental practices – at least in the UK – are becoming saturated with a concern for private and domestic lives. For example, parenting and becoming a parent has become a site of intense government intervention in the UK (Gambles), while government programmes such as Sure Start 'link community and neighbourhood development to spheres of family life and childcare' (Jupp, Chapter Six, p 77). Interventions around young people in her study were often based around activities associated with the domestic or private sphere such as cooking, gardening and small-scale arts and crafts – what she terms an 'extension of family life' into the wider public realm. However, she also demonstrates the significance of the 'contact zones' in which personal resources are mobilised for public projects, and demonstrates the ambiguous 'public' potential of the liminal spaces in which public, private and personal are entangled.

Chapters Four, Six and Seven all show how new governmentalities of the self are mediated through particular technologies (the web, community governance and schooling). These chapters highlight the ambiguity of new governmental practices that supposedly pursue a public interest – for example, in Chapter Seven, Jessica Pykett asks whether the introduction of personalisation strategies in schools signals a retreat from the notions of schools as public places that have a role in addressing spatially specific structural inequalities. In Chapter Three, Richenda Gambles shows how web-based mediations bring personal issues into the public/political domain, but also how the anonymity offered by the web can offer a means of being privately public. The web, she suggests, enables personal disclosure, but at the same time 'promotes self-responsibility through an emphasis on personal empowerment and the therapeutic' (p 37) – an approach that can 'reprivatise' issues and close off attention to wider socio-economic factors affecting 'personal' experience.

We are not, it seems, simply talking about how things previously public are becoming private, or vice versa, but about how the meanings of the terms themselves are being renegotiated. And the reworking of these understandings offers new spaces of mobilisation through governmental programmes of empowerment, training and development. These top-down governmental projects are, of course, shot through with contradictions and ironies. For example, Pykett identifies the paradox produced as the individualising logics inherent in 'personalisation' strategies in schooling in the UK coexist with a new focus on citizenship education as a means of producing what may be thought of as 'public' selves. These sorts of paradoxes need to be scrutinised in order to unfold the forms of contentious agency of which they are an index and the forms of proactive agency that they, more or less intentionally, help to facilitate.

These analyses of personalised registers of public address and engagement generate a first set of questions that may throw light on the normative evaluation of processes of public emergence: when does this process indicate a steady accommodation of new identities and forms of political practice; and when does the slippage between public, private and personal undermine the collective possibilities enshrined in the vocabularies of publicness?

Representing publics

One key task of 'rethinking' the public that has been widely acknowledged elsewhere is the multiple ways in which claims on behalf of the public or specific publics are being voiced, that is, the public realm cannot be viewed as a domain in which a single entity is spoken to or spoken for through conventional representative channels. Theoretically, the concept of representation has been reconfigured around understandings of contested claims-making (Spivak, 1988; Saward, 2006; Parkinson, 2009). Saward (2006) demonstrates the aesthetic features of formal processes of political representation: how elected and non-elected representatives draw on symbolic practices to constitute, rather than reflect, their constituencies. Young (1990) and Phillips (1993) have highlighted the symbolic role of embodied actors whose presence in formal decision-making forums has been limited through exclusionary practices. An understanding representation as a performative process (Barnett, 2003) draws into view the importance of non-discursive modes of representation in processes of public address and assemblage.

Our contributors have highlighted something of this proliferation of claims-making practices through which publics emerge. Chapters Two, Five, Nine and Ten have traced representative claims articulated by social and political movements. Chapters Six and Seven show actors such as community workers and teachers speaking on behalf of young people at the same time that young people are encouraged and 'empowered' to speak for themselves. Chapters Four and Five show the significance of print cultures in projecting urban publics to themselves and beyond, and emphasise the importance of the ways in which textual artefacts are enacted in situated practices. We have shown the significance that abstract figures or non-human figures can play in articulating claims of public legitimacy: in Chapter Eight, Liza Griffin traces the slippery role of fish in complex processes of negotiation around access to, and potential depletion of, fisheries as a global commons. She shows how notions of the public interest are brought into being through governance arrangements that speak to differently imagined publics, and how different representations of publics are summoned up by different stakeholders, from 'vulnerable fishing communities' to environmental campaigning groups. Some of these speak on behalf of a wider concept of civil society that includes unborn populations, and each mobilises fish themselves as actants. In Chapter Nine, Clive Gabay focuses on how the Millennium Development Goals serve as a kind of 'immutable mobile' drawn on by varied governmental and non-governmental actors in assembling transnational networks of policy and activist action. But he also shows how the naming of publics is itself a political act that can prematurely close down other possible becomings.

The chapters also highlight the significance of governmental practices of representation, promulgating images of desired public subjects, from good parents (Chapter Three) to good citizens (Chapter Seven) and responsible communities (Chapter Six). But they also demonstrate the ways in which governmental practices shape the possibilities and practices of claims making. Mahony's analysis of a participative budgeting exercise and Jupp's ethnography of community practices both demonstrate the increasing significance of the local as a site of governance *and* contention in the UK. Pykett shows how pupils may be able to make claims within the classroom in the context of citizenship classes, but this may be subordinated to other governmental processes that close down the idea of pupils as members of a collective entity.

This is the key issue in reframing of the concept of representation (as a process of claims making) as central to process of public formation. Any representation, any claim, cannot guarantee its own 'felicity conditions' – it is just as likely to generate dissent, argument, refusal and counter-representations. So, for example, Gambles shows how Mumsnet claims to represent the interest of mothers to government while also representing exemplary practices of mothering to other mothers. It forms a kind of clearing house for developing, disseminating and refining representations of mothering, but emerges as a space of contention in which lay voices and personal experiences compete with various professional perspectives in ongoing disputes about what counts as good mothering. In Chapter Ten, Simon Hutta shows how the failures of representative processes to speak for a particular public in Brazil produced claims for autonomy; in the process, an emergent public itself had to engage in the work of alliance building to be able to legitimately engage with more formal political processes. What he calls 'heterogeneous processes of political world making' – of rational deliberation, affective bonding and disruptive confrontation, of dissidence and party organising – are combined in this movement to generate various forms of effective representation. And in Chapter Five, Gurpreet Bhasin shows how the relationship between colonial authorities and colonial subjects in India was worked through competing representations in the proper place of 'Indians' in public space, representations that circulated in both public cultures and in private communications. Colonial authorities made claims about the colonised through a set of representative practices positioning the colonised as potentially disruptive of public order. But she also shows how colonised subjects spoke back in struggles to represent themselves, by generating innovative styles of public communication in urban space, or by projecting representations of pan-Islamic publics through transnational print cultures.

The chapters as a whole suggest that processes of representation are dynamic and reflexive; those represented may take up the positions offered to them but may then speak back, seeking to represent themselves through counter-claims to autonomy, authenticity or legitimacy. But they also raise a normative set of questions. How, and in what ways, might claims-making practices 'fix' an emergent public by assembling or aligning it with existing institutions and practices, or indeed, in Gabay's terms, simply by naming it as a collective entity? How might material objects and non-human actants – whether these are discursive figures or material media – figure in representative claims, and with what consequences? Griffin's analysis suggests that where publics are indeterminate and rarely visible, we should be extra cautious about claims to protect the 'common good'. It also suggests the need to ask, when issues of the 'commons' are at stake, what particular interests are mobilised, who or what is being excluded in accounts of problems and how far 'publics' respond to interpellations inscribed in public governance discourse. Such questions point us towards our third theme, the importance of understanding the processes of mediation through which publics are formed.

Mediating publics

The emphasis on emergence and becoming that we have emphasised in this volume is not meant to suggest that publics have no background, no rootedness in given configurations of social relations, material infrastructures or institutional arrangements. Quite the reverse; the idea that publics emerge around objects and issues of concern implies precisely that cultural sedimentations, governmental practices and institutional legacies shape the possibilities of emergence and deflect, incorporate or suppress new forms of publicness. It is this relationship between the given and the emergent that brings into view the importance of attending to the mediating practices through which some issues, and not others, are made into objects of public action through the agency of particular subjects and in particular registers.

One thing the chapters in this volume do is challenge the image in much discussion of the public realm of the media as a mere medium, by placing media practices into the contexts of situated public action. Chapters Two, Three, Four and Five take us beyond a binary conception of 'new' and 'old' media, challenging any excitement about the potential of new communication technologies to revolutionise public communication and action. And across the volume as a whole, the contributors offer an expansive conception of *mediation* that goes beyond attention to 'the media', old or new. Chapters Three, Six and Seven illustrate how processes of mediation stretch across what is normally understood as a public–personal or public–private boundary. Several chapters suggest the significance of institutional and professional practices that mediate emergent forms of publicness. Chapter Four traces the ways in which new media practices and technologies enter into so-called old media organisations, focusing on the work of editors – work that is understood both as a set of rules, routines and shared sense of purpose, and as a set of material arrangements of bodies, object and technologies; Chapter Eight demonstrates how 'the public interest' is mediated by governmental institutions in order to maintain the legitimacy they require to govern; and Chapters Nine and Ten emphasise the mediating practices through which movement and campaigning networks extend themselves and seek to exert influence on governmental and corporate actors.

As with the processes of representative claims making discussed earlier, processes of mediation bring into view the different forms of power that are at stake in the formation of publics. But while issues of representation give rise to questions about power with reference to issues of authenticity, authority and legitimacy, issues of mediation disclose other modes of power to be at work. They suggest more anonymous modes of power, such as the power of material technologies to configure particular possibilities of action and lines of sight while occluding others, or the power provided by particular discursive figures or specific technologies of reaching out across time and space and assembling extensive publics. There is, then, what Mahony terms a 'politics of mediation' embedded in the practices by which new and old formations of the public are assembled through institutional, organisational, discursive, professional, material and technological assemblages. Understanding this type of politics requires shifting attention away from static contrasts of publics and markets towards understanding processes of performing publicity and enacting publicness. The sense of the unanticipated powers exercised through processes of mediation, and of the more-than-intentional effects of particular assemblages, throws us forward to our final theme of thinking about the emergence of public forms.

Emergent publics

A recurring theme running through the book has been a focus on emergent publics – on the processes, practices and events through which publics are made, summoned, sustained and contested. The emphasis on emergence was the focus of a research seminar series funded by the Economic and Social Research Council and directed by the editors that ran through 2008–09, and around which the group of early career scholars who have contributed to this volume was formed. The theme of 'emergence' has diverse sources and is going through one of its regular periods of revived interest, informed by Deleuzian-Spinozan readings of 'emergent causality' (Connolly, 2008) and picking up on discussions in the life sciences and philosophy of mind (Clayton and Davies, 2006). But our guiding sense of 'emergent publics' has slightly more prosaic references, taking its guide from Raymond Williams' (1977) three-fold distinction between *residual, dominant* and *emergent* formations. The attraction of thinking with Williams' sense of the emergent is that it is associated, in his own work, with a sensitivity to thinking about the newness of new forms as full of contingent potential, without slipping back into romanticism of the past or thoughtless celebration of novelty.

It is in this spirit that the collective endeavour of rethinking the public collected together in this volume has been undertaken. This sense of emergence offers several resources for research on public formations. First, it challenges the simple alternatives of decline or proliferation of publicness. The chapters here do not take as their starting point the idea of a singular public domain or set of institutions in retreat in the face of neoliberal pressures and the corruption of public culture. Nor do they straightforwardly celebrate innovative forms as realising the classic promise of the public sphere. They focus instead on *processes of becoming* rather than on the decline of sedimented institutions and cultural practices (see Chapter Eight, in particular, on the play between assembling and convening publics, and the different acts of representation invoke by each). Chapter Two offers case studies of three 'innovative' sites in which 'new' publics – including the supposedly politically disaffected – are mobilised for the purposes of participation. Chapter Three shows how the web can offer new possibilities of becoming a public, albeit that such a public is infected by ambiguous interweaving of public, private, personal and political identifications and relationships, while Chapter Six highlights 'community' as a potential space of becoming. Chapter Five offers a historical perspective on how print media contributed to the formation of an urban public in colonial Delhi, and on the emergence of a transnational Muslim public. Chapter Nine shows how global justice movements offer a means of inculcating 'a notion of unification with distant others' (p 136) or 'a sense of global responsibility for issues that affect most people who live on the planet' (pp 136-7) and Chapter Ten suggests that a 'desire for new affective forms of subjectivity and sociability' can open up the possibility of 'a new worlding ... where different becomings conjoin' (p 152).

Second, the focus on emergence is meant to reposition the emphasis on multiplicity and plurality in any attempt to 'rethink' the public. For at least two decades, a feature of debates around publics – public space, the public sphere, public services – has been a concern with transcending overly unitary, singular understandings of the public that flatten out difference and erase multiplicity (Duggan, 2003; Cooper, 2004). However, incorporating notions of difference and multiplicity proves difficult, in theory and practice, without seeming to undermine the sense of collective, shared purpose from which the topic of the public derives its normative force in this first place. The proliferation of publics, in response to a politics of difference, tends to be presented as a threat to the unity of purpose presumed to be necessary for effective, legitimate public action; but this unity of purpose is always regarded suspiciously as more than likely based on exclusion, silencing or selectivity. Rather than trying to provide another theoretical solution to this conundrum, the contributors to this volume have focused empirically on the fact that publics are assembled and summoned in multiple ways, and indeed, how multiplicity and plurality is an important resource for the emergence of publicness, rather than a threat to public formations. For example, Hutta examines heterogeneous publics, but also focuses on the plural strategies of representation, advocacy and expression generated by these formations. Likewise, Gabay demonstrates the ways in which a complex transnational network is woven from multiple strands, and in turn uses this constitutive multiplicity as a normative guide for developing a critique of how this particular formation weaves together its different strands. The emphasis in this volume, then, has been on bracketing the question of what the place of difference should be in public life in favour of exploring empirically the difference that multiplicity and pluralism make in practice to how publics are formed and function.

In focusing on processes of emergence, our contributors have been informed by the initial theoretical framing presented in the Introduction – of the entangled emergence of public subjects, the emergent objects of public concern and emergent processes of public mediation. These are not distinct categories, and each chapter has worked across each of these aspects. The focus on emergence calls for theoretical approaches that enable an understanding of processes, practices and performances of publicness. In this enterprise, our contributors have engaged with the work of various writers, including John Dewey, Michel Foucault, Nancy Fraser, Felix Guattari, Bruno Latour, Michael Warner, Raymond Williams and Iris Marion Young. Theoretical resources drawn from feminist, gay and lesbian, post-colonial and queer traditions have been particularly important in providing ways of working through the challenge of thinking about the emergence of new forms of publicness in non-reductive ways. Such theoretical engagements have opened up analyses of the multiple ways in which publicness is practised or performed; the different affective and normative rationalities within which publics are constituted; the proliferating forms of mediation that shape the conditions of possibility for becoming publics; and the governmental processes that open up and close down spaces of emergence.

Conclusion

The contributions to this volume have challenged normative claims – optimistic and pessimistic – about how the public has changed, its sensibilities shifted and its modes of performance and thus capacity for political engagement transformed. But at the same time they have been cautious about the political possibilities offered by new cultural and social formations, new communicative technologies and new spatial imaginaries of public identity and action. The focus has been on identifying tensions, paradoxes and possibilities, and how these are contained, resolved or displaced. Many of our contributors have been inspired to engage in their studies precisely because of political and personal commitments to understanding these issues. Our focus on emergence flows from such starting points on the part of contributors and editors. As such, we have attempted to capture something of the multiplicity of new subjects, objects and mediums of publicness in ways that emphasise potentials without lapsing into naïve celebration of novelty.

Tracing the emergence of subjects, objects and media of publicness may not satisfy the demand for clear-cut normative standards by which to judge whether publics are on the wane or are entering a new age of proliferation. There is no doubt that the early 21st century has seen a marked shift to modes of public life shaped by anxiety, fear and insecurity (Berlant, 2008; Barnett, 2009). In response to this emergent, fear-full rationality of publicness, we certainly need analytical tools and conceptual resources to understand the processes that help to form public concern around certain objects, through particular media, and appealing to specific constituencies and registers of engagement. But these tools need to be rooted in careful study of how public formation happens and why. The politics of publicness coalesces around the combination of practices of representation, material attachment and identification that are mobilised in these processes of formation. As we noted earlier, 'emergence' is a concept in vogue in the critical social sciences and humanities at the moment – and it is often assumed that 'emergence' as such carries normative value, that the appearance of the 'new' and the 'unanticipated' automatically qualifies as politically desirable and publicly valuable. The chapters in this book have departed from the voguish understanding of *process* that denies the significance of stubborn, sticky attachment to things and identities; of *performance* that ignores the importance of scripting and staging; and of *flow* that disregards the durability and potentials of territory. They have shown how important existing formations, sedimented identities and inherited resources are in enabling the emergence of new formations. The chapters have, therefore, underscored the significance of the cultural and material forces that shape the formation of publics and practices of publicness in specific places at specific times. This is why the focus on empirical work has been so significant for this project – not only do we want to 'rethink' the public, to invent wholly novel understandings, but also to demonstrate the value of combining conceptual and empirical analysis in the task of developing new ways of approaching what have often become stale, predictable debates and evaluations.

References

Barnett, C. (2003) *Culture and democracy*, Edinburgh: Edinburgh University.

Barnett, C. (2009) 'Violence and publicity: constructions of political responsibility after 9/11', *Critical Review of Social and Political Philosophy*, 12(3), pp 353-75.

Berlant, L. (2008) 'Thinking about feeling historical', *Emotion, Space and Society*, 1(1), pp 4-9.

Clayton, P. and Davies, P. (eds) (2006) *The re-emergence of emergence: The emergentist hypothesis from science to religion*, Oxford: Oxford University Press.

Connolly, W. (2008) *Capitalism and Christianity, American style*, Durham, NC: Duke University Press.

Cooper, D. (2004) *Challenging diversity: Rethinking equality and the value of difference*, Cambridge: Cambridge University Press.

Duggan, L. (2003) *The twilight of equality: Neoliberalism, cultural politics and the attack on democracy*, Boston, MA: Beacon Press.

Fraser, N. (2009) 'Feminism, capitalism and the cunning of history', *New Left Review*, 56, pp 97-117.

Lister, R. (2003) *Citizenship: Feminist perspectives*, London: Palgrave.

Mansbridge, J. (2003) 'Rethinking representation', *American Political Science Review*, 97(4), pp 515-28.

Newman, J. (2009) 'Working the spaces of governance', Paper presented to Canadian Association of Anthropology conference, Vancouver, July.

Newman, J. and Tonkens, E. (forthcoming) *Active citizenship and the transformation of social welfare*, Amsterdam: Amsterdam University Press.

Parkinson, J. (2009) 'Symbolic representation in public space: capital cities, presence and memory', *Representation*, 45(1), pp 1-14.

Phillips, A. (1993) *Democracy and difference*, Philadelphia, PA: Pennsylvania University Press.

Pykett, J. (ed) (forthcoming) 'The pedagogical state: education, citizenship, governing', *Citizenship Studies Special Issue*.

Saward, M. (2006) 'The representative claim', *Contemporary Political Theory*, 5(3), pp 297-318.

Spivak, G.C. (1988) 'Can the subaltern speak?', in C. Nelson and L. Grossberg (eds) *Marxism and the interpretation of culture*, London: Macmillan, pp 271-313.

Williams, R. (1977) *Marxism and literature*, Oxford: Oxford University Press.

Young, I.M. (1990) *Justice and the politics of difference*, Princeton, NJ: Princeton University Press.

Index